The Bat House

The Bat House

A Montana Memoir

by Michael B. Riley

*
WordsWorth Publishing

Copyright © 2024 by Michael B. Riley
All rights reserved. No part of this publication may be copied, reproduced in any format, by any means, electronic or otherwise, without prior consent from the author and the publisher of this book.

ISBN: 978-1-7334897-6-8
First edition paperback

Cover photo of author by Becca Dailey.
Cover illustration by R C. Tafoya, from a photograph of Mike and Theo's "Bat House" courtesy of the Walter B. Dean family.

WordsWorth Publishing
Cody, Wyoming
www.wordsworthpublishing.com

To my grandchildren,
Sydney, Mason, Oliver, Alexander, Melissa,
and to Theo,
who loved me through all my craziness
and taught us all how to love well.

Theo and Bill

Despite my wife's misgivings, we bought an eighty-acre farm on the Yellowstone River in eastern Montana fifteen miles from where I grew up. I had not looked in the attic of the 1917 brick house until two years after the contract was paid and the old man we'd bought it from was dead. When I crawled up the built-in ladder under the attic access and pushed on it, I vaguely thought the little black pellets falling to the floor was mouse dung until I pushed the access to one side and tiny ebony capsules cascaded like a coal shower onto my arms, face, and shoulders. The stench was unbearable, pungent like sweetly rotten cabbage. I climbed far enough to poke my head into the odorous space and illuminated the dark with my flashlight. I saw something moving directly above me. It chittered and flickered. Wings unfolded and closed. Heads turned and tiny eyes glimmered.

Bats.

A cluster of them the size of a football hung directly above my head. They began nervously flitting their wings and chittering more at the interruption. I could see four more clusters hanging from the rafters in the belly of the Union style roof. The guano was eight inches deep, and the smell nearly made me vomit.

I had agreed on a handshake in 2007 to buy the place while hunting pheasants with a lifelong friend, Jack Ferguson, when we stopped to ask an old timer if we could hunt his land. He had a big ditch lined with Russian olive and cottonwood trees. It held a good stand of cattails, perfect habitat for pheasants, especially since Jack, who leased the land, had planted corn in the fields around the ditch. I had never met the owner, but according to Jack, he was a good old guy in his nineties and tough as they came. Jack also allowed, with a hint of keen enthusiasm, that the old bird had the best apples in the valley, so we pulled off the pavement onto his dirt lane.

I was familiar with the house, a monolithic, union roofed, two-story red brick icon along the Carterville Road north of the river. It stood close to the old Milwaukee Railroad bed, where I had worked on a steel gang before the company pulled up the rails and ties. I had driven by it a thousand times. But as we rattled in Jack's pickup down the lane toward the river, the wild grapevines climbing the fence, the chokecherry trees and the plum tree thickets forming a high wall along the dirt road conjured a spectral memory of the house, the apples, and the thin, lovely woman in the kitchen there.

About fifty years before, I had run telephone books from my mother's car up to the doors of rural homes, and she paid me a nickel a book. She was moonlighting for Bell Telephone, where she worked as a switchboard operator. She said she never listened in on conversations, but I knew she did because I overheard her recounting several scandalous dialogues to her sister, my Aunt Eunice. The night she placed a call to Switzerland for one of the town's two doctors was a stellar moment for her, her self-worth rising noticeably because of how she had handled her first international call.

When the new phonebooks were printed, it was much cheaper for Bell to pay her twenty-five cents per book to deliver them to rural customers than to mail them. We drove around in the country in the evenings after her regular day shift on the switchboard.

I had to get the books past territorial and often vicious cattle dogs. Usually, I could just talk to them, not move too quickly, and never take my eyes off them, but dogs are reflections of wolves, and I got my share of nipped calves and ankles before the owners would come out and yell at them. This house, I remembered, had a beautiful auburn dog, a dog that wagged his tail as he approached me and nuzzled my hand. It was the first golden retriever I had ever seen.

It was a vague memory, but I knew the place, and when Jack parked his truck at the house, I vividly recalled the apples in the kitchen while I had stood at the open door as the dog wagged his tail and bumped my elbow. Cardboard boxes and wooden bushel baskets of big red apples, smelling like everything I knew about the sharp goodness of autumn, occupied the floor, the counters, and the tables. Five or six women were in the kitchen. They were full of energy, moving between the apples steaming in huge pots to the counters, and they were smiling. The thin woman offered me some — no, not one, she laughed, take a whole box — and I carried it back down the steps to my mother's car.

"Haralson's," my mother said. "The best apples in the valley."

She waved at the smiling, aproned woman who stood on the steps, thanked her for the apples, and promised to return for a Sunday visit. As we drove back up the lane with its gigantic cottonwoods supremely golden, we both bit into the fruit, and the tart, sweet juice poured out. My mother laughed as she wiped her chin with her hand. It was the best apple I had ever tasted.

"We came at the perfect time," mother had said. "Right after a good frost."

The woman was Winnifred Lloyd, Bill Lloyd's wife, Jack told me, and she died in 2001.

"Bill is awful lonely without her," Jack said "Talks about going to be with her all the time. I'm afraid every time I go into the house that I'll find him dead. He's a tough old guy though, and he just keeps living."

He told me how Bill had slipped on wet grass when he was eighty-five and fell backwards onto a concrete irrigation head gate. Jack didn't know for sure, but he thought Bill was unconscious for a while, and when he came to, he crawled out and made it to the house. Winnifred had gone to town, so he wrote her a blood-spattered note that he'd had a little accident and had to go to Miles City, and not to worry. He drove himself to the Vets' hospital, where they told him he'd broken three vertebrae and cracked his skull open. They flew him to Salt Lake City, where a doctor inserted a stainless-steel pin in his neck to stabilize it.

"Now I guess he has skin cancer on his head," Jack said, "and the county nurse comes out twice a week to clean up the bandage on it. It just oozes blood all the time."

"Won't the cancer go into his brain?" I asked.

"I don't know," Jack said. "You'd think it would. Eventually."

I braced myself to meet this tough old survivor as we walked into the back porch — the door was open — and I was aware of an acrid odor, like the smell from the scrap woodpile in my garage, from what I thought must be mice. I thought they must be nesting in the porch under the stairs — a blue plastic sheet, weighted with bricks and two-by-fours, covered a coffin size door to the basement, and I imagined Grand Central Rodent Station under it. A stack of cottonwood limbs covered in cobwebs rested in the corner. Buckets of agates and petrified wood lined the walls. A pick, a maul, a shovel, and a spike bar leaned in the corner by the door. A cowbell hung above my head, obviously supposed to clang when the door opened, but it was too high.

A rooster pheasant, in rigid flight for at least twenty years, was nailed against the east wall. A cat's bed with "OLD ADMIRAL" painted on it lay on a platform at the top of the handrail. An empty box of D-Con sat in it.

The mice around here probably eat that stuff for dessert, I thought as Jack opened the spring-loaded screen door. And they probably ate the Old Admiral.

Jack knocked on the inner door's window, opened the door and yelled, "Hello, Bill!"

"Hellllooo?" I heard from inside. "Who is it?" The voice was slow and low. A very comfortable voice.

"It's Jack!"

"Ohhh, come on in, Jackie. Come on in."

We took off our boots just inside the door, the kitchen to our left, a dining room table and a piano in front of us, and the living room beyond it where I could see Bill's legs on the other side of a bookcase. The house was sweltering. I shucked my coat, but I was instantly sweating in my fleece top under a wool Pendleton shirt, which I unbuttoned all the way, pulling its tail out of my Levi's.

It must have been ninety degrees in the house, and I smelled pipe tobacco over too many other odors to recognize. Mice, I believed, were dead behind the cupboards, alive in the walls and ceiling, and I wondered about the old golden retriever, Maggie, that woofed at us. Obviously blind and crippled with arthritis, she could barely get up and waddle toward us, but I did not detect dog urine or feces in the aromatic blend.

The smell was ambivalently familiar to me. I'd known it as far back as I could remember, its personality so mixed with the peculiarities of old men in my life, that I found it both comforting and nauseating. It wafted up from childhood days of visiting Norwegian great-uncles with their brunost cheese, snuff tobacco and wet wool coats, iron strong coffee, smoked whitefish and dead mallards on pine counters, head cheese sandwiches and uncorked bottles of whiskey. Ultimately, I loved it with a nostalgia and sentimentality that testified more to my respect for these old men and their uncompromising ways of life than for the modern sterility I found so prevalent in suburban sprawl.

Bill was sitting in an overstuffed chair in the corner of the living room. He wore blue long-underwear and thick wool socks. He was a tall man, big boned and long armed as he reached to shake my hand when Jack introduced us. His grip was strong, his wrist thick, and his smile revealed five or six teeth as he said in a surprisingly formal voice, "Well, I am pleased to meet you. Sit down. Make yourself at home. Sit right there."

He pointed to a small, overstuffed chair at a right angle in front of him. He seemed a bit hard of hearing, so I sat turned in the chair, and after a while, my neck grew stiff from cranking it around to face him. On a shelf to his left, he had a can of Prince Albert tobacco, an ashtray with a corncob pipe, and a small cassette tape deck. Behind him, a .22 bolt-action rifle leaned in the corner.

He was flanked by books and became visibly animated when he learned I taught English and journalism. He wanted to know what books I was reading with students and who my favorite authors were. To his right, half of a sectional sofa was stacked three feet high with paperbacks, hardbacks, and a raft of Readers Digest Condensed volumes. Jack sat on the half that appeared to be Bill's bed.

From his stories, I learned he served in the Navy from 1930 to 1955. He traveled up and down the east coast hunting German U-Boats, all the way to South America, and he was in the Pacific, mostly Saipan, and in Korea. He whipped the light heavyweight champion boxer of the Sixth Fleet by what he called "a lucky punch." He told the story as if it happened last night.

Lucky punch, my ass, I thought. I wouldn't want him taking a swing at me.

He told several hours' worth of stories, but I especially related to the time he went overboard in an atmospheric diving suit, the heavy helmet-with-a-hose type, in Saipan, where he was harbor master. At the last minute before he went over the side, he decided to leave the boot weights on deck. When his hose kinked, stopping his airflow, he was glad he had because he had to rocket to the surface. He would have drowned if he'd put on the weights.

As a Dive Master in scuba, I appreciated the severity of the situation, but there was a secondary element to the story. Rising to the surface that fast could have killed him too.

"How come you didn't get the bends?" I asked.

"Maybe I did," he said. "Maybe that's what's been wrong with me all these years."

Jack and I laughed, but then he got serious.

"I do know that ever after that," he said, "I can't stand to be in closed places. Like in a theater, I must sit by the aisle at the end of a row."

"Claustrophobic," I said.

"Yes, a severe case," he said. "Worse than you'd think from something like that."

He told the story of walking by Jack Dempsey's bar in New York City, how even though Dempsey had been his hero ever since he was a kid, he couldn't go in.

"I just walked past it several times," he said, "looking inside from the street. Too crowded."

He knew the history of boxing like no one I'd ever met, reciting round by round the famous fights of the thirties and forties, and I realized it was dark out, my pheasant hunting kaput, but I didn't mind. We talked of dogs, birds, and guns.

"Go upstairs," he said. "Look around. I've got some good guns up there."

I was midway up the stairs when he said, "Why don't you buy this place, Mike?"

I stopped to look at him. He was lighting his pipe. Jack was still sitting on the couch where Bill slept, the pile of books between them.

"Don't your kids want it?" I asked.

"No," he said. "And I'd rather sell it to you than some damn Californian."

"I couldn't afford it," I said. "I'm just a teacher."

"Make me an offer that you can afford," he said.

"I wouldn't want to insult you," I said.

"You won't insult me."

"What are you asking?"

He told me.

"I would like to buy your place," I said, "but it's a bit sudden for me. Besides, I couldn't afford that."

"What could you afford?"

"About seventy thousand less."

He was quiet for a moment, and I thought he must have been insulted, even though he said he wouldn't be. He puffed at his pipe, re-lighting it with a kitchen match.

"How about sixty-five thousand less?" he said, waving the match out.

"Sold," I said. I walked back down the stairs and extended my hand. Bill reached up and smiled his ragged, toothy grin as he gripped my hand again.

"Pending the approval of a loan, of course," I added, the weight of the deal I'd just made hitting me in the back of the head like a two-pound maul.

"OK," Bill said. "Let's give it a month."

"I think I can manage that."

I realized I had not been upstairs yet. Or in the basement. And I hadn't even talked to my wife Theo about it. I wondered with panic how I'd convince her to go along with me on this because she'd been talking about retiring from her psychology practice for several years.

I could just hear myself sounding like a realtor's ad: "Eighty acres of the best farmland on the Yellowstone River," I'd say. "Two story brick house with a full basement. Twenty-seven hundred square feet at the end of the road. Secluded hunter's paradise. Geese, ducks, grouse, pheasants, turkeys, whitetail, and mule deer. Fruit trees. Catfish, sauger, walleye, sturgeon, smallmouth bass, northern pike. Fifteen miles from town."

I could see her scowling.

"Why would we want that?" she would say.

We lived in Cody, Wyoming, about 200 miles from the farm, where Theo was a clinical psychologist. She was a frugal Scot, her grandfather having borrowed a thousand dollars from the Mother Masonic Lodge in Dalry, Scotland to emigrate to America, where he found work in the Rock Springs, Wyoming coal mines. He brought his five-year-old son Matthew with him while his wife, Theo's grandmother, stayed on the other side of the Atlantic until he could provide transport and lodging. A tall, strong, no-nonsense fellow, he quickly rose to Safety Inspector and paid his debt to the Lodge with $40 interest, which the Masons gave to his wife, who shortly arrived in The Equality State to live in a tar-paper shack among the other miners, a propitious transfer from the Miners' Row poverty of Dalry.

Theo had refused agreeing to several real estate investment opportunities I had found that would have been golden during our marriage. She loved free things like hiking in the mountains, cross-country skiing, throwing out a bedroll under the stars, fields of wildflowers, and swimming in lakes. She seemed born with the ability to make one chicken feed an army for three meals, and if the chicken was too expensive, she would find a pot roast on sale.

I was thunderstruck at the realization of the deal I had just made as I rode with Jack on the darkened lane, the trees looming shadows now, the inside of Jack's pickup all a swirl. My only hope was to convince Theo of the purchase as a sound investment opportunity.

"You can't go wrong," Jack said. "It's some of the best farm ground in the valley. And you're getting it for a damned good price."

"Why didn't you buy it if you knew it was for sale?" I asked.

"I've got too much land as it is," he said. "But there are four or five people who would buy it in a minute if he'd sell it to them. He likes you. He wouldn't have offered it to you if he didn't."

Within a month, I had convinced Theo that we might as well invest our earnings in real estate as the stock market, where we were seeing a meltdown caused by some skullduggery among bankers re-selling unsecured loans. Real estate values had dropped as steadily as November leaves in the breeze, and our investment agent believed we could not go wrong.

Theo trusted him, if not me, and I had also brought my nephew, H.R. Coe, a contractor in Cody with several renovations under his belt, to the place to get his opinion on buying it, his advice on how to start renovating it, and an estimate of the cost.

"You never know about renovations," he said. "But I think I could make the place comfortable for fifty thousand dollars. For a hundred thousand, I could make it damned nice. But you never know once you tear into things. It could be twice that."

He assured me the house was structurally sound, but he recommended replacing the heating system, tearing out the lath and plaster, framing the walls, insulating them, rewiring, and installing new plumbing. He stopped at the chimney on the east side, looking up at it and shaking his head.

"This has got to go," he said.

I looked at it and wondered why. It looked fine to me, but he was on the Cody Volunteer Fire Department, and I figured he knew more about chimneys than the average contractor.

"Do you see how it snakes up the building?" he said. "It's crooked as my dick. And did you notice the ninety-degree stovepipe out of that wood burner in the kitchen? I'm surprised it hasn't burned the place down."

I told him how Bill had not used it since his chimney fire. His wife Winnifred was standing in front of the refrigerator when the stove's door blew open and shot a column of fire across the room. It scorched her dress and terrified them. Bill had just bought a couple of fire extinguishers, luckily enough, a few days before it happened.

H.R. looked at me with wide eyes and said, "Well, don't worry about it yet. Start at the top of the house and work down. The roof is OK for a few years yet, so go in the attic and begin by ripping out the ceiling. That old bead board is too rotted to keep."

Theo loved H.R., her sister's oldest child, and when he told her it would be a great place to take the grandkids hunting and fishing, and that she would love it there once we renovated it, she agreed to the purchase. So, on December 6, I was back on the Yellowstone at Bill's place with two checks from different bank accounts.

Bill didn't like it. He thought there should just be one check from one bank.

"I don't know if that'll work," he said, but I assured him it would be OK, and I helped him into my Toyota Tundra. We drove to town, and he began to enjoy himself. He couldn't remember the last time he was in town. It was like taking a kid to the carnival.

In the bank, he told them he wanted three Certificates of Deposit, and he was nervous about my two checks, but they cleared, and when a smiling young girl handed him the CD's, he finally relaxed.

We went to the title company, the courthouse and the Feed and Seed Store, where he wanted to sit and chat for a few minutes with the old men who sit there every day. They discussed the price of cattle, the cost of electricity, the warm winter, and politicians' empty promises. Then we were on our way back to the Rosebud house.

"You never told those guys you sold the place to me," I said in the pickup.

"It's none of their business," he said. "Besides, they'll know soon enough. You can bet on that."

In the contract, I had my lawyer allow him to live in the house for as long as he was able.

"I only have about a year left," he said.

"Hell," I said, "you'll probably outlive me."

Bill laughed and then said with a wizened certainty, "No, I only have about a year left in me. I know that."
    Before I drove back to Cody, he handed me a rent check for $200. I told him no, that was not in the contract, but he insisted he pay rent while he lived in the house. I argued with him until I saw refusing his offer was not the right thing to do, finally telling him I would put it in a special account in case the place needed repairs. He smiled and said that would be fine.
    Then he wrote me another check for $700.
    "You shouldn't have to pay all those lawyer fees and closing costs by yourself," he said.

Home on the Yellowstone

In my corn field 200 miles from home and Theo, I spread goose decoys in snow on a January morning, the earth lit by a wolf moon, so close I thought I could walk to the end of the row and polish it with my hat. My black Lab, Rookie, stared at it and howled seconds before the sun began its magic act, and I thought of my father, how far he had been from me because of his addiction to alcohol, and my mother, who died at forty-eight from cancer a month after I graduated from high school.

When I looked at the old brick house across the road, I understood I was drawn back to the Yellowstone Valley by my love of the river and its life. For more than forty years, a melancholy had weighed on me when I left the Valley, and I did not understand that, except that I knew I'd suffered a terrible loss I could not regain. I knew the feeling was anchored in the succession of deaths in my immediate family while I was young, but the land itself remained aloof, unrequited, never offering me the fulfillment I needed, no matter how beautiful I found it.

I had come to realize the river didn't care about time or people. Since boyhood, I had spent many days watching and listening to it from sunup to sundown, sitting on its banks, fishing or hunting ducks and geese from a blind. Mistaking my decoys for the real thing, a bald eagle had once swooped through falling snow to flare in front of my face, and a bobcat had walked into my driftwood blind. Deer had passed so close I could have touched them.

The river, almost silent, has a silken sound to its flow. It is fed, and it feeds. It is much like the wind. It cuts away and it rebuilds. It can take your life in seconds and it can nourish you however long you can stand. It always moves. It always changes. Millions of years ago it flowed a hundred miles north of its present channel. Dinosaurs, buffalo, Indians, trappers, horse soldiers, railroads, towns, highways: all merely a riffle in its 692-mile relentless run.

The house I had bought was empty, dead. I owned it and I knew I must begin a dream of not being alone on the river, of creating a refuge in a place I loved that I could share with those who loved me. I thought the house would prove me. I thought renovating it would deliver me, the unkempt, skinny little kid who lived with his grandmother in the tiny house by the river and whose father was the town drunk. I would restore it to the mansion it once was, and I would claim it as mine.

Theo and our two boys stood foremost in my heart with this reclaiming. I felt I could bring to them the joy the Yellowstone had offered me and fulfill myself by doing so. Our lives had not been easy before our marriage, and with no good father model in my own life, I had struggled at fathering her two boys, always believing I never did well enough, though Theo had stalwartly supported me through personal difficulties, and I imagined this place would bond us with what I felt was its idyllic nature.

Theo was by no means a stranger to personal difficulties. Her grandfather died an early death of pneumoconiosis, black lung disease, when her father was eighteen. Her grandmother remarried shortly after his death to another Scot who voiced such a thick brogue Theo could rarely understand him, but he was a merry man who loved to sing while under the influence of "the water of life," Scotch *ouiski*, which Theo's grandmother begrudgingly allowed and furtively enjoyed, especially on formal occasions like Christmas and weddings. As a little girl, Theo was tutored in The Highland Fling and The Sword Dance, both performed in the traditional aboyne dress with velvet bodice over a white blouse, knee high stockings and ghillies, soft ballet like shoes. She inherited her grandfather's coal black hair and piercing green eyes, which stopped me in my tracks the first time I saw her.

I was twenty-seven years old, walking in the hall of the high school where I taught with my colleague Doug Price who was a few strides ahead of me. As I passed by the open door of a classroom, I looked in and saw a woman, a substitute teacher, sitting with straight back and hands folded in her lap at the teacher's desk on the far side of the room. She turned her head to look at me, and like an iron filing obeying the force of a magnet, I couldn't move. I knew in that instant she was the one true love of my life. She turned her head back to look at the students, and I stood there breathless.

Doug stopped walking, saw me staring into the room, came back to take hold of my forearm, and began pulling me down the hall.

"Forget it, Riley," he said. "She's married. And besides that, she's Mormon."

As he dragged me down the hall, my feet could hardly move one in front of the other, the pain in my gut so deep it swirled up into my brain, which maintained against all odds that this could not be true. My heart said it was not.

I taught photography classes then, along with English, and about a month after seeing Theo substitute teaching, I was surprised to see her walk into my classroom. She held a Nikon camera, said she was getting it in her divorce, and wondered if I would show her how to use it. Two weeks later, I asked her to marry me. She said I was crazy. Her divorce was not even final, and she had two young boys. She needed time and space, she said, to sort things out.

I told her to take all the time and space she needed, that I would wait for her, and I wouldn't change my mind. She took a job as a Title I counselor at the high school, so throughout the next year, we continued to occasionally spend time together—a trip with the boys to camp by the ocean on the Olympic Peninsula, cross country skiing, backpacking into remote mountain lakes, pheasant hunting and fishing, movies and talking about books. I learned about her life, the character she had developed, and became consumed.

Her father, William Strannigan, an All American in basketball, had become an athletic legend in Wyoming. Curt Gowdy, his college roommate who became the noted national sportscaster, called him "the best all-around athlete I've ever known" in his memoir *Cowboy at the Mike*. After serving during World War II as a Navy Ensign in Norfolk, Virginia, where Theo was born, he coached at Colorado State University, Iowa State in Ames, and the University of Wyoming.

Theo showed me the *Sports Illustrated* magazine from 1957 with a full-page photo of him jumping off the Iowa State bench when a last-second shot beat Kansas by one point. Wilt Chamberlain played for Kansas then, and Theo, an eighth grader, had the game program with all the players' autographs.

She had loved Iowa. They lived across the street from a park where she roller skated in summers and ice skated in winters. She excelled in school, had many friends and was active in drama. The local paper featured her dad and her on a Girl Scout camping trip. But her parents' marriage was beginning to fall apart. She was told to close the windows of the house when they argued so the neighbors wouldn't hear them. Her mother suffered from depression and anxiety and began to excessively drink alcohol. She had grown up in Colorado and wanted to go home. She hated Iowa and all the pressure of being the wife of a high-profile coach in the Midwest.

Her mother was a beautiful woman, tall, refined, quiet and extremely intelligent. She was Welsh and English, coming from a family of judges and newspaper owners. She had grown up climbing the 14,000 feet mountains of Colorado as a matter of course.

She played a concert piano and ice skated like an Olympian, once taking Theo to watch Sonja Henning perform in Chicago.

When a Wyoming Senator and the Athletic Director at U of W urged Theo's father to return to coach, he accepted, thinking his wife would be happier there among her family and the mountains she loved. Theo, a high school sophomore, was extremely upset and horribly reluctant to leave. She asked her dad if there was a city park in Laramie, and he said yes, right across the street, just like in Ames. Upon arriving at their house on the edge of town, she could see no park and asked her dad where it was.

"Right there," he said, sweeping his arm out at the sagebrush, rock, and high prairie with a horizon that melted into sky. "You can play out there to your heart's content."

Her mother took her to climb Long's Peak, on hikes in the Medicine Bow Range and camping in Estes Park. For a while, Theo's life was stable and content. Her father bought her younger sister Marty a horse. Susan, the middle-aged girl, became a genius of sorts in school, "the smartest of us all," as Theo said. A brother, Matt, was born and would follow in his father's footsteps as a renowned basketball player and coach.

Theo and her two sisters became well known as "The Strannigan Girls" at Laramie High School and the University of Wyoming. Theo was almost Queen of Everything. She led parades in her Angle Flight uniform and presided as royalty at formal dances. She graduated with a degree in English and was awarded Teacher of the Year in her first year at Laramie High School.

Her mother had begun to drink heavily again and left in her car for extended times. She was given shock treatments for depression, and when Theo was twenty-two, teaching in Cody, her mother got up from the dinner table in their Laramie home, went into the bathroom, locked the door, and hung herself in the shower.

Theo married a local Cody man shortly afterwards, had two

boys and drove a hundred miles to Billings, Montana every day during the week to acquire a master's degree in counseling.

After seven years of marriage, she decided to divorce. The Nikon she brought to me was one her husband had used to take pictures of automobile accidents and fires. Her sons, Bart and Matt, were four and two then. I immediately fell in love with her and her boys and made my proposal to marry her as soon as I could. As I said, she wanted time and space, so I backed off, telling her if she ever changed her mind to let me know. I had relationships with several women, but she was always floating in the back of my mind like a white cloud with a piece of my heart in it.

The lightning and thunder in this cloud was that she dated other men, and when I saw her with them in our small town, I didn't think my heart could take it. I medicated that feeling with marijuana, cocaine, and alcohol. I didn't let up even when she moved to Logan, Utah to pursue a Ph.D. in psychology. I began to deal to my friends to finance my habit, buying coke by the kilos in Steamboat Springs, Colorado, and selling it to break even with a free stash for myself.

We stayed in touch with letters and occasional visits in Logan and Jackson Hole campgrounds for the next two years.

Then in the spring of 1980, she called and asked if I still wanted to marry her. I told her yes, and she said she would travel to Cody that weekend so we could talk about it. In the morning, I dumped a quarter of an ounce of coke in the toilet. I never used the magic white again.

I sent my letter of resignation to the School Board that month, and in August, I moved to Logan, where Theo and I were married. I cashed in my retirement fund and we bought an old house in the country surrounded by dairy farms on the Bear River, and I worked at a cheese factory and K-Mart while Theo finished her Ph.D.

We just broke even selling the house and moved to Austin,

Texas where Theo interned at the University, and I taught woodshop to multi-handicapped students at The Texas School for the Deaf. Theo and I and the boys attended John Prine and Willy Nelson concerts, swam in the Pedernales, and fished from a canoe in the Colorado under the Congress Street bridge where thousands of bats emerged at sunset. I thought they were beautiful, and I never wanted to move from Austin.

Theo could have had a job at the University or anywhere in the country, and she chose Chester, Montana, a town of 840 people on the Hi-Line, about thirty miles from the Canadian border, where wheat farming, severe weather and isolation were the order of the universe. True to her nature, she wanted to serve a diverse population with great need and little support. She worked closely with, and became highly respected by, the town's one doctor, the sheriff, and police. Her clients ran the entire gamut of mental illness: depressed farmers and wives, alcoholics, drug addicts, abused Hutterite women, schizophrenics, sex offenders, and children. I never knew this until much later in our marriage. During her entire career, she never once told me the identity of a client, and only after 41 years of marriage did I realize the deep scope of her secret life.

Saying that it was her turn to support me, Theo encouraged me to apply to the MFA program in fiction writing at the University of Montana in Missoula. I had taken classes there from Richard Hugo and William Kittredge during my Bachelor of Arts years, and I had continuously written since, but was reluctant to be away from Theo and the boys. Theo cajoled me into doing all the paperwork to apply, and after being accepted, I decided I would drive to Chester, 172 miles from Missoula, on weekends, and she would occasionally bring the boys to Missoula.

It worked out well the first year. I won the Trans-Atlantic Henfield Award for short fiction and published several poems, but I tore my Achilles tendon while playing basketball, and during the six weeks I had to sit around in a cast, I began to drink heavily and smoke pot. It got worse during my second year, and by the time I had the degree, I was using marijuana and hitting a bottle of Irish whiskey every day. I won a Fellowship from the Montana Arts Council for the first two chapters of a novel, and they hired me as Writer-in-Residence for the State. Traveling to schools across Montana for the next year didn't help. I became intimate with every Podunk joint that served alcohol in the State, and I nearly killed two highway workers one night by slamming into their pilot car head-on. I'd been stopping at every bar between Kalispell and Lincoln. Fortunately, by the time a Highway Patrolman arrived, I had sobered up enough that he didn't even suspect I'd been drinking. Theo came to get me, and our car was hauled to Great Falls.

When we moved to Choteau, about a hundred miles from Chester, on the eastern front of the Rockies, I met A.B. Guthrie. He had won the Pulitzer for *The Way West* and had written the screenplay to *Shane*. I had taught *The Big Sky*, which I thought was his best book, in my Western Literature class at Cody High School, and a neighbor on Deep Creek gave me his first novel, which was horrible. A.B. had bought up all the copies he could to keep them out of circulation. I was smoking pot all day, every day, believing it helped the creative process. His failure encouraged me to hack out my novel without the smoke. When he died, his wife gave me a five-cent slot machine he had stored in a shed before the law raided the Elks Club in Great Falls during the Forties, and I was invited to be on a panel of writers honoring him with Richard Ford, Bill Kittredge, Ralph Beer, Mary Clearman Blew, and Jim Welch. I made one appearance and then skipped out to go pheasant hunting because I felt so unworthy and out of place.

I went to work for a wilderness outfitter in Augusta as camp cook, and when I came out of the Scapegoat after a month of hunting camp, I stayed drunk for three days, winding up in Helena. Theo felt our relationship was doomed and suggested we go to a drug and alcohol counselor. After taking his tests, I agreed to in-patient treatment for twenty-eight days. I never even realized I had a problem. Everyone else had a problem. But I entered the hospital for the duration because I didn't want to lose Theo and the boys.

During treatment, I was made aware of all the loss in my life up to that point. I counted thirteen close family members who had died, including my mother, father, and brother, and I found that I'd never learned what the grieving process was or that there was such a thing as healthy grieving. I'd just known that real men didn't cry.

I emerged wobbly, but with a new perspective. I attended AA meetings twice a week and started writing without the pot. It scared the hell out of me, but I soon found I could write just as well, if not better, without the weed. I took a job teaching at Blackfeet Community College in Browning, eighty miles north of Choteau.

I found a house on top of a mountain bordering Glacier National Park where I could live free of charge. Grizzly bear claw marks decorated the heavy wood front door, and I carefully walked around the place, especially at night and early morning. Again, I was driving back to Theo and the boys on weekends, but it wasn't that far, and I was attending AA meetings in Browning. The stories I heard there made me realize my problems were miniscule compared to the challenges many Native Americans face. I became good friends with several colleagues, attended religious ceremonies in sweats, and traveled to International Native American Education Conventions where I ran workshops and lectured. The students I had were older and grateful for help. Many were trying hard to remake their lives, just as I was.

I made the mistake of selecting Native American literature for my classes. We were reading *Love Medicine* by Louise Erdrich, and I could not prompt any discussion of it from the class. It's a powerful novel that starts with a rape at Easter and gets even more powerful as it proceeds. I finally said, "What's going on? Why don't you want to talk about this book?"

A woman said, "Well, no offense, but why do you want us to read it? There's nothing to say about it. It's just normal life. This stuff goes on all the time."

I realized I should have had them read *One Flew Over the Cuckoo's Nest* or *Stay Away Joe* and showed them the movies. Both would have given them something to say about Indian and White culture.

It took me a long time to get used to the wind there. I had compiled and edited anthologies of student writing from Arts Council residencies, the title of one coming from a poem a Browning fifth grader had written called *The Day the Wind Blew My Brother Away*. His brother had opened his coat at the top of the outside stairs before entering school, and the wind picked him up and threw him on the other side of an eight-foot fence next to the school.

But I had no idea of the wind's power until one of my colleagues told me it had blown a train off its tracks. I didn't believe him, of course, but it happened again below my house on the mountain. From my experience working on railroad gangs, I couldn't verify that faulty rail rather than wind had caused the wreck, but grain spilled from upturned cars and fermented, getting three grizzlies drunk and killed by another train.

One day a student came into class late, and I asked him what had happened. He was usually there early.

"Sorry," he said. "My house blew away."

He was not joking. When I went out to see where his home had been, nothing remained but a concrete pad and twisted pipes and wires. The rest was scattered for miles across the prairie.

I came to admire and respect the Blackfeet people and their countryside so much that I asked Theo if she would consider moving to Browning or East Glacier. We were thinking about it when a Cody hospital board member called her to ask if she would consider moving back to Cody. She turned him down twice without asking what her salary would be. and finally accepted when they told her it was more than we were both making. I got a job teaching English.

Theo worked as the hospital's psychologist, but sexual harassment charges against an administrator came to a lawsuit. Theo could have been in on the settlement, but she chose to stay out of it except as a witness. I had strongly urged her to keep a record of incidents that she had, and she did. Her boss moved on, and a psychiatrist she worked well with was hired, but problems there eventually emerged. After eleven years of this, Theo came home one night and shook her index finger at me. This was serious. I had seen it before.

"In one year," she said, "I want to be out of the hospital and doing something different."

I had started a newspaper class and a television production class at the high school. My students were winning national awards at every Journalism Education Association Convention, and I became the JEA's director of Broadcast Journalism. But Theo wanted out, so I began looking at overseas schools online. Kwajalein popped up. It turned out to be one of the Marshall Islands in the Pacific where a battle had been fought in WWII, and was now used as a target for Reagan's International Missile Defense.

They fired dummy missiles from Vandenburg Air Force Base in California that flew eight miles per second at the largest lagoon in the world, and the physics brains on Kwajalein tried to shoot them down. When I was twenty-one, I made a list of twenty-one things I wanted to do in life, and living on an island for a year was one of them, but I was also intrigued by many other schools who wanted a psychologist and an English teacher. When we went to an international job fair in Waterloo, Iowa, the Superintendent at Kwajalein took us to dinner and offered us both jobs before the fair even started. After interviewing at five other schools, we had offers at each one, so we drove to Ames to think over our possibilities, and Theo showed me the house she had lived in across the street from her park and the old gym where her dad had coached basketball. Big pillars stood in the middle of the stands, and Theo said she used to sit behind them with her fingers crossed behind her back. That brought her dad good luck. Now, as we looked down at the gym floor, it was sectioned into computer cubicles where ISU employees worked. We attended a woman's game in the new gym, and when I talked with a few old timers wearing Cyclone shirts, they remembered her dad well and directed us to a bust of him in one of the alcoves above the stands. As we stood there, Theo said she wanted to take the Marshall Islands offer.

I was granted a one-year Leave of Absence from the high school, and Theo resigned from the hospital. One of the Marshall Islands, where the first hydrogen bomb had been detonated on Bikini Atoll, Kwajalein is a crescent shaped island a half mile wide by two and a half miles long, at the bottom of one of the largest lagoons in the world, 839 square miles. It sits 2,100 miles from Hawaii and another 2,100 to Japan, surrounded by 2.5 million square miles of Pacific Ocean. We had to undergo intense background checks by local law enforcement, the FBI, the CIA, and I don't know who else. Men showed up in Cody to interview our neighbors. I thought that with my past, there was no chance in hell I would pass.

But I must not have posed too much of a threat, because we were soon flying out of Hickam Air Force Base on a C130 Hercules in seats facing the tail that dropped down to unload pallets of supplies and vehicles. I walked up to the cockpit where the pilots handed me headphones and gave me a seat with a view that changed my whole perspective on the world. Theo and I had flown across the Pacific to New Zealand, but the view from that flight had not given me the overpowering sense of awe at the earth the C130 did.

My classroom was open windowed to the lagoon. Lizards and geckos ran across the floor and up the walls. Students wore shorts, tank tops and flipflops. With a hundred inches of rain on the island a year, my students covered their feet with plastic grocery sacks as they pedaled their bicycles to school so the coral dust and rainwater would not splash onto their feet and legs. They were rocket scientists' kids, and any misbehavior on their part would get their entire family kicked back to the U.S., but even though the security at the airport was tight, they figured ways to smuggle in marijuana and drank alcohol by the quarts on weekends. They were bored out of their minds.

But they were brilliant. Under my supervision, the students started a weekly newspaper called *Enan Eo*, *The Talk* in Marshallese, which engaged their creativity and brought excitement and compliments from everybody on the island. People said it was better than *The Hour Glass* which was published every week by the Public Affairs Office of the Army.

At seven degrees latitude, every morning at six Theo and I walked with our coffee to the beach to watch the sun come up over the ocean, and most evenings at six, from our hammock between two palm trees, we watched the sun go down. Quite content with snorkeling in the lagoon, Theo was afraid to scuba, but I convinced her to get her Open Water Certificate, and after receiving her Advanced Certificate, it soon became her favorite sport. She was the best dive partner one could ask for, always attentive to her surroundings, hardly using any air and enjoying the calm floating feeling of neutral buoyancy. She was more relaxed than I'd ever known her to be. She especially enjoyed night diving, when the coral lit up in our underwater lights like a million Christmas trees. She did not like sharks, and would get behind me, grabbing onto my tank and moaning through her regulator whenever they got too close, but she overcame that fear after we made over a hundred dives.

After two years there, the island became too small for us, though we made trips to outlying islands, Hawaii, and the Continent. We returned to Cody in 2001, where my job was waiting for me, and Theo went into private practice. The World Trade Center was attacked in September, and we learned that Kwajalein went into a lockdown.

She enjoyed great success in private practice after returning from Kwaj, and I had my old job back, continuing to be active in State and National scholastic journalism associations. We had saved quite a bit of money, and we bought the Yellowstone farm in 2007.

In 2018, when Theo was diagnosed with Stage 4 metastasized breast cancer, I asked her what the happiest years of our marriage had been, and she said without pause, "Kwajalein."

Regrets

Bill lived about a year and a half after he sold the place to me, off his prediction by six months. I was not entirely sure what happened, but as best as I could piece it together, he tripped on his dog, and after driving to town "to get checked," he was advised to stay in the hospital overnight. During his recuperating stage in the hospital, as I heard the story, he tried to get out of bed on his own to go to the bathroom, and his wheelchair rolled away from him, causing him to fall and break his hip. It was downhill from there, with pneumonia setting in, and he died on April 5, 2009. I regretted that I did not make it to his funeral. I was responsible for fourteen of my students who had paid for a trip to a national journalism convention in Phoenix several months before. The best I could do was send flowers and a note to the family, although I felt like it was a measly effort.

During the time Bill lived in the house, I visited him at least once a month, but I never felt like I should start work on the place while he was living there, even though he told me to go ahead, and I never stayed in the house, even though he always offered me a bedroom.

"After all, you own the place," he said. I did not want to invade his privacy. Although it was clear that he enjoyed my company, often telling me how lonely he was, I also got the distinct feeling he just wanted to be left alone.

I only ate one meal with him, a breakfast of sourdough pancakes and my home-made chokecherry syrup, with a few antelope steaks his son Dan had given him. I was surprised at how little he ate and came to realize much of the pheasant, elk liver, trout, and goose I brought him just stayed in the freezer, or he gave it away, while he lived mostly on oatmeal and canned Vita-milk.

In June of 2008 I brought five video production students to the house to tape an interview with him. We were producing a documentary on the Matthew Quigley Long Range Buffalo Rifle Shoot, held every Father's Day at the Lee ranch north of Forsyth. Among the students was Chynna, a senior whose talent ranked her as the most popular anchor in the history of "CHS Wired," a TV news show I started in 1997. Bill had no problems with the cameras and lights — he warmed to Chynna quickly, reciting poetry, telling war stories, and like a true sailor, playing his harmonica.

About halfway through the interview, I noticed that Chynna was crying, but I didn't say anything until afterwards, when I asked her what had happened.

"He was so sad," she said. "I mean he was so cute, and he reminded me of my grandpa, and the whole thing was just so sad."

I never saw anything sad about it. It was the most animated I had ever seen Bill.

He told several boxing stories, one of which entailed walking several miles to the Mees brothers' place to box them because they were rich enough in those Depression days to have gloves. I knew the family, several of their clan living in Cody, and they were all big and strong. The brothers would invariably punch the hell out of Bill, creating in him a competitive desire to return. His toughness and determination reminded me of James Braddock, so one weekend I brought my laptop computer and a DVD of "Cinderella Man".

I cued the DVD and handed him the laptop. He took it, holding it in the air as if I had given him a newborn alien.

"What is this?" he asked.

"You can watch the movie I told you about on it," I said. "Just set it on your lap."

After I pushed "Play," he sat engrossed and unmoving for the entire film, afraid to move or touch the computer. At the end, I asked him what he thought of it.

"It's the darnedest thing I've ever seen," he said, handing the laptop back to me as though he were a priest offering the Eucharist chalice. He had just jumped light-years in technology. He had been born in 1911.

"But what about the movie?" I asked. "What did you think of it?"

"Well, it was a fine picture show," he said. "Braddock was a slugger. He had no style. Just a tough slugging dockworker. But I don't like the way they portrayed Max Baer. He wasn't that way."

"What way?"

"He took care of the widows of those guys he killed in the ring for the rest of their lives. He paid for their kids' education and sent them checks every month," he said, visibly irritated by the philandering image Ron Howard had given Baer. "He felt terrible about it, but his punch was just so devastating."

I didn't want to argue with him about the historical accuracy of Baer's life, so I told him I had sat next to Max Baer, Jr. on an airplane when I was a sophomore in high school. He had played Jethro Bodine on the "Beverly Hillbillies."

"He wore a lime green V-neck sweater," I said, "and he smoked a long thin cigar."

Bill looked at me as though my swerving in the conversation had gone a hundred miles south of the road.

"He didn't mean to kill those guys," he said. "He wasn't that way."

I knew then Bill was familiar with haunting regret, that he might have identified more with Baer than I knew, and he was a forgiving man because of it, although he was as tough minded as they come. While captain of the guard at Montana State Prison, rioters broke through several cellblocks into his office and demanded the keys to the outside. Bill pulled the keys out of his desk drawer and threw them out the window rather than give them up.

After reading about the episode in several Montana newspapers, I wondered why they hadn't killed him and heard from a reliable source that they had liked him too much. He evidently had established various recreational venues for them that they greatly appreciated, and he treated them as fairly as he could.

In my last conversation with him, Bill asked me several questions about my wife Theo, how her psychology practice was going, how we met, and how we got along. He had met her only once, and he liked her, as everybody did.

"I hope you are good to her," he said. "I have nightmares about how I treated Winnie." And then after a long pause, he said with a tone mixed with disgust and sadness, "Of course, when I got out of the Navy, I was half psycho."

I waited a while to hear if he would say anything else, but he was silent. From what friends who knew him well had told me, he had never physically abused Winnie, so I assumed his regret resembled my own painful awareness of my past with alcohol and drugs during the first seven years of my marriage. Remembering Theo's unswerving loyalty and support, I said, "Well, everybody who is human has regrets."

He sighed, and after a few minutes said, "I shouldn't have sold this place to you."

"Why?" I asked.

He didn't offer anything more.

Ghosts

When the family came to the house for Bill's possessions, they left the appliances, which were in the contract as part of the sale, some furniture, and miscellaneous collections of sporting goods, canned foods, and tools. They didn't venture far into the buffalo hunter's cabin, the little shed next to it that served as Bill's shop, or the chicken coop constructed of railroad ties, all three packed wall-to-wall and six feet high with years of aggregate Bill could not throw away. They gave me several of their mother's paintings, perfect Americana pieces I felt honored to have, as well as Bill's Stetson and one of his knives. The women were trying to clean the kitchen when I told them not to spend the energy — my plan was to gut the house and start from scratch anyway.

I made myself scarce, leaving them to the privacy of whatever family dynamics had long ago been established. It was none of my business.

Dave, the oldest, a retired teacher, superintendent of schools, and author of several historical books about Montana, was the most talkative. Dan, the youngest, lived and worked in Forsyth, and I garnered that he occupied a particularly soft spot in Bill's heart because of Dan's "terrible experiences in Viet Nam," as Bill had offered to me.

After the family left, I found Dan's Marine trunk with his uniform, medals, and Life magazines from 1968 in the attic, and I took it to him, but he didn't want it.

"Mother kept that stuff," he said. "It doesn't mean anything to me."

I told him I'd give his uniform and medals to his daughter, but that I would like to have the Life magazines for my Mass Communications class.

"They've never seen any magazines from that era," I said. "They'll love them."

"If you can get some good out of them with those kids," he said, "you are welcome to them."

"Don't you want to look at them?" I asked. "The pictures of Khe Sanh and Pleiku are incredible."

"No," he laughed. "I was on Hills 881 South and North at Khe Sanh. I have plenty of pictures in my head."

I'd read about the 1967 Battles for Khe Sanh. In a siege that lasted almost three months, 20,000 North Vietnamese Army troops had surrounded about 5,000 Marines. The valor shown by the Marines struck me as nothing but monumental, and while talking with Dan, my old feelings of ambiguity, confusion, sadness, and anger from those years washed up in me. I'd been attending college on a basketball scholarship while he'd been caught in a meat grinding hell I couldn't imagine.

"Why didn't you want the Rosebud place?" I asked.

"Too many memories," he said. "Too many ghosts."

I wondered if they were just his ghosts, or if they were waiting for me too.

The Attic

"Start at the top and work down," H.R. had said. "Go in the attic." Good advice, I discovered.

At the apex of the roof, directly above my head, the football-sized brown clusters of the furry little critters pulsed and rippled. I closed the access door and backed down the ladder. I looked closely at the black droppings. Their elongated and segmented shape, tapered at the ends, would become too familiar.

Now what? I thought. I have no idea.

After a few minutes of telling myself no one was coming to my rescue, I crawled up again with my flashlight, pushed the access door aside and scanned the whole attic while holding my breath. I saw at least five clusters, and the guano rose several inches above the joists, blanketing the attic floor like a black quilt. Several bats became agitated with the light and fluttered around their communal mass. They squeaked and chittered at an increasing rate.

I knew nothing about bats. My grandmother told me they could get caught in my hair. I caught one on a fly line once while fishing at night. On my back cast, there was a thunk. I thought I had hooked a tree at first, but it was different. I beat it to death by grabbing the line and whipping it on the rocks, then cut the tippet. I used to find dead ones in windowsills of the old Alexander house in Forsyth before they tore it down. Alexander was one of the town's forefathers. He died from a lightning strike, which augmented the common belief that the abandoned Victorian house was haunted, so we kids had to go in there. I picked up a few dead bats and took them to school, where my second-grade teacher told me I could get rabies from handling them.

Bats had flown within inches of my face while fishing in a float tube as evenings arrived at various ponds, and they had flown around Theo and me as we watched Shakespeare plays in an outdoor theater in Ashland, Oregon.

That was about all I knew concerning bats. Except for the vampires. When I was in Mexico, I heard about vampire bats sucking the blood out of babies and goats at night. I never verified it, but several farmers I met claimed it was true. One old Mayan told me the story of Popol Vuh, how he was decapitated by a bat named Camazotz, a big meat eater with blades on its wings.

I asked around, "How do you get rid of bats in your attic?"

One local told me he'd go up there and suck them into a big vacuum cleaner.

"That'll be fun", he said, "I can just hear them plunking into that canister."

Several people told me to put mothballs up there. "They won't come back," they said. "They hate mothballs."

"Sulfur candles. That'll get 'em."

"Use electromagnetic ultrasound."

A woman who knew my mother told me to spray them with water. "They'll leave in a hurry," she said.

One old timer who grew up out north by my dad had a biologic strategy. "Get a bull snake," he said. "Put it up there, and it'll eat all of 'em. Take care of the mice too."

After listening to these and several other remedies, I was skeptical and called about ten pest exterminators, finally finding one who would handle bats, a guy I called Batman Biff.

At first, he tried to talk me into waiting until after July because of the baby bats.

"It's still a bit early," he said, "but if they have pups in there, they will die. You don't want a bunch of dead baby bats on your hands."

I told him I needed to get started on renovating the house, that I didn't give a damn about the baby bats. I just wanted them all gone as soon as possible and asked him about the various methods I'd heard. He scoffed at them.

"I don't know about you," he said, "but I don't think I want to be in an attic with a vacuum cleaner or a hose and a bunch of pissed off bats."

"So, what's the strategy then?" I asked.

"Well," he finally said, "the first thing you need to do is find where they are exiting the house in the evening. There might be several spots. Try to get a count on how many leave. Watch the place for three or four nights."

I couldn't be there, having commitments in Cody, so I enlisted my niece, her husband and their son and daughter, to go on Bat Patrol. I also asked my friend Jack Ferguson if he'd give it a looksee.

During the first night of standing around in the tall grass, they were covered with ticks, and they counted at least sixty bats flitting out of the attic around the chimney Bill had built on the east side of the house, the one H.R. said had to go. About ten or fifteen more crawled out and flew from the screened porch where the ceiling had rotted and fallen. They used flashlights, and the bats did not like that. They paused and chattered when they emerged. One winged Jack in the shoulder.

"It came right at me," he said, "whacked the top of my arm here on my shoulder." He was wearing a Levi jacket, so nothing penetrated his skin. I told them to stop the Watch and called Batman Biff.

"That's unusual," he said of Jack's incident. "They're incredibly expert flyers, so it must have been highly irritated to brush him like that. They have a claw on their thumb they use for climbing, handling their food, and grooming. It might have brushed him with one, or it might have been trying to bite him. A lot of people never even know they are bitten. Lucky it didn't hit him on the ear."

He had a look around the house as I showed him the exit points the Bat Patrol observed, and after looking in the attic, he said the good news was he didn't see any pups yet or sick ones flopping around erratically. The bad news was there were a lot of them. He got his ladder off his truck, and we carried it around to the east chimney.

"The majority of them are using this chimney point," he said, showing me the pile of guano at the base of it. "And they've been in this house a long time."

After getting on the roof, he told me whoever built the chimney did not flash it correctly. There was a three-inch gap between it and the roof.

"All they need is a three-eighths inch gap," he said, "about the width of a pencil."

I thought of Bill. He must have built the chimney after he had the roof replaced, or the roofers did not flash it right.

Biff began duct taping around the opening and ran a two-inch flexible hose from the opening into a little box with a plastic, S-shaped tube inside. The box had small circular screens on the sides, and he nailed it to the roof.

"They follow airflow," he explained. "The screens on the box allow for that. They'll crawl out their regular access, down the hose and fall through the plastic tube. Once in the box, they won't be able to get back up the slick tube."

"They don't like change," he said, "but a lot of them will come out tonight. You'll hear them plop into the box through the tube, so stand out here just before sunset and count how many plops you hear for a couple hours."

He fashioned another box on the outside of the porch and taped several holes so they would have to use the only opening available.

"Call me tomorrow to let me know how many we have in the boxes," he said, and got in his truck.

"DO NOT try to remove those boxes yourself," he warned, "just count how many bats you hear going into them."

"Don't worry," I said. "Messing with those boxes is the last thing I'd do."

I sprayed myself with insect repellant to ward off the ticks and mosquitos and stood at the southeast corner of the house just before sunset. It was only a few minutes before I heard the first plop in the box by the chimney. Then more in a staccato beat — five, ten, up to thirty-two, and it stopped. A few fell into the porch box, then six more. I shined my flashlight on the box, and I could see them through the screens. They chattered and flapped around.

I'll be damned, I thought. *It's working.*

Biff returned the next day and slid a gate over the opening to the hoses, removed the boxes and brought them down. He showed me the night's catch — they lay motionless for the most part, crawling a bit and chittering.

Hairy little devils, I thought. *We got your asses.*

He put on thick gloves, opened the gate to one of the boxes, shook it and caught one in his hand, then closed the gate.

"Look at this," he said. "See the blood on her vagina?"

He held her by the back, stretching a wing with his other hand. I saw the drop of blood around the opening in her fur and wondered what menstruation would be like while hanging upside down.

But Biff said it was most likely not menstruation. Bats copulate in September or October, just before hibernation, or even during hibernation for some, and the female holds the sperm in her uterus until spring, when fertilization occurs as the sperm becomes motile and the eggs are ovulated. Delayed fertilization or ovulation, as the bat experts call it, allows for about a two-month gestation period so the pups are born in early summer, when insects are abundant. The blood on this female was probably from a failed pregnancy or a recent birth, both very rare at this time of year.

"They'll start having their pups in a few weeks," he said. "And will continue into July. I didn't see any pups in the attic yet, and that's good, because they can't fly for several weeks, and the mothers need to nurse them."

"How are you going to kill them?"

"It's up to you," he said. "It's not illegal in Montana, but it's the wrong thing to do if you can help it. This little thing will eat up to a thousand mosquitos in an hour. And she only weighs about seven grams."

"And from the looks of the attic," I said, "she can shit fourteen grams."

He explained how he could set up a bat house close by, so the maternal colony wouldn't be more stressed than it was, and I would still have the benefits of their being around.

"I need to find a south facing pole or tree with plenty of sunlight," he said. "You might have them hanging from your soffit for a while, but they'll eventually use the houses."

"I don't want them hanging anywhere but from a noose," I said. "Get them the hell out of here."

"Well, if you feel that way," he said, "I'd have to take them at least fifty miles from here. They can easily fly that far in a night, and they will be back otherwise."

"Take them to Alaska," I said.

"They might just become a problem for other people if I displace them," he said. "And they'd be messed up."

"Messed up?"

"Disoriented. They wouldn't know where they are."

"I want them dismembered," I said.

He laughed and said, "Yes, I understand. They have to come out of there. You most likely have a problem with your roof beams too."

"What?"

"Their urine. It softens the wood."

Well that's just great, I thought.

"And remember this," he said. "Once a bat house, always a bat house. No matter how clean you get the house, you must make it tight as a drum or you will have them back."

Over the next few days, he managed to get about sixty bats out of the house, and there were no pups yet. He guaranteed that no more would get in the attic, but he didn't know about the porch. He said they could use too many entry points there, with the torn screens on the windows and the house's south chimney running down inside it.

"You might have a real problem with that chimney," he said.

Bill had tightly covered the fireplace in the living room by taping plastic around it and covering it with rolls of pink fiberglass insulation. I hadn't taken it off yet to see what was under it.

"I think something broke in there," Bill had said. "It started pouring smoke out one night when I had a fire going, so it must be blocked or something."

"And one more thing," Batman Biff said. "I noticed bat bugs around the opening they were using."

"Bat bugs?"

"They're a parasite on bats," he said, and he took me upstairs to the bedroom Bill used before he couldn't make it up the stairs. He searched the wall by the ceiling, directly in front of where the east chimney went up the outside of the house.

"Right here," he said, picking a bug off the wall. "This is a bat bug, and it's full of blood."

It was about the size of a big tick with a red abdomen. He pinched it between his thumb and forefinger, the bat blood popping out. Almost identical to a bed bug, the bat bug never evolved to dine primarily on humans like the bed bug did after the humans left the cave, or so the theory goes, he explained, and while they certainly might not be averse to a few sips of Homo Sapiens protein, they prefer Chiropteran's.

"How do I get rid of those?" I asked.

"Spray everything with Tempo SC Ultra," he said. "Wear goggles, a good respirator mask, rubber gloves, and a full bio suit. Do NOT get it in your eyes. Wait at least twenty-four hours before you go in the room again. I would spray the entire upstairs and attic, and after you tear out the ceiling and walls, spray it again."

"And where do I get that stuff?"

"Most feed stores. It is about forty-seven bucks a pint. Double the recommended strength — five ounces to a gallon."

Wonderful, I thought. *The blood in my head fell to my feet. How much more of this will I need to fight?*

"And I'd get rid of those swallow nests under the north soffit," he added. "They can carry as many pests as bats. People think it's cool to have a bird nest next to their window, but they don't realize how many pests can invade their house from it."

I did not admit I liked having about thirty Cliff Swallows' mud-daubed nests on the north side of the house. I'd always admired their fighter jet acrobatics, and I loved watching them swoop into the nests' openings.

"One more thing," he said. "I would call a disaster restoration company to remove all that guano in the attic."

"I can just vacuum it out myself," I said.

"Not worth it," he said. "It's rare in Montana, but you can get histoplasmosis from a fungus that grows in the guano. You need a mask that filters at least two microns, and the amount up there is just too much for you to handle. You'll take the mask off every time you come down with a full vacuum canister, and that will increase your risk of exposure. Hire the pros to do that — they have the big equipment, and they follow the correct precautions."

"Histoplasmosis."

"Yeah. Dry cough, fever, vision problems, organ failure

sometimes, and death."

Now I was afraid, I realized, but I had always told my students not to be afraid of being afraid, and that idea fortified me. I would learn how to deal with this.

I called my stepson Matt, who had become a virologist doing post-doctoral research at Princeton, to ask him about the Batman's suggestions.

"What do you think?" I asked. "Histoplasmosis?"

"Not only that," he said. "Eighty viruses have been identified in guano. They've traced the Ebola virus to a bat cave in Africa. It's bad shit, no pun intended."

I saw that Matt had not lost his sense of humor since his immersion in academia, but it sobered me. I did not want to pay somebody to run a vacuum. But Ebola?

"It's a simple virus," Matt said, "but a subtle one." He talked about genomes and glycoproteins, how Ebola tricks cells into making them produce the proteins it needs — ones that trigger the immune system to create what he calls a "cytokine storm" — blood vessels leak, organs fail, blood pressure and core temperature drop, and the body goes into shock.

I'd always been amused at Matt's love for and admiration of viruses. "They are the smartest things on the planet," he would say. Ever since he was a little boy, he exhibited a brilliant mind, so it did not surprise me that he chose to study what he considered the most intelligent life form.

"Ebola actually was first found in a nun's blood sample from Yambuku," he told me. "But the Antwerp virologists named it after a local river, the Ebola, to keep from stigmatizing Zaire."

"Well, that helps," I said. "Remind me not to become a nun in Yambuku."

"It's not funny," Matt said. "Get the pros to take care of it. Bats carry more zoonotic viruses than rodents."

Zoonotic?

"Animal diseases communicable to humans," he said. "But rodents have twice as many species, so you should be careful of them too."

"How many species of bats are there?"

"I'm not sure," he said. "I think somewhere between nine and twelve hundred."

I readily accepted that he knew what he was talking about. I realized how smart he was when he was about eight and claimed he couldn't afford the time to mow the lawn. It was during my time in graduate school in Missoula all week, coming home on weekends to Chester, where Theo worked in Community Mental Health. She'd asked me to talk to him about shirking his chores, which included mowing.

"So, your mother tells me you refuse to mow the lawn," I'd said.

"Yeah," he said. "I don't have time."

"What do you have to do that is more important?" I asked.

"Practice basketball," he said.

"You think practicing basketball is more important than doing your chores?" I said, using the paraphrasing-rather-than-blaming skills I'd recently learned in a parenting class. "How is that?"

Well," he said, as though trying to explain to a dummkopf, "you played basketball in college, didn't you?"

"Yes," I said.

"And you wanted to play pro, didn't you?

"Well," I said, "of course, but I wasn't good enough."

"And you mowed lawns when you were a kid, right?"

"Yes," I said. "That's how I earned any money I had. That and shoveling snow."

"Well," he said, "that's where you went wrong. You should have practiced basketball more instead of mowing lawns and shoveling snow. Then you would have been good enough to play pro."

I eventually won that Socratic dialogue, but I decided to take his advice on the guano, so I hired a restoration company out of

Billings to get rid of it. Three guys brought a vacuum on the bed of a one-ton truck, and they ran six-inch hoses through an upstairs window to the attic. Two of them wore bio-suits, rubber gloves, goggles, and masks. I couldn't see any part of their bodies. The other guy ran the hoses into bags twelve feet long and three feet in diameter. They filled four bags and got ready to haul it away.

"You have to have a special permit to dispose of it," the guy on the ground said.

One of the boys in the suits told me the rafter joists were discolored from bat urine, and they would need to be sanded down to the bare wood or replaced, depending on how deep the rot was.

"I scraped a couple of them just to see, and they weren't too bad, but who knows about all of them?" he said. "Do you want us to take care of it?"

"I imagine that would get pretty pricey."

"Oh yeah," he said. "It would be what they call labor intensive."

I decided to use a hand sander and do it myself. I thanked them for a great job, paid them $1,500, another deposit in the money pit, and they left me with a half-way clean attic, at least one I could enter.

I realized after they were gone that I needed a porta-potty, one of those fiberglass outhouses. Every time I took a crap in the grass around the place and buried it, squirrels or raccoons dug it up, and I had ticks crawling up my legs. Anyone who worked on the place would need one too, so I rented one from Miles City at a hundred dollars a month. I figured each dump would cost me about five dollars and fifty cents.

That night at the poker table in Buff's Bar I told the story about the guano. Two notorious potheads in the game responded.

"You got guano?" one said. "Why didn't you tell us?"

"It's the best fertilizer in the world for weed."

"They sell that stuff on the internet for ten bucks an ounce."

"Maaaaan, why didn't you tell us? We would have done it for

nothing!"

"How about the stuff in my porta-potty?" I asked them. "What will you give me for that?"

They wondered about it for a few seconds, and finally one said, "Nah, too many chemicals in it."

I told them I was hurt that they did not appreciate my efforts to help.

Kenny

H.R. gratefully noticed the porta-potty's addition when he arrived from Cody, but he wondered if any wasps had established residency in it, so he carefully opened the door to peek inside before committing his trust to it.

He brought a kid named Kenny to get the demolition started before we renovated. He lined out the work we needed to do, left Kenny with me, and I paid for our motel rooms in Miles City at the Red Rock. I was buying his meals and paying him fifteen dollars an hour.

"He's a great worker," H.R. said. "He's had some trouble, but he's getting his life straightened around, and he'll work like hell for you."

A skinny, dark haired twenty-three-year-old, about five feet, seven inches tall, Kenny was oddly handsome, like an emaciated Errol Flynn, a few years past being a dashing swashbuckler. He had that strong Flynn jaw and quick energy, but just as Errol's self-destructive drunkenness left him dead at fifty, Kenny's visage made me wonder how long he had left. He sported a thin, scraggly goatee and ran everywhere he went — up the stairs, down the stairs, from the pickup to the restaurant, as if he were on a mission to rescue some damsel in a castle keep. I didn't know of what mother his energy was born and suspected methamphetamine or a desire to escape thought.

He said he had been a meth head, as well as an alcoholic. Most of his upper teeth were missing, and the ones intact were rotted down and black.

"I haven't had a drink in three months," he said, grinning at me.

He was sent to reform school at fifteen for burglarizing cars, and he talked like he might be a good mechanic — he loved old cars and wanted to restore them.

I took him to breakfast at Gallagher's for sausage and biscuits, but he just drank a Mountain Dew and wasn't hungry until 8 p.m. after working hard all day.

Miles City was celebrating its 125th anniversary that weekend with a parade, a street dance, and all kinds of picnics. Two rodeo queens, a blonde and a brunette, gorgeous girls with glistening hair, big hats, sparkling belts, champion buckles, tight Wranglers and fitted western shirts, walked into the 600 Café while we were eating dinner. Kenny bounced in his booth bench as they walked by and craned his neck and torso around to follow them with his eyes.

"What do you think you'd need to get into that?" I asked.

"A little vodka," he said.

"Is that all?" I laughed. "I thought maybe you'd need a yacht or a big ranch."

"Well, money helps," he said.

"Would you need the vodka for you or for them?"

"For them. I don't have any confidence anymore, vodka or not. Now everybody's into real white teeth, and I don't have anything but black nubs," he said. "I just don't even try with women anymore."

He said he had smoked meth every weekend for about a year. His teeth began to hurt, and he chipped at them with his fingernails. He raised his upper lip so I could see — they looked like Indian corn in several stages of rot.

"I can't believe how stupid I was," he said.

When I asked him how he got started on it, he said it was a long story, but it involved long-haul trucking and a twenty-three-year-old stripper.

He was working on a dental credit plan to get his teeth pulled, "saving my money," he said, "no cigarettes or booze in three months. Thirty days in jail for my second DUI made me think how I didn't want any more of that. I did NOT like that place."

He admitted to still smoking a little pot, "but only at home because I get bored, and it helps with my anger."

"I'm workin' on it," he said, "but I still don't know why I get so angry."

"I'm pissed off about ninety percent of the time," I said.

"At what?" he asked.

"People," I said. "I feel like killing someone just about every day."

"Why?"

"Read the news," I said. "Just read the paper."

"Maybe you should stop reading it," he said, laughing. "I'm a bad reader. It's just not something I do. But I have a pit bull, and I love spending time with him. He's the best thing in my life."

"Is he mean?" I asked.

"People whose dogs are mean are just plain stupid," he said. "Like the guy in Cody whose pit bull chased a horse around until it died. I love dogs, and if you love them, they won't be mean."

When we got back to Cody, I stopped at my house for a copy of *Call of the Wild* for him. I explained the plot, and he grew excited, saying he would start it that night.

At his house, he showed me his dog, Kato Kaelin, who must have weighed as much as Kenny and acted like a puppy, all wag, licking my hands and face and wanting to cuddle.

"Why Kato?" I asked.

"After that O.J. Simpson dude," he said. "Some dumb ass friends were feeding beer to my first dog named Kato, and he fell off a cliff and died. So, I traded this dumb ass woman a quarter ounce of weed for this one — that's how much she thought of him — and I just named him Kato too."

He had a Camaro he put Lamborghini doors on — showed me the 350 engine — and a Suburban jacked up with huge tires. The battery was dead in the Camaro, and the Suburban needed a new transmission.

I saw several young girls smoking on the porch of his mom's trailer and asked who they were.

"I don't even know who's in there," he said, "and I don't even want to go in. I can see I'm going to take a long walk with Kato."

Julie and the Buffalo Hunter

At home, I read an e-mail from my principal that one of my former students had died. At nineteen years-old, she collapsed in front of her house after midnight. A strikingly beautiful girl with extremely high intelligence, she had taken three classes from me. She was born with heart and lung problems and needed transplants for both. When she found that most heart-lung transplant patients only lived an additional one to two years, all of it bedbound, she opted not to get on the waiting list.

"I was struck by the pride and courage in that," a colleague who knew her well said, "but I was affected more by the fierce realism in it, probably bred from the painful cycle of hope and disappointment she must have experienced so many times."

She was not to do anything remotely strenuous in my classes — not even carry her books from class to class. She was supposed to take the elevator, not walk the stairs.

I was always fearful for her and scolded her several times for carrying her backpack full of books, which weighed more than she did. I was supposed to pick her up and carry her out the building during a fire drill, which I did, and she joked about carrying her across the threshold before we were married. Her mother always accompanied her on field trips, and I often took her out of class because she was too pale and exhausted.

But she downplayed her condition, and when I asked her how she remained so optimistic and cheerful, she shrugged her shoulders.

"I just live one day at a time," she said.

"You mean one minute," I said.

She grinned, her smile and eyes model perfect.

She didn't want to do the video autobiography assignment in Mass Communications and was willing to take a zero on it, even though she was a straight-A student. I finally understood she didn't want to have the other students in the class know about her condition, so I made a deal with her that only I would watch it. She kept the only copy. I still remember her face looking straight at the camera and saying she just didn't think about bad things in life.

I was more seriously depressed about her death than I understood. Back at the farm, while cleaning out the old buffalo hunter's cabin, I was thinking the existential nihilists had it right, that life has no meaning or purpose and that I was insignificant. I was overcome by those old feelings of isolation, uselessness, and despondency so familiar to me from my high school years. Even though I'd been a decent athlete and excellent student, taking care of my invalid grandmother and paying our expenses with only our Social Security checks took its toll. My brother had cashed in the AT&T stock my mother had accumulated for me to attend college, laughing in my face when I asked him to pay it back. I could not afford a ten-dollar pair of shoes for basketball my senior year, so I was ready to go to work after school and not play, but I found an old pair someone had discarded in the locker room, and I repaired them with athletic tape. My coach finally bought me a new pair.

The struggle I had then seemed nothing against Julie's, which contributed to a greater sadness in me rather than awakening a gratitude for what I had. I suppose I was ashamed of myself for falling into self-pity, but in the buffalo hunter's cabin, the weariness in my heart circled back to those years. When I scooped a Santa Claus pillow into my shovel, it fell apart, rotten, wet, moldy, and covered in mouse or rat or bat dung, or a combination of all three, and thousands of little plastic beads spilled out of Santa's belly off the scoop. His head collapsed onto the dirt floor, and I acutely wondered for the first time what in the hell I was doing. I was fifty-nine years old, and I could barely endure the utter frustration of the task, let alone the risk of contracting Hantavirus, or any of the various parasites and viruses associated with bats.

I was wearing a mask, the Darth Vader type Batman Biff recommended, goggles, a white, full-body biohazard jumpsuit and leather gloves. I had sprayed the whole corner where Santa lay with a strong solution of chlorine and water, but Biff the Batman had told me, "Hantavirus lasts FOREVER."

"Treat every turd like it has Hantavirus," he had said, "and you'll be OK."

There were piles of turds mounded like the Taj Mahal on everything in the cabin. It was a sixteen by twelve-foot, pine-log frontier cabin, eight logs high. I had to duck to go under the cross logs. The outside had been worked flat with an adze, and the corners were double dovetailed. It was in amazing shape, with a huge river-stone fireplace and the original bubbled glass door with an iron handle.

According to Bill Lloyd, a buffalo hunter named Alexander Spencer, or Spenser, built it around 1880 and died in it in 1895. Bill's father found Alexander and buried him about a hundred yards to the north, but when the Milwaukee railroad came through in 1905, they had to move him.

"Go out directly northwest of the house at a forty-five-degree angle," Bill told me, "and you'll see a sandstone slab about six feet long. He's buried under it."

I found the sandstone, which was broken almost at the halfwaypoint, a pile of raccoon poop ignominiously punctuating Alexander's marker. I wished I knew more about him, but his history remained buried with him. Several cabins like his still stand along the Yellowstone, and many of their builders were killed by

Indians, died of typhoid, or just left the country once the bison were gone. I could only imagine what life was like for Alexander, and most often, I found myself thinking it was quiet, stifling hot or freezing, and Spartan. He haunted me when I turned on a sink faucet, flipped a light switch, adjusted a thermostat, or opened the refrigerator door.

He had been one of about 4,000 buffalo hunters who arrived along the Yellowstone in 1881 and 1882, lured by two to four dollars a hide. Most of the hunters could manage at least 1,000 robes a year in an era when the average farmhand made about forty dollars a month plus room and board. The bison herd within a hundred-mile radius of Alexander's cabin numbered somewhere around 500,000, and by 1884 the entire northern herd, which modern estimates place at about 30 million, was almost decimated.

Someone had re-roofed the cabin with tin plates for offset newspaper printing from the 1970s, but it looked like debris going back as far as Alexander's time had been stored inside. Everything I picked up had little black droppings on it, along with mysterious stains of varying colors, perhaps urine, maybe chemical. I removed several broken glass jugs with red skulls and crossbones and the word "POISON" on them. A fifty-gallon drum with the same inviting label was buried under DDT sprayers, half-full cans of pesticides, herbicides and other cides I had never heard of.

I used a diamond willow staff that was leaning against the cabin to gently lift, poke and probe each item before picking up any piece of the collection with my hands. I knew a rattlesnake the size of the Australian Rainbow Serpent was lying fat with mice somewhere there or crawling in the roof just a foot above my head, ready to drop on my shoulder because of the dust I was stirring up. I thought at least a bull snake as big as an anaconda would suddenly recoil and hiss at me, causing me to fill my pants on the spot. But no snakes, thank the Lord, Kierkegaard, Nietzsche, or Camus, just a rotten old Santa Claus pillow whose tiny beads of stuffing I swept with my gloved hand into the scoop shovel, then into an old washtub that I dumped into my pickup bed.

"You will wash the bed of the pickup, won't you?" Theo had asked in Wyoming. She wanted to use it the following week to haul her and our two boys' camping gear to the Grand Canyon, where they were hiking rim to rim.

"Of course," I said, "and I'll spray it down with Clorox." I never said anything about the ticks I'd found crawling on the cab's white upholstery. The grass around the old brick house was knee high, and the mama ticks were bursting with millions of babies.

The Jacobsen

"Mow the grass," Batman Biff said. "That will help a lot with the tick problem."

I didn't have a mower for an acre of grass and weeds, so I bought an old Jacobsen which the Gillette, Wyoming golf course had used for years. It was a zero-turn with three blades and a fifty-four-inch deck that rose about a foot. I paid $400 for it, and the owner said, "It just needs a little work, but it cuts fine."

I took it to a small engine mechanic who said he charged forty-seven dollars an hour. I told him to go through it to make sure it started easily, which meant a new battery, new choke cable and a new hose, and to ensure that it cut well, which meant sharpening the blades.

The bill was $312. Three hours labor. He said it was running fine, and he loaded it into my pickup. I had to find a bank to unload it off the Carterville Road, so I drove down in the ditch in four-wheel drive while Kenny ran around in the tall grass to find where we could unload it. We used two planks, and it came off fine. I drove it back to the house, hit the power take off switch to run the blades, and went over some weeds.

I was excited to be able to finally cut them, but when I looked back, some of the weeds were bent a little. That was all, except for being flattened where the tires rolled over them. I was cussing the "mechanic" when Kenny came out of the house where he was tearing out the attic ceiling.

He looked over the Jacobsen for about a minute and said, "The belts are shot."

He lay down in the dirt, pulled one off and showed it to me.

"Look," he said. "It's cracked and slick, and there's not even any tension. Besides, the blades are duller than hell. They look like they've been mowing rocks. How much did you pay that guy?"

The next day we went to buy new belts, and I stopped at the mechanic's shop.

He said he wouldn't give me any money back because it was running fine when it left his shop. I called him several names and threatened to kick his ass when his wife came out blabbering about calling the police if I didn't get off their property immediately. I told her to go ahead and call them. I was explaining how small claims court works to the "mechanic" when Kenny tapped me on the arm and said, "Let's go."

"Why?" I asked.

"We don't need cops," he said. "Nothing good will come of it. I'll fix the mower myself. You can settle this another time."

"He's right", I thought. "Damned if the little tweeker isn't right."

We drove back to the house, and he began working on the mower, found a tick crawling on his back, and then another one a few hours later, "in the same damn spot," he said, "right where I'm sweating."

He wanted to look at the agate pile Bill had collected after I explained they were dendritic agates used for gemstones in jewelry, but he had to go through tall grass to see them. He stood contemplating the danger of more ticks for a minute until I walked over to the pile of agates, and then he leaped into the grass, picking his feet up high as he bounded over to me as if he were running on hot coals.

I showed him the agates, which ones were worth more, which ones less, and he understood. I told him they were only found in the Yellowstone River valley from Huntley Project to Glendive.

He looked up in the cottonwood tree next to us and saw a hole in the trunk about ten feet above.

"What do we have goin' on there?" he said, bending around to look at it, as if something might fly out of it and stick to his neck.

"Looks like a raccoon could fit in that hole," I said.

Kenny bounded off through the grass to the truck, both hands swiping wildly at his head as though a swarm of bees were after him.

"As long as it's not bats," he said. "They give me the creeps."

I went to the chicken coop made of railroad ties to salvage several bundles of cedar shakes in there, thinking there might be enough to re-roof the buffalo hunter's cabin. Mosquitos buzzed up out of the grass in clouds, and Kenny swore at them.

"They've finally emerged," I said. "Now you have to worry about West Nile virus as well as Rocky Mountain Spotted Fever from the ticks, Hantavirus from the mice, and who knows how many viruses from the bats."

"I want biohazard pay," he said, and laughed.

He got the old Jacobsen running in the afternoon, had Jack Ferguson sharpen the blades at his shop, and it mowed like a beast. I went through thick weeds with the deck lifted, then lowered the deck and went through again. It turned on a millimeter.

Friends

After spraying the attic with chlorine and water, Kenny and I set up a deck of H.R.'s scaffolding on planks across the joists to attack the rafters with power sanders, masks, and wire brushes. It was worst at the apex, where the largest part of the bat colony used to hang, the spot directly over my head when I first opened the access. Although we worked early mornings and late at night, the temperature quickly rose to at least 96 degrees. I set up two box fans to move the air, but they offered little relief. It took us three days to get all the rafters down to the bare wood, past the soft, whitened mush into which the bat urine had metamorphosed the fir. We took breaks from the heat to drink gallons of water, and Kenny, fueled on Mountain Dew, worked with Satanic fervor, cursing the bats in a mumbled scream under his mask.

I bought three gallons of oil-based paint that was supposed to kill any mold, fungi, and bacteria, and we took turns with H.R.'s power sprayer. The fumes from it reached lethal proportions, so we traded off every ten minutes or so. I had rented a "roll-off bin" as Jodi at Miles City Sanitation called it, a thirty cubic foot trash bin they roll off the truck, and had it placed on the west side of the house so we could throw everything into it through the upstairs windows.

I was tearing out lath and plaster between the walls of the upstairs bedrooms and throwing it into the bin when I heard a crash in the attic.

"Kenny!" I yelled. No answer.

I ran up the ladder to the attic and saw him lying on the planks below the scaffold where he had fallen. He slowly rose and looked at me, his mask askew on his face.

"Are you OK?" I asked. "What happened?"

"I think so," he said, shaking his head. "Man, that shit is worse than meth."

When I opened the upstairs door a few nights later to check on Kenny's work, a snowstorm fluttered in my face. Millers. Thousands of millers, Noctudidae, commonly known as cutworm moths, had infested the house and come out of hiding. They speckled the windows like jigsaw pieces, almost completely filling the frames, and flew crazily around my light by the thousands. We hauled the Shop-Vac upstairs and began sucking them into the canister. It took two hours to get most of them, and I decided I'd had it with these bugs. I would spray the upstairs and attic with Tempo SC Ultra.

I wore a hooded bio-hazard suit, goggles, rubber gloves, and the Darth Vader mask. By the time I had sprayed the windows and the top bricks, just below the attic line, which was now exposed since we'd torn out the ceiling, I had sweat out everything I'd drunk in the past five years. My shirt and pants were totally soaked after an hour in the 110-degree attic.

At one point, while I was at the maximum height on a twelve-foot ladder, something large and brown dropped to eye level an inch from my head, and I thought *bat!* I jerked away, causing the ladder to tilt, and I lost footing, landing crookedly on my right ankle, but only sprained it, nothing as bad as it could have been. I lay there with my sprayer tank and wand still in hand, thinking of my friend George, an electrician who broke his ankle so badly in a fall from an eight-foot ladder that he was six months recuperating.

And I thought of Jack, who just a few days before lay pinned under a horse in a muddy ditch while his six-year-old granddaughter tried pulling the reins to get the horse off Jack's leg. The horse had landed on its back when it slipped. Jack finally told her to go get help, but she wasn't big enough to catch a stirrup on her own horse, so Jack beat the horse's head with his fist while she pulled the reins again, and the horse eventually moved enough so Jack could slip out from under it.

I asked him if he'd been hurt by the incident, and he said, "No, no. I'm fine because I sank into the mud, but my hand hurts like hell from beating on the horse."

I didn't know what I'd do without Jack as a friend. He and most others in the county epitomized community spirit, and I don't mean bake sales, picnics, and parades. When he leveled the old railroad-tie chicken coop with his D3 Caterpillar and pushed it into a pile west of the house, he also pushed in an old barn, the outhouse, and the wood pile Bill had created during forty years of cutting cottonwood and scavenging shingles, poles, posts, and stumps. It was varmint heaven.

Before we set it afire, Jack loaded about twenty railroad ties on his truck to use as fence posts, and I hauled fifteen bundles of the cedar shakes into the buffalo hunter's cabin. I had no idea what I'd use them for, but I couldn't see them burn. I called the Rosebud County Fire Department to see if they might bring a truck out in case the fire got out of control.

"Do you have a truck available for that?" I asked the Fire Chief.

"Yeah," he said. "I can loan you one."

"Loan me one?" I asked.

"Yeah. Meet me at the station at noon."

So, I did, and he showed me which switches to flip, how to start the pump and handed me the keys. He never asked to see my driver's license or to had me sign any kind of formal release.

"Is there a particular station you'd prefer me to use to fill it with diesel when I bring it back?" I asked.

"Oh, you're only going to use about three gallons of fuel out to Rosebud and back," he said. "We won't even worry about it."

"Do you have a college fund for your volunteers' kids, or anything like that?" I asked.

He laughed. "Well, we have a benevolent fund," he said, "for people who lose everything in a fire. You know, we get them a motel and enough food until they can get settled."

I got the address from him and sent him a check for $25, but later I thought it was too little, that I should have sent him at least fifty.

We never had to use the truck. With an extremely wet spring, the grass was never in danger of catching, and Jack had created a berm around the fire with his Cat, but his wife Julia was especially worried about flying embers getting on the roof of the house.

I had to get back to Cody while it was still burning, and Jack said he'd keep an eye on the fire and return the truck to the Chief. I asked him how much I owed him. He had brought two hired hands who had previously helped Kenny and me get a cast iron bathtub out of the upstairs bathroom and move huge wooden boxes Winnie used to ship her art around the country, the Cat, and a front-end loader tractor.

"Nothing," he said. "I've got those guys working for me anyway, and I get paid with those ties. They're thirteen dollars apiece."

"Hell, you can't do that," I said. "I've got to pay you for this."

"No, no, no," he laughed. "I'm glad to do it."

He had agreed to lease the place to grow alfalfa and corn, and I told him he could farm it for nothing. I felt fortunate to have him working it because I would never know how, even if I'd had the equipment. He scoffed at that, saying there were fifty guys in the valley who would be happy to have the lease on such good ground.

A close friend once told me I depended a lot on my friends. Perhaps I did, but if true, I was never conscious of it, having grown up with absence and scarcity, so since then, I had been careful not to be. I liked to think my friends could depend on me, no matter the circumstance.

On my way home, I gave Jack's grandson Neeko an envelope with three $100 bills in it.

"Give that to your grandpa," I said. "And don't lose it."

When I came back to fight the millers, I found the envelope with the bills still in it on the seat of my pickup.

Insulation

I couldn't sleep in the house yet, so I was staying at the Red Rock Village in Miles City. Upon arriving one night, a slim girl with big eyes and long black hair was swaying around to Bob Marley's "Buffalo Soldiers" on the veranda in front of my room. She wore a thin top-cut blouse tied in a bow under her breasts, no bra, and white shorts about two inches long, her arms, shoulders and belly deeply tanned. Several bicycles, not the road bikes of long-distance cyclists, but the fat-tired, rugged mountain bike breed, tennis shoes and beer bottles lay on the walk in front of the rooms on both sides of mine.

"*Oh shit,*" I thought, "*what kind of gypsies am I going to have to put up with tonight?*"

"What's happening?" I said to the girl as I carried my clothes toward my room, number five.

"Weer gine ta tone," she said. Or something like that. She smiled hugely, flopping her forearms straight out at her elbows, ninety degrees from her sides. Her hands bounced at the end of her arms as if controlled by puppet strings.

"You what?" I said. I figured she was mentally challenged, on drugs, drunk on the beer, or a foreigner.

"Weer gowin' ta tawn."

"You're going to town?" I said.

"Yeeesss," she said, still smiling. "Are you stying here?"

"Yes," I said. "And you too?"

"Yes, in dat room." She pointed to number three. "Cout you haf a beer?"

"Oh my God," I thought. "She looks like she's sixteen. What in the hell kind of set-up is this?"

"Thank you," I said, "but no." This was difficult, despite a long hot day of work and my desire to accept an authentic, friendly offer. I'd quit drugs and alcohol in 1987, and as alluring as she was, I had followed too many old paths like this that ended up in twisted jungles. Still, I was interested.

It turned out she was an industrial designer from Germany, an intern on an Earthship crew building a self-sustainable house made of garbage: tires, cans, glass bottles, and plastic, for a couple in Miles City. About fifteen interns from all over the world were led by a guy named Phil, a long-haired architect who said he had built these houses in several countries.

Phil and I talked for a while about solar and wind power, collecting and recycling rainwater, sewer systems, maintaining temperature, and green houses. I told him about my project, and he said he would love to look at it before he had to go back to Taos. They rotated crews every two weeks. He invited me out to the site to have a look in the morning. Before they left for town, they picked up all their beer bottles to use in the house.

The next morning at six I drove out to the bluff overlooking the Yellowstone River where the owner gave me a tour. It was close to ninety degrees and the crew was already working. The German girl wore a gargantuan wide brimmed hat as she slopped mortar with her hands onto a wall of beer and pop cans.

"Goot morgnign," she smiled. Two petite Norwegian girls, one an engineer and the other an architect, were pounding dirt into tires with ten-pound sledgehammers.

"How much do you pay them?" I asked.

"Nothing," the owner said. "They each pay twenty-five hundred dollars for a four-week internship."

"They pay?

"Yes, it's part of their class."

"I'd like to get this crew to work on my place," I told her, and she didn't laugh.

"Talk to Phil," she said. "I'm sure he'd arrange it for you."

"Too late," I thought. "I already have Kenny."

That week the grasshoppers buzzed up in clouds everywhere I walked. They ratcheted out of what little grass and weeds that survived and even found some kind of perverted pleasure in the dust, as if they were created from dust, invisible until I almost stepped on them. Clicking and whirring around me, they rose with fat multicolored abdomens, their wings blurring and clattering like rattlesnakes. They ate the grass to bare ground, leaves to stems, and cannibalized their dead. My grandmother had told me they'd even eaten clothes she'd hung out to dry during the 1930s.

In my dream that night, they started to take over the world. They talked a secret language and ate racoons, coyotes, and horses, growing to tyrannosaurus proportions. Three of them started munching the house, and I yelled at them that they had forgotten their manners.

"This is my house," I screamed, "and I make the rules!"

They flew away laughing and burst into a million bats.

I awoke, but soon fell into another dream in which a man was following me through a maze of stores in a mall. The storekeepers were closing, and this man in a grey trench coat grew more obvious in his pursuit. I advanced my pace, stepping quickly into an elevator, but as the doors were closing, he jumped inside with me and pulled a knife out of his pocket. I awoke again, and struggling to make sense of these disparate dreams, nodded off again, only to find myself standing on a platform in a bar with the patrons watching a butt-grinding contest.

Girls came up on the platform and stood in front of me to grind and shake their booties in my crotch. The volume of the crowd's applause scored the contestants' talents. The clear winner was an old high school pal's girlfriend, a cute, short, amply endowed girl who, with her hands on her knees, worked her rear like a jackhammer. This was enough. I got out of bed and made coffee at 4:30.

At 6:30, I called Theo to recount this trio of surreal scenes and get her take on making sense of them.

"Why would I bring this girl up?" I asked her. "I was never attracted to her. She was just a friend. I haven't even thought about her in forty years."

"Well," Theo said, and I could tell by the drag in her voice she hadn't drunk much of her morning coffee, "Freud would say she was part of your shadow side."

"Oh no," I said. "What does that mean?"

"She was part of your consciousness that you never acknowledged."

She was quiet then, obviously bored by this, as if any six-year-old could figure it out.

"I wonder how many others are going to pop out of my shadow side," I said.

I got a bemused laugh out of her, and she said probably quite a few.

She offered no explanation for the other two dreams, so I called Matt to tell him about them, and his son Oliver, who was six-years old, answered. I told him about the guy in the elevator dream.

"He drew a knife on me," I said.

"Where?" he asked.

"In the elevator."

"I know," he said, "but where did he draw the knife on you?"

"In the elevator," I said again. "He drew the knife on me in the elevator."

"I knooow," he said, "but did he draw it on your arm? Or your face? Or where?"

"No," I said. "He pulled a knife out of his coat pocket and was going to stab me."

"Ohhh," Ollie said. "I thought he took a marker and drew a picture of a knife on you."

I admitted that would have been more in line with the other two dreams, and suddenly I wished Kenny were there so I could discuss them with him. He would have some kind of metaphysical twist in his interpretations, but he had gone back to Cody to work for H.R. after finishing most of the demolition. I missed him, and the bats hung all over the house at night, crapping in piles below. I kept checking the attic to make sure they hadn't found a way in. I could still smell the guano, though, and I knew something wasn't right.

I talked with an Insulator in Miles City about spraying insulation on the inside of the roof. Several people assured me this would be a huge mistake, that the house would not breathe, that I needed soffit vents, and that the roof would buckle in the heat. The Insulator laughed at their objections and gave me several references in Montana and Wyoming. Even H.R. didn't think it was a good idea, but he told me to call Leah in Bozeman, and if she said it was OK, then it would be. She had been one of my former students whom even the skeptics of the practice believed was the best architect in Montana and Wyoming.

"Of course you should do it," she said. "I don't build a house without it anymore."

After the Insulator sprayed it over the rafters that Kenny and I had sanded and painted, going through the access was like opening a door to heaven — big soft clouds of white puffed above me, and I could not smell guano, but I still could on the second floor. I soon found out why.

The upstairs floor had three bedrooms off a landing, where the attic access was in the ceiling. Four doors, one to each bedroom and a bathroom, surrounded the perimeter of the landing. When

I tore out a panel in the bathroom where a doorway to the porch roof used to be on the original house, I found guano packed six inches deep, three feet wide and five feet high next to the north chimney. I looked out on the rotten porch roof at the chimney and saw gaps a half-inch wide between it and the house. The bats were crawling in there, and obviously, always had been. I put on the Darth Vader mask, vacuumed what I could see, and took it to the alfalfa field to dump it. Then I crawled out on the porch roof again with several cans of spray foam and filled the gaps, wondering if any bats were trapped in there and how Phil's crew would have responded to that job.

The Mystery Well

I could not find the well anywhere on the property, and the pipes in the basement did not make any sense. One came in from the west, and another from the north. The pipe from the west went up the wall and ran around in the basement like a maze. An artesian well west of the buffalo hunter's cabin had a plastic pipe in it carrying water out to the drain ditch. That wasn't it. It had to be to the north. That pipe had an in-line pump in the basement, but looking for hours showed me nothing on the surface. I called Dave and Dan, but they didn't know where it was either.

The old Jacobsen was smoking as if it were on fire, and it was going through two belts every other time I mowed. I sank a tire into a four-inch hole in the lawn, and after getting the Jacobsen out, tried to fill the hole with dirt. It kept falling into the hole, so I started shoving bricks into it. It just got bigger, swallowing the bricks, and I started digging with a shovel to see what was there. Water. I'd found the well, and it was leaking.

Upon the recommendation of Dr. Dean, a chiropractor friend, I hired Craig Nile, or *C. Nile*, which everyone mirthfully called him, to come out with his excavator to dig. He showed up with a 1962 Bantam excavator that looked like a yellow brontosaurus on a flatbed trailer. Its battery was dead, so we removed the old Jacobsen's, transplanted it into the brontosaur, and C. Nile brought the beast to life. It awakened reluctantly, but lumbered and jerked, its chain drive squealing and clanking off the flatbed, into the twenty-first century.

As soon as the dinosaur sank its teeth into the hole the Jacobsen had fallen into, the hole filled with water, and after C. Nile coaxed the behemoth's jaws down four feet, he pulled up the reins.

"We've got to get a pump," he said, "and run the water over to the ditch."

The Insulator was watching and happened to have a submersible on his truck. He dove into the job as though I had hired him to do it. Soon they were both down in the mud, shoveling around the well-head, C. Nile welding the cracked pipe, and the Insulator directing the water out of the hole. They used a five-gallon bucket as a form around the pipe and filled it with concrete. The Insulator made a run to Miles City, returning with a nine-foot length of four-foot culvert insulated with his spray foam on the inside, which he placed in the hole. They cut the pipe to the house and put a valve between the well-head and the culvert, then cut a hole in the culvert for the pipe to run through.

"Now," the Insulator said, "all we need is a lid." He soon fashioned one with two handles and insulation under it. I beveled the insulation with a carpet knife, and it fit perfectly. I shoveled about a foot of gravel into the bottom of the pit so I wouldn't be standing in mud if I ever had to go down to work on it or shut off the valve.

"How much do I owe you?" I said to the brontosaurus rider.

"Oh," he said, scratching the side of his head and shifting his weight to one hip. "How does a hundred-fifty sound?"

"God bless, you, C. Nile," I said.

Finally, I knew where the well was, and it was fixed.

The Cesspool

The next thing I needed to do was figure out the sewer system. About thirty feet from the well, eight plywood sheets were nailed in a sixteen-foot square to a two-by-four frame on the ground. It covered what Bill Lloyd had told me was a cesspool. I had never seen a cesspool, but I knew it was some sort of underground container for temporary storage of sewage. A pump in the middle of the square had a hose that went down through a hole in the plywood. A couple broken plastic chairs, a few lengths of garden hose, a bent-up TV antennae, a rusted unused pump and various pipefittings littered the plywood square.

Bill had given me instructions about when to have the cesspool pumped out and when to schedule treatments. He also had the information with dates written in faded pencil on a piece of cardboard in the main floor's bathroom. Treating it with bacteria broke down the sewage, but it was necessary to pump out the waste at regular intervals. It was a step up from an outhouse, which fills sooner and needs relocating, but I had no idea about the container, its size or structural material.

I wondered how healthy it was to have it so close to the well, and my cousin Leon, a plumber in Billings, said I needed to re-plumb the house and install a septic tank. I didn't know how deep the cesspool was, or how wide it was, but I didn't think I wanted to die in it, so I tied a rope around my waist, secured it to a vertical railroad tie that served as one end of a clothesline, and tentatively stepped out onto the rotted plywood square toward the pump.

If I fall through, I thought, I'll be able to pull myself out.

The plywood broke after my third step onto the frame. My foot went through and hit solid ground. I backed up, untied the rope, and began tearing up the wood frame that surrounded the pump. When I got to the center after tearing up about ten feet of the frame, I got the rope and harnessed myself again. The boards creaked and sagged as I lifted the pump out and walked away, pulling the hose out of the hole. I carefully tore away the rest of the cover and saw that the cesspool was shaped like a bell jar and constructed of brick. The top of it was about ten feet in diameter. It curved sharply away from the top, opening about six feet out and went down at least twenty feet to the top of the sewage. I was surprised that it did not stink, and it looked like watery beef stew.

I dropped a large rock into the sewage water, and by the sound of its impact, I guessed the bottom at another ten feet. Given the bell jar shape, if I had fallen into it without a rope, I would have had to be Spider Man to escape. I would have swum around in sewage, my Navy survival stroke only taking me from one side to the other, unless I went in circles, until I drowned. Perhaps the fumes alone would have killed me. At best, a neighbor would have come along and heard my screams for help. That story would have made its rounds long after I was dead.

If I had fallen into it with the rope, I'd have been dangling with the rope around my waist, probably with a broken back, with no way out other than hand over hand up the rope, which I never was any good at in P.E. or Boy Scouts.

I stood there wondering what the original cover had been before the plywood, and if any bodies were in there. *Why did they build it like a bell jar, and how many bricks did it take?* I briefly thought it would be a good place for my old Jacobsen's "mechanic" and a few high school principals I'd had as bosses. *Throw them in alive.*

But the immediate problem was what to do next.

My cousin Leon-the-plumber said to fill the cesspool in with dirt and to contract a guy he knew who was good at installing septic tanks. In the meantime, I finished gutting the upstairs of lath and plaster, wires, pipes, and radiators, and began pulling a million nails from studs.

The repetition of popping out nails kept my mind from dwelling on the impending cost of the septic tank. My finances were getting as low as the cesspool.

Willie

I was upstairs on my knees with the Shop-Vac, chipping at plaster in a one-inch channel between the flooring and the wall studs. I was using a screwdriver to lift the plaster before vacuuming it up, when I saw something round underneath the plaster. It was a 1912 V-Nickel.

I thought it must have fallen out of a carpenter's pocket as he was filling the channel in with plaster, but that didn't seem plausible. It was in the south closet, and I briefly thought clothes, but the closet was built before anyone hung clothes in there. After all, it was underneath the plaster.

I was more careful about what I vacuumed from then on, and in the north closet directly diagonal to the room from the V-Nickel, I found a 1911 Lincoln Wheat penny under the plaster in the same channel.

No one I asked knew why carpenters would deliberately place these coins in their work until I told Dr. Dean, my geologist-gone-chiropractor friend.

"Oh yeah," he said. "It was common practice to place coins above the lintel or under the threshold of a new house so it would never be without money."

"How do you know this shit?" I asked.

"I don't know," he said. "I guess I was just born a walking compendium of bygone trivialities."

"Something your mother ate."

"More likely something she didn't eat," he said.

"Like what?"

"Tomato soup," he said, "no lycopene equals no dry matter."

Assuming he was on a tangential circuit I did not want to navigate, or that he was just dispersing nonsense, I gave this one to the wind. After a few seconds of his baiting smile, he told me he knew a fifteen-year-old named Willy who was looking for work, and he thought it would be good for him to help me on weekends.

I put Willy to work pulling nails from the studs where the lath and plaster had been upstairs. He was a good-looking kid, starting to muscle up and about five-feet-eight. He bragged about his prowess with the girls, his skill at soccer he played in the East before he moved to Rosebud, and his abilities in basketball.

"I can shoot the eyes out of three-point land," he said, "and I even dunked it once."

I left him upstairs alone while C. Nile and I considered the conundrum of getting an ancient Ben Hur chest freezer out of the basement, a mammoth that must have weighed half a ton. C. Nile suggested I use it as my coffin, which was not a bad idea, but I reminded him that we would still need to get it out of the basement unless my family wanted to keep me there.

"And they would need to clear the legal channels," he said. "The county coroner might frown on it."

When I checked on Willy after an hour, he was standing with the hammer in one hand and texting on his cell phone in the other. He had about four studs clean.

"Do you mind if I ask whom you are texting?" I asked.

"Some girls," he said. "We're planning a party for Saturday night."

"How much did I say I'd pay you?" I asked.

"Ten dollars an hour?" he said, as if guessing at a question from a history teacher.

"From now on I'm paying you by the nail," I said. "A penny a nail."

He looked at me with widened eyes and a half smile.

"For reals?" he asked.

"No, but I'd like you to put the phone away while you work and not get it out unless your mother's calling."

"OK," he said, and put the phone away.

"Young, dumb and full of cum," C. Nile said.

After a few days, I found that Willy could be a good worker, but I had to closely direct him and check his progress often. He was at his best when I worked with him, like when we tore the roof off the front porch. It was full of guano, so I made him wear a mask and goggles. He looked like a character in the Star Wars bar scene, but the gear didn't slow him any, and I had to tell him several times not to run and jump everywhere. He had broken his back playing football and had a metal rod in it. I was terrified he'd re-injure himself.

He finally jumped on a rusty nail that went through his tennis shoe and into his foot a half-inch, and I took him into town for a tetanus shot.

"Do I have to do this?" he asked. "I hate needles."

"Your mom says you haven't had a tetanus shot within the last five years," I said, "and believe me, you don't want lockjaw."

"Lockjaw?" he asked.

"Yeah," I told him. "Your jaw locks up so you can't talk or eat, and your testicles fall off."

"For reals?"

"Damned straight. I knew a guy once who got lockjaw. His balls just shriveled up and fell off and he couldn't even tell anyone about it."

"How do you know he had it?"

"He showed me just before he died," I said. "Nothin' but little black nubbins."

"What happens to women who get lockjaw?"

"Don't know for sure," I said, "but I imagine their vaginas just close. Attacks the jaw and the genitals for some reason."

"I guess I better get the shot," he said.

Before the nurse gave it to him, he asked her if she thought he'd get lockjaw.

"I hope not," she said. "Especially after this shot. You can die from it."

"Worse than that," Willy said.

The Chemistry of Crazy

Willy couldn't help me on the weekend, so I tore into the main floor demolition. In the kitchen, a firebox to the crooked chimney stood in the east corner. It was open to the dining room, off the east side of which was a bathroom with a toilet and sink, and the dining room was separated from the living room by bookshelves. On the other side of them, Bill used to sit in his chair, and the fireplace he had covered with fiberglass was on the south wall. Stairs to the upstairs bedrooms were on the east wall. I started in the kitchen by ripping out cabinets, where I found a rat's nest four feet long and two feet wide under the counter in the northwest corner of the house. It had a child's cut-glass ring in it, bits of tinfoil, cat food, fiberglass insulation among other types of bedding, and a pair of reading glasses.

"I wonder what it was reading," I said aloud.

Billy Currington was philosophizing about how "God is great. Beer is good, and people are crazy" on KIKC, the Forsyth radio station. The old man in the song leaves him a fortune because Billy talked to him at the bar.

"From now on," I thought, *"I'm going to talk to every old man I see at the bar.*

"Wait a minute," I realized. "I am the old man! And I don't have a fortune."

I couldn't get anything else on the radio. Music on NPR during the weekday sounded like death by burial in a fire ant mound. I wondered what had happened to the good music, and why I didn't have my favorite CD's there: Credence Clearwater, Etta James, Jerry Jeff Walker, Muddy Waters, The Righteous Brothers, Robert Johnson, Chet Atkins, Leadbelly, Billie Holiday, and so many more.

I guessed it was the getting old. I had told myself when I started teaching that I never wanted to end up like the soured teachers close to retirement I had known. I promised myself that if I ever caught myself complaining about "kids today," I would recharge, and so far, it had not happened to me, but I seriously began to wonder why I found modern country music sentimental, melodramatic tripe.

I decided I was being overly judgmental, but I was going mad listening to the inane lyrics of KIKC's country music. "My Achey Breaky Heart" repeated in my brain like a rusty gate swinging in the night wind. "Play Something Country" twanged like a cat's claws on a chalkboard, and I was so overjoyed when Brad Paisley told me "I'm Still a Guy" that I moved the refrigerator and the stove out and hauled them to a storage unit I'd rented in Forsyth. I had filled it with a collection of things you see hanging on the walls of restaurants that sport a country atmosphere, things I did not want to throw away because of the history they represented, things Bill's kids didn't want or didn't know were there. I put an ad on KIKC's morning show, *The Country Store*, and sold most all of it to one collector.

Still feeling like a guy, I gently pushed on the bricks of the fireplace Bill had sealed with plastic and fiberglass, and most all of them fell on the floor. After hauling them to the Rosebud dump, I pulled out the wood stove and end-over-ended it out the door. It had at least three inches of creosote built up inside. Behind where it used to be, I found a steel shroud almost as heavy, so I end-over-ended it out the door too.

When I looked inside the fireplace, the whole cavity was filled with guano. Bricks lay helter-skelter as if they had fallen from inside the chimney. I called my chimney sweep in Cody, and he came to look at it.

"It's a double drafted chimney," he said. "It has two chambers drawing air, one from each side. You don't see them much, but this one has caved in about halfway down on the west side. I can see why smoke wouldn't rise in it."

As much as I liked a wood burning fire, I decided to put a propane fireplace in it, the fake logs type I'd always hated. No mess and much safer.

I vacuumed as much guano as I could from it and decided to wait for H.R to build a foundation for the propane one.

Next, I began cleaning the basement. I rolled up five rugs Bill had on the floor, each one with a different color of mold. When I got to the bare concrete, all the colors of each mold greeted me. I mixed a few bottles of different cleaning compounds into one bottle to spray it down, but the solution began to bubble and fizz out the top, smoking and fuming at me.

"Bad idea," I realized. "Where was my high school chemistry?"

I was going crazy, walking around the yard talking to myself, wondering how I was going to pay for all the renovation, dreaming of dinosaur bats, collapsing chimneys, dying in cesspools and mold, and forgetting I had to teach on Monday. I had spent more money on the renovation at this point than I had paid for the place, and there was no end in sight. I didn't think I'd be able to stay in the house for another year. Theo was funneling her work money into it, taking care of business at home, and she only had a vague idea of the work I'd done and what I still needed to do. I felt like I was betraying her good trust.

The only thing I could think was that it was time to play some poker. I knew well that it will drive a crazy man sane, and a sane man crazy.

Sixty

On my sixtieth birthday, Theo made me lasagna, salad, garlic bread, and a German chocolate cake. We invited my sister Lynette, her husband Curt, and their son Nick to the feast. Theo gave me two shirts, and Lynette gave me a cribbage table with my initials outlining the peg holes. I felt like doing something life-changing at sixty, re-inventing myself, as they say. At thirty, I got married. At forty, I quit using drugs and booze. At fifty, I moved to the Marshall Islands and learned to scuba dive.

As we dug into the cake, I told everyone I might become a Chip & Dale stripper. I'd have the two little chipmunks tattooed on my butt-cheeks.

"That would be Sneezy and Dopey," Theo said, "not Chip and Dale."

"I can think of somewhere else you could have them tattooed," my sister said, "but they might look kind of wrinkled."

"Ouch," Nick said. "I don't even want to think about that. Why don't you just become a pilot or something? Build your own plane. I'd even help you."

"Oh dear," Theo said. "Don't encourage him to do that." She knew that when I was twenty-one, I made a list of twenty-one things I wanted to do in my life. Among the three unaccomplished was to have my own plane and landing strip. At the farm, I now had the landing strip.

"Why?" Nick said. "It would be fun."

"It would be much too dangerous," Theo said.

"Not necessarily," Nick said. "They make some awesome kits now."

"I'm not worried about the plane," she said. "I'm concerned about the pilot."

Everyone looked at me in a bum-foozled turn.

"Why?" I asked. "You don't think I can learn to be a good pilot?"

"No, I think you could be a good pilot," she said. "I just wonder about the mental stability of someone who considers tattooing chipmunks on his rear."

I laughed, but I was wondering about my mental stability notwithstanding the tattoo joke. I had a vague idea then that I had bought the farm in the metaphorical sense. Turning sixty in the middle of a renovation that was breaking us seemed to augur a broken man who was trying to prove something he didn't need to prove. I thought one night while listening to owls that I had never felt good enough in my life, and that buying and rebuilding the iconic two-story brick house in the country where I grew up would somehow make me good enough. It was folly upon folly. I realized in the first third of the renovation that I had been trying to prove my worth since I was about twelve years old.

Pieces of Father

I ate breakfast one Sunday morning at Fitzgerald's Restaurant with Paul Kanta and Harold McCaskie, both in their eighties. The summer of my senior year in high school I worked with Paul when my geology teacher got me a job with Hallett Minerals mapping deposits of bentonite by Vananda.

Paul drilled core samples to find the depth of the deposits I mapped, and we had lunch together almost every day, sitting under a pine tree on a ridge overlooking Mission Valley. I hadn't stayed in touch with him through the years, but since working on the house, I'd come to enjoy this ritual Sunday breakfast with Harold and him.

Harold grew up north of Vananda, where the bentonite mine was. After a frozen rope baseball bruised his shin, the leg injury degenerated, and when he was fifteen, a doctor told him he had bone cancer and amputated his leg below the knee. Soon after, in church one Sunday, the preacher railed about God's vengeance on sinners, pointing at Harold and naming him aloud as an example of God's displeasure.

"I got up and walked out," he said. "If that is the way God acts," he told his parents, "I don't want anything to do with him."

He'd never been in a church since. His prosthesis to his knee easily slipped off, and he said he wanted to find a bar with a low enough ceiling where he could bet the house that he could stand with one foot on the floor and one foot on the ceiling at the same time.

Harold knew my wife was a Scot, as he was, and as much as I admired his sense of humor about his handicap, I loved his ability to joke about the Scots' fiscal tightness because it echoed the ethnic stereotypes I had grown up hearing but were frowned upon by modern sensibilities. The humor was meant as light-hearted fun and often self-denigrating, a quality in men I found more attractive than the braggadocio I'd experienced in athletics and bars.

I also enjoyed Paul's and Harold's company because they had known my dad well and told me many stories about him. That day, Harold told me about the time my dad floated down the Yellowstone at night, holding onto a cottonwood log as he took his bath in the moonlight, while Harold was fishing for catfish. He drifted up to Harold, let go of the log, walked out of the river stark naked, visited with him a while on the bank, then swam back upriver.

Several of the stories I heard about my dad were semi-fictional, but I believed this one fully, primarily because his mantra was "Keep swimming upriver." He would say this as his goodbye when I was in my pickup loaded with antelope and deer meat, ready to head back to college after a weekend of hunting the Froze to Death ranch he managed, as well as when he was half conscious after a four-day drunk.

One of the more painful memories I had of him was a Christmas morning when a bartender called recommending that I come pick him up. I found him in the frozen alley behind the bar. He wore no shirt and one shoe as he sat on the concrete steps to the back door. Three different sized TVs with variously shaped antennae were lined up on the step above him. He had bought them from three different bars so back at the ranch he could watch three channels at once. As he dazedly looked around for his other sock and shoe, I asked him how much he had paid for them, and he didn't know, but he thought he'd gotten a good deal on all of them.

"Keep swimming upriver," he said, over and over, as if the alley were the river and he would survive it.

I knew the bartenders must have royally cheated my dad for them to take down their bar TVs and sell. I wanted to go call them out for taking advantage of my dad, but I was too ashamed of him to do that. It was the central emotion I had about my father, instilled in my early years from the few experiences with him after my mother divorced. Besides, I didn't feel like I was responsible for my father any more than he had been responsible for me. I hadn't known him much from the time I was four until I was in high school, and I hadn't known my dad while he was sober until the last ten years of his life.

I found his shirt, his other shoe and sock below the garbage bins, loaded the TVs in the back of my pickup, and drove him the forty miles to his house on the Froze to Death, then back to town. The next day, I had a friend drive his pickup to him, dropped it off, and returned home. He offered to write a check for gas, which I refused.

All I wanted was a thank you, but he never offered it for any of these kinds of episodes. They were like just another Tuesday to him, and if he had any regrets about his behavior, they didn't last long. It was on-with-the-day-there's-work-to-be-done soon after any of them, and his generous, easy humored nature engendered a mix of pity, forgiveness, and baffled respect in people for his ability to accept his weakness and bounce back with alacrity and physical energy.

For me, anger and disappointment were more the norm, and I limited my visits to hunting and fishing forays. I had stopped coming to help him butcher a steer, a hog, or chickens because the process would invariably end with my doing all the work after his frequent trips to his house for a little nip of Irish whiskey. Sometimes they turned into disaster—a mechanical failure on his front-end loader holding up a beef carcass, or his freezer burning up, a dead battery, or just a missed .22 bullet aimed at a pig's brain, and his inebriated state prohibiting him from effectually dealing with any problem. His knives were always dull, so I customarily brought a sharpening stone which I had to use for an hour before we even started. In my own later treatment for addiction, I came to realize that much of my desire for perfection, and my anger at not achieving it, came from my frustration with his sotted incompetence.

My feelings were enmeshed with what he could have been, especially since they were born of stories I heard from my mother and others like Paul and Harold about his former reputation, before alcoholism, as an incredibly hard worker, a powerful swimmer who regularly used the Yellowstone River as a bathtub, and a formidable fighter if a wrong toward anyone close to him had to be righted. There were several stories about his losing his mind in fights and nearly beating men to death until he had to be stopped. None of my own childhood memories of him were good, but perhaps there was one.

I must have been about three, standing on the bank of the Yellowstone River as he stood waist deep in the relative calm of an eddy where he was working on an irrigation pump. It must have been June because the river was full, muddy, and swift. Great cottonwood trees were being swept along and spun in its roiling current. For what reason, I have no idea, I yelled, "Geronimo!" and jumped into the river. I remember the wonder (I cannot call it fear because I had no sense of what would happen) at being carried downstream at an alarming rate, and the next thing I remember, and I remember it vividly, is sitting on his broad, tanned back and holding onto his long thick hair as he swam upriver to safety.

The memory of his heroically saving my life and the feelings of shame and fear from other memories created a mixture of confusion and guilt. Compassionate understanding and forgiveness of his disease were as far away as the moon. Once during my elementary school days, I was with friends and saw him drunk on Main Street. They never knew he was my father and made fun of him as he stood reeling in a daze, and they eventually asked him for money. He turned his pant pockets inside out and handed them fistfuls of change. I stood watching a half block away, and when he asked them if they knew me, I turned to walk the other way. They followed me, catching up to tell me he wanted to see me and wondering why I wouldn't go back to him. They just thought he was great fun, but I had memories of him that terrified me.

One was shortly after my mother's divorce when we had moved into my grandmother's little house when I was four. My sister and I were asleep in a bed with our mother on the closed-in porch while my brother slept in two chairs pushed together. It must have been around midnight when my father knocked on the door of the porch and pleaded with my mother to let him in. At first, his voice was gentle, cooing, and soft. I asked my mother to let him in, and she told me to be quiet and not to move. I remember her stiffening and hugging me. Then his voice changed.

"I know you're in there," he said. "For Chrissakes, let me in!"

Then he pleaded again, saying how he loved her and how things would be all right again if she would give him a second chance, how he would change. And then he banged hard with his fist on the door and threatened to break it open.

"Do you think this little door can keep me from coming in?" he yelled.

He was silent for several minutes, and I thought he had gone, but my mother again whispered at me not to speak. He changed his voice back to mournful pleading, promising he would change and apologizing for his mistakes in their marriage and asking her forgiveness.

After we lay there quiet for what must have been a half hour or more, we relaxed. He had probably left, and I went back to sleep. Years later, Mother told me she had tried living with his alcoholism until he had hit her in the face, and she had packed us up and moved in with my grandmother.

It must have been shortly after that night when he picked me up in his 1953 Chevy and drove me with a friend of his to our farm in Mission Valley, about thirty miles from town, mostly on dirt roads. Maybe I'd been playing in my grandmother's yard, and he put me in his car, I don't know, but I couldn't have been more than five years old. When we arrived at our farmhouse, I vaguely knew where I was, somewhat comfortable in the kitchen, where I had sat on his lap at the table while he held his mouth open, and I used a toothpick to flick the specks of black chewing tobacco from between his teeth. He poured me a glass of chocolate milk from a quart carton, and when I took a sip, I almost threw up and told him I didn't want it.

"What the hell's the matter?" he had said, "I thought you liked chocolate milk," as if I had offended him by refusing it.

His friend picked up the glass, smelled it, and told my dad it had soured. My dad cursed, loud and angry, and put me to bed. I knew they were drinking from a bottle of alcohol, but only had a nebulous notion of its importance. Sometime in the night, my mother arrived. I have no idea how she knew I was there. Perhaps she had telephoned him, but I remember her anger, her threats, and her carrying me in a blanket to a car she must have borrowed.

A few years later, Mother told me he had driven back to town that night, and on his return to the farm, hit a bridge abutment and suffered a brain injury. She said thank God he hadn't wrecked while I had been in the car with him. When I was in college, his sister, my Aunt Emma, told me she had taken care of him, and said that for weeks when he went outside to work, he walked in wide circles until she yelled at him to "get on track."

There had to have been a period when Mother trusted him enough to allow him to take me with him, but it must have been four or five years after his accident. I walked with him to the rodeo one summer, and I remember his attempt at conversation with a woman walking alone out of the Fairgrounds.

"Are you going to ride the broncs?" he asked, smiling at her.

"Not likely," she said, and kept walking. He turned his head to follow her with his eyes, and even as a young boy, I recognized his clumsy attempt to pick up a female. His behavior made me feel uncomfortable, and when we entered the rodeo, I became unbearably uncomfortable when he left me in the unshaded area of the grandstand, where no one else was sitting, while he walked down to the beer stand. I sat by myself with my light skin and no hat, baking in the sun until I saw him staggering in front of the crowd in the shaded area of the grandstand, stopping to look up in the bleachers, talking to himself and waving a can of beer at the audience. I walked down the unshaded bleachers and ducked under the metal supporting structure to find my way out.

My mother also let him take me fishing with his brother Kenny and Kenny's son, Jimmy. It was my first-time fishing. My cousin and I caught bullhead catfish by the bucketsful while Kenny and my dad drank whiskey. When we returned to town to clean the fish, I was afraid to gut them with a knife. I tried but was repulsed by the blood and slimy entrails.

"What the hell?" he yelled. "You think your goddamn hands are made of gold?"

He grabbed my hand and slapped a fish in it, the spiny barb of the bullhead's dorsal fin poking into my palm. I cried out in pain, and he said, "Oh Jesus! I'll clean them myself, you little sissy!"

I had other memories. In my fourth-grade year, I was inside during recess working on an art project when an older boy came running in to tell me a man sitting on the steps of the school had asked him to find me and bring me to him. He had told the boy he was my father, and that he was going to cut my throat.

I hardly knew the boy, but I remember his eyes were wide with excitement as he urged me to go outside. He wanted to know if the man was really my father, and I'm certain he wanted to see if he'd cut my throat. I went to the doors at the top of the long stairs and looked down. My dad was sitting there, as the boy had said, surrounded by my classmates, waving his arms in the air in some kind of entertaining animation. I turned around, terrified and ashamed, and returned to my classroom. I looked through the second story window to see the school's principal go out to talk to him, and watched as he staggered down the stairs and into the street. Nothing was said to me by other students, my teacher, or the principal. I don't know if I or anyone ever told my mother about it.

Another memory involved talking to Dad through the bars of a screened window in the town's jail. It was at ground level. The grass was green, and several Native American women sat on blankets on the lawn. Who told me he was there, why I went to talk to him, or what was said, I don't know, but I remember sitting on the lawn above him and talking to him as he looked up at me through the window. I know one or two of my friends sat there with me. Years later he told me of having delirium tremens in jail, of a huge spider that danced in a semi-circle in front of him as he curled into a ball in the corner of his cell, covering his face with his arms and howling in terror. I wondered if it might have been that day.

Paul and Harold were two of the few people still around who verified and patched fragments of memories like these, and I relied on them, scant and painful as the memories might have been. What they and others found comedic about my father's eccentricities, I found tragic, disgusting, and shameful, and I viewed his history as I heard it with a heavy dose of objectivity.

I left the restaurant before Paul and Harold that Sunday, paying for their breakfasts at the counter, and told the waitress to inform them I'd had a brain aneurism, and that they had better appreciate my generosity while they could because it would never happen again.

Art

When I got back to the farm, Jason, my cousin Leon-the-Plumber's son, had put in the basement drains after jackhammering the old concrete out. He was one of the hardest working kids I'd ever seen, and he was always good natured and smiling no matter how crappy the job was going.

While Jason worked in the basement, Willy and I tore the roof off the north entryway. It was caked with bat shit two inches thick along the walls, so I had C. Nile tear them up with his yellow brontosaur and drop them in the roll-away dumpster. He chained the Ben Hur freezer and hooked the other end of the chain to the brontosaur's bucket. I lay some two-by-fours on the stairs going outside, and he pulled it out, carried it over to the roll away and mashed it down.

"What about the Freon?" I asked him. "Do you suppose any is left?"

C. Nile said, "Hmmm," and scratched his head. "Do you want me to call the Environmental Protection Agency?"

"I don't think so," I said. "They'd probably declare this whole place an environmental hazard."

Using a Sawzall late that evening, I cut into the pipe coming into the house through the west wall, and water began to shoot out like an elephant pissing. I thought I had hit a live well pipe, another well I had not found. Willy and I immediately went into frantic panic mode, running around to get the wet vac, calling

Frank Askin in Miles City, my well man, who said, "Get some duct tape and see if you can stop it that way — anything to stop the flow. I'll be there in thirty minutes."

I thought the basement would fill with water and my whole project would be ruined, literally down the drain.

I was looking for duct tape when Willy said, "Hey! It's going down."

He was right. The pressure had eased off and the spray soon quit. I immediately called Frank back and told him not to come. The water had been caused by a poorly taped plastic pipe that flowed out to the drain ditch from the west well. When the box around it filled with water, it drained into the pipe that ran to the house. When I cut into it, the pipe drained to below the full box and stopped. I realized the builders had used this well at one time, then re-plumbed the house from the north well.

I had C. Nile dig to the pipe from the house to about twenty feet out, and I cut that section out, then filled the hole through the concrete foundation into the house with black fountain-foam. The adrenaline rush of thinking the house would fill with water from the live west well slowly subsided, and as relief replaced it, I found myself grateful for the men who were helping me now, and in the past.

I was dimly aware that I had always searched for a father figure in the men of my life, but none of them ever took up the challenge for long. I had tried pleasing them in every way I could, but mostly with humor, at which I became quite accomplished. In fifth grade, my teacher asked us to write what we wanted to be when we grew up, and I had written "Archeologist or Comedian." I didn't know what an archeologist did exactly, other than find mummies, but it was a big word I thought would impress her, while my real idols were Frank Gorshin, the first Riddler in *Batman*, and Red Skelton, both consummate impressionists. I began impersonating all kinds of famous people, having my greatest success with Igor, John

Wayne and Ed Sullivan. I thought I could make myself worthwhile as a funny kid. I was looking for a father figure who might become a constant source of guidance. I had been chasing a phantom all my life, and renovating the Bat House was just on another plane. Making it into a mansion of my ego would never make me feel any more worthwhile. That had to come from something I had not discovered, and I felt like I should have Jack Ferguson bulldoze the house into an enormous brick pile, but Theo and I had too much money in it already, and as Biff the Batman had said, "Once a bat house, always a bat house."

My adolescent life had been filled with men I admired, from judges and lawyers to broken old cowboys and garbage men. That fall, while I was working on the house, one man I always respected — my closest neighbor at the Bat House — died.

Art was Julia Ferguson's dad. I used to set bowling pins when I was thirteen, and Art would limp up to the foul line with an elevator shoe on his left foot and loft the ball about four feet into the air before it crashed to the lane and wobbled toward the pins. He had lost most of his foot in a B-17 over Marseilles in 1944. He was a waist gunner, and he said they were only a little way out when they got hit. Shrapnel came through the belly of the plane and knocked him down.

He radioed the captain while his foot was spurting blood, and the captain came back to the fuselage to tell Art he would have to tough it out, that they couldn't turn back before they dropped their bombs. He lay on his back, holding his foot in the air for six hours.

"I think it was the cold up there that kept me from bleeding to death," he said. "We wore those electric suits, and it got down to fifty below."

That spring I paid $450 for a half-hour ride over Billings in a Flying Fortress just to get a glimpse of what it might have been like for him. With four 1,200 horsepower engines, the planes were stripped to the bare metal and the waist gunners shot fifty calibers out of open windows. I grabbed a gun Art would have had in the fuselage and imagined aiming at a Messerschmitt. When I sat in the glassed-in nose as we flew down the Yellowstone, I imagined gunning down geese on the sandbars.

Art told me he was sure of only one kill.

"You had to lead them so far out," he said, "you never knew if you or somebody else got 'em, but I could see the eyes of one German I hit. And the last thing he saw were mine."

He flew thirty-six missions, and when he got home, they gave him an elevated shoe and told him good luck. That was it. I don't think he was afraid of anything after that. In the face of disaster, he would just laugh like a magpie on speed.

He loved his children and grandchildren with implacable patience and forgiving heart, and he didn't seem to be afraid of anything. Julia told me the story of a friend's finding him asleep in the sagebrush with a rattlesnake next to his ear. She was on horseback, moving cattle north of town. She found him sleeping in the dirt.

"Art," she'd said quietly, "don't move. There's a snake right next to you."

He awoke, looked at it and sat up. "Oh hell. It's just a little rattler," he said, and got to his feet, leaving the snake to sleep.

If I could model myself after men like Art, I didn't think I could do better.

Keep the Change

In a Friday poker game at Buff's Bar, we kept swatting flies. They never diminished. I couldn't understand why they were so prevalent until I looked at Arvin, a paraplegic who had been in a wheelchair since an auto accident just out of high school. Both legs had been amputated, and he had a colostomy bag.

Scooter Strong had drunk a little too much, and had been going to sleep at the table, not bothered by the flies, and all night we had been waking him to tell him to check, bet, raise or fold. He was being a real pain in the ass, but we tolerated it because most of us would have done anything for him. He had been an excellent basketball player who had tutored me on the court as well as off. He had a kind heart that spread to his sense of community, and he never shied from expressing his opinions about anything, which usually rose from a liberal caring about the welfare of the less fortunate. Some said he suffered from a "South Side Complex," which was probably best interpreted as not feeling as socially and economically respectable as the population who lived on the north side of the railroad tracks. This led to a sort of high-minded view of injustice in the world, and if anybody in town could have been called a socialist, it was Scooter. He paid attention to people, their plights in life, and offered what he could to help. After years of working on the railroad, he had become a Union Representative, the perfect job for him.

When I was a sophomore in high school, he was a senior. With his help after regular basketball practices, I had become a starter on the Varsity. One night after a game in which I had performed particularly well, he waited for me outside the locker room to give me a ride home, and on the way, which was only a few blocks, he asked me why I never went out to the Froze to Death Ranch to see my dad. I don't know what I said, but he told me how proud of me my dad felt, how he listened to every game on the radio and wondered how I was doing since my mother had been diagnosed with breast cancer that year. He urged me to go see him, offering to drive me out there if I wanted.

It surprised me that my dad even knew I was alive, and it changed my attitude enough to begin making trips with my cousin Jimmy to hunt and fish there, and of course, to visit with him. It started a relationship with him, however frustrating and painful it was until he stopped drinking, but in the end, I was grateful to Scooter for it.

He had also made regular poker games available at his house. They were nickel-dime-quarter games, but I had been tutored at nine years old by a former professional player named George Avalos who had worked on my uncle's ranch, and I learned different games than five card stud, which George called "pure poker," at Scooter's. I also made enough money in his games for gas money, and I owed my later ability to win in bigger games to George and him.

Since those years, Scooter had changed considerably. He was overweight from drinking too much and not exercising. His wife had died of cancer, and I thought he'd never pulled himself out of his grief, as little as I knew about it.

Playing poker in Buff's Bar that night, when Arvin released the gas from his colostomy bag, we all gagged and shoved our chairs back. All except Scooter.

He rolled his head up from his sleep, and with half open eyes, said, "Who's been eating cabbage?"

"That'd be me," Arvin said, laughing.

"I can live with that," Scooter said, and laid his head back down.

When I went in the front porch of the Bat House the next morning to begin tearing it out, I saw four bats hanging from slats of beaded ceiling that had fallen. I got a sponge mop, bent a glue-pad for catching mice around it, and stuck them to it, then drowned them in a five-gallon bucket of water. I found they can hold their breath for a long time — over a minute.

Cousin Leon was there working on the upper floor, and he noticed that the chimney was buckling away from the house, leaving an inch gap six feet from the porch floor. H.R. said he could fix it by running rods with plates on one end through the ceiling joists. I wanted to tear it down, but H.R. said it would add $10,000 to the value of the house. My Chimney Sweep concurred when I called him.

"You'd be amazed at how people love a fireplace," he said. "It's the first thing they comment on when they see one in a house."

I had a bad headache, and I never got headaches. I didn't think Theo and I could afford a fireplace. I didn't even know where we'd get the money to pay for what we'd done.

When I told Theo about my fears, she rode up with me that weekend to see the progress on the place. She had a bloody nose in the pickup, and when I stopped at Laurel for gas, she was tilting her head back and putting pressure on her nose with a tissue paper. I asked her if she wanted anything, and she said a Chai tea from the coffee shop next door. I filled the tank with gas, washed the windshield, and went in to check my lottery tickets. I had bought one for twenty dollars on every trip and had lost about three hundred dollars, but I had paid for them with poker winnings and didn't feel guilty about it.

Linda, the cashier, took the tickets to her station and said, "Oh my, I think you hit the big one."

"Are you kidding?" I said.

"No. It says here to contact Helena."

"How much?" I asked.

"Ninety thousand," she said. "But it looks like a woman from the Hi-Line also hit it. So you'll have to split it with her."

"Happy to," I said, and she gave me the ticket.

"Write your name and address on it NOW," she said. "You can either go to Helena or mail it."

"I don't like Helena," I said. "Too many bureaucrats."

"Whatever," she said, rolling her eyes. "Congratulations though."

I went back to the pickup where Theo was still nursing her nose.

"What took you so long?" she said.

"I hit the Montana Cash lottery," I told her. "Took some time to do the paperwork."

"Right," she said, not moving her head.

I threw the ticket with the paperwork on her lap and walked over to get her tea.

We ended up getting $29,200 of it. The day of the drawing, the fourteenth, was my dad's birthday. I was convinced either he or Bill had something to do with it. It was nice of them, whoever it was — perhaps both.

It's amazing how drastically a little luck can change one's attitude. I now believed in God again, higher powers we only catch glimpses of, and besides, it was Halloween, my favorite holiday. It was on a Saturday that year, but even with my freshly found ebullient spirit, I felt the Cody Chamber of Commerce had ruined it for me. When it fell on Saturday, I expected all kinds of kids at the door, all kinds of fun shenanigans, and a late night for all under a full moon. I used to go through about $200 worth of goodies every year, offering a huge bowl of peanuts, tangerines and chocolates to each little monster who knocked on the door. I'd tell them to take at least three handfuls, and my Scottish wife would call me crazy. Their responses ranged from shock and incredulity to ravenous greed, and surprisingly, I found the tangerines were the favorite.

"Oh, look! Little pumpkins," some kids would say, having never tasted a tangerine. I used to buy them by the case for the night, but in the past few years the merchants downtown had freely offered miniscule pieces of colored, hard candy in their stores to get people downtown. At four in the afternoon, Cody's Sheridan Avenue was flowing with parents taking their kids store to store. They finished before the sun went down, just when I felt things should begin on Halloween, the night for making fun of fear.

When I was a kid in Forsyth, we trick-or-treated until 7 P.M. and flocked with our spoils to the school auditorium, where the Lions Club showed Charlie Chaplin, Buster Keaton, The Three Stooges, and Abbot and Costello movies with a scary flare. I still remember the laughter, and I found when I showed Chaplin or Keaton to my high school students fifty years later, they had not lost their appeal. After the movies, we would hit the streets again to replenish our sacks of homemade caramels, popcorn balls, peanuts, apples, and chocolate bars until people who answered the doors were in bed, clearly irritated and telling us it was time to go home.

That Halloween, my neighborhood sidewalks were empty. Lights were out, and only I had carved pumpkin jack-o-lanterns lit by flickering candles on my doorstep. I got thirteen kids, most of them my nieces and nephews, when I used to get sixty. I pretended to fear them, invited them in to meet Mac, our black Lab who wagged his tail, sniffed at them, and let them stroke his silky ears. I took their pictures, asked them why they chose their costumes, and wished them Happy Halloween as they trundled down the sidewalk in their glow of make-believe.

"Happy Halloween!" they replied.

But they stopped coming by 8 P.M., and I watched *Nosferatu* and *Young Frankenstein* one more year, never hitting "Pause" for the doorbell until 11 P.M. when suddenly it chimed.

Who in the hell can this be? I asked myself. It must be students.

A Ku Klux Klan member in full hooded regalia stood on the porch with a chain attached to a collar around an African American male in tattered pants and a ripped T-shirt. The "slave" stood with his head down, mumbling, "Yassuh, massa. Yas suh, Masta!"

"Quiet, nigga," the Klansman said, and I had no idea who these two were. I stood there with my mouth open and the big bowl of treats in my hands.

"Trick or treat, fool," the Klansman said, and I knew from his voice it was Kenny.

He pulled off his hood, his African American friend straightening and pointing his finger at me as both split their guts over how good they got me. He still didn't have his teeth fixed, and after they'd left, I thought how appropriate the bat was as a primary symbol of Halloween.

I told C. Nile the story of Kenny and his slave when I got back to the farm, and he took off his hat, rubbed his balding head and chuckled like a gnome, his shoulders jerking up and down and his blue eyes sparkling.

"I hope they didn't trick-or-treat the NAACP," he said.

He awakened the brontosaurus with the battery from the Jacobsen again and began lifting its neck and slamming its jaws down on the edges of the cesspool's opening, trying to cave the top bricks in. It didn't work.

"It's way too strong," he said. "We'll have to fill it with dirt."

He went to get his dump truck, but he said it would take him a while because he had a flat tire on it, and he needed to find a used one to replace it.

After three days, we got the cesspool filled, and C. Nile put the yellow brontosaurus to sleep under the cottonwoods again where a light blanket of snow soon covered it. Things were changing.

2010

When people came by the house to look at my progress in April, they routinely nodded at the work, but went nuts over the big windows that Bo, one of H.R.'s men, had installed, and they always wanted to know where I got them.

"From a Russian girl," I said, and they thought I was joking.

"Is she good looking?" they'd ask, laughing and waiting for a punch line.

"A knockout," I said, and it was true.

Julie-the-Russian showed up in the United States with no money and about fifteen words of English, and she now ran her own windows, doors, and cabinet shop in Cody. She just learned as she went, she said. She thought most Americans don't realize how fortunate they are to live in this country.

"Americans live in the honey pot of the world," she said, "and they don't even know it."

Julie's optimism and determination comforted me when I believed everything was wrong with my efforts on the Bat House. The front porch was totally torn out except for three brick pillars that had supported the ceiling and the deck on the second story, and I was in waiting mode while H.R. finished his mother's house in Cody. I'd had the water tested to determine the best way to get rid of the sulfur, which was at 0.76 mg/liter, too strong for me to drink. But if I looked at the longevity of people in the valley, I had to think it might be one of those secrets to ripe old age everyone is always seeking, like mashed carrots and turnips, a handful of peanuts a day, red wine, fish oil, or a firm reliance on the protection of Jesus.

In January I had the upper floor wired, framed, and plumbed, now ready for the State Inspector. The Insulator sprayed foam insulation for $1,300 per floor. The main floor and part of the basement was framed. The furnace and gas fireplace were installed, fueled from a used, thousand-gallon propane tank I bought from a dealer in Miles City. A woman had ordered it from him, but he accidentally scratched it for about five feet when he unloaded it, and the woman wouldn't accept it. I gave him $1500 for it, feathered the scratched paint with wet sandpaper and repainted it. I paid another $1500 for the septic tank, which now accepted deposits fifty yards northwest of the well.

By the middle of April, during the Journalism Education Association's convention in Portland, I found myself wondering why I didn't live there, close to the ocean, slurping down oysters on the half shell at Dan and Louis', choosing fresh vegetables at the river market, and chomping brioche-based doughnuts at Blue Star. On returning to the Rosebud place, I even more seriously considered it while I cleaned up limbs from a big windstorm. It had blown the porta-potty over and rolled it about twenty feet, and birds of all kinds, many I'd only seen in the east — Baltimore orioles, cardinals, hummingbirds, indigo buntings, rose breasted grosbeaks, purple finches — flew confused among the trees. According to a meteorologist friend, they were blown off course in the gigantic storm. It was wonderful to have them there, but I couldn't imagine they knew where the hell they were, lost in eastern Montana, kind of like me with the bats.

I took this phenomenon as a bad omen when my chainsaw's starter rope broke. I couldn't manage the uncoiling spring to fix it, and then the steering tire on the old Jacobsen went flat. I bought a new tire in Miles City for forty-five dollars, and when I started mowing, I hit a steel cable I'd used to pull down broken tree limbs. It wound around the blades and smoked the belts.

I could pay these bills in cash most of the time because I'd been doing well at poker, winning second in two good tournaments and a substantial amount in cash games. If I paid attention to my subconscious, or gut feeling as some call it, I usually came out way ahead, but if I didn't, I'd do something I regretted, like a recent tournament where three of us were left. I was chip leader and not in the blinds. The other two went all-in pre-flop, and my gut told me to call, but I didn't with 8-9 off-suit. The flop came 7-9-9. The turn was a 9, and the river was a king. I would have had four 9s if I'd called. Those hands haunted me. I knew I should follow a course of action, but I didn't. Sometimes I wonder what's wrong with me, but most of my friends in the poker circuit tell me they do the same thing — call or fold when they know they shouldn't.

I'm not sure what to think of this curious behavior, other than to call it denial of the subconscious. We know we are beat, but we call another's bet anyway, like throwing money in the river. It's like we must see the other player's cards to ensure we have not been bluffed, an excruciating injury to our egos. Better to swallow our pride in these cases and admit defeat, but it's more difficult to do than one would think. Even the most seasoned players struggle with it, as one of them admitted to me, and he reasoned that the behavior also carries over in our personal lives.

When Theo became ill, I found that it works both ways. If I'd vacuumed the house, mopped the floors, washed our clothes, changed bedsheets, mowed the lawn, cooked a good meal, exercised the dog, written a satisfying number of words, paid the bills, practiced yoga, and administered Theo her scheduled medicine, I could confidently decide to play poker or not. But I rarely did during those years, desiring to be with her every minute I could. Still, she encouraged me to host my home game, delivering her professional lecture on the stress of being a caretaker. If I did play, and I had a subtle feeling I would win, I usually would. But if I was tired, hungry, or not satisfied with myself for not having accomplished anything that day, or if I felt guilty about leaving her upstairs in bed alone, I would make wrong decisions and feel like a rabid bat. Every decision seemed to compound itself for better or worse.

The same set of circumstances seem to influence my personal relationships now, and I think that's what my professional poker player friend meant. I've learned I need to pay attention to present details, and the future will take care of itself. If I recognize that moment between stimulation and reaction, that pause needing careful consideration, like at the end of an exhale, and choose from experience, it is usually the right choice.

I love poker, believing it is the best game invented, its propensity for engaging with people socially, psychologically, economically, and fatefully like no other, and I still host a Thursday night low stakes game. We bring smoked fish and goose, cheese and crackers, chocolates, and most guys drink a few beers. Lynn Ackerman, a Hall of Fame softball pitcher from Michigan, football coach John McDougall and I started it in 1974 in John's garage. It was a Mormon klatch, mostly. One night, Mac's wife popped her head in the room to say, "John, the Bishop is here." The table cleared. Everybody cashed out, leaving Lynn and me staring at each other as if the game had been raided.

A barrel-chested Scot with a nose like Mike Tyson's, Mac always ate popsicles at the poker game in his gym shorts, even in the winter when the rest of us were freezing, and we had to coax him to turn up the heat. His dad had been the sheriff of Fremont County in the wild years, and we played with chips he confiscated from an illegal Riverton game. Mac was a Golden Glove champion boxer; his unofficial fights began when he was fifteen, and from BYU he launched into Las Vegas fame.

I began playing poker in the eastern Montana bars when I was fifteen. It was solely five-card stud or five-card draw then, and

I used my money from selling the jack rabbits I had hunted all winter to get in the bigger games. I stored them in an old coal bin attached to the barn until March when they began to thaw, then took them to Miles City Pacific Hide and Fur where in 1964 they brought eighty cents each. That year a hired hand named DL who was fresh out of the Army, and an old cowboy named Stubby drove me into town with my rabbits in the pickup bed.

The two couldn't have been more different. DL was all square jaw, shoulders, and legs, muscled hard as a shoeing anvil, and Stub was so short he needed a milking stool to mount his horse Troubles, a big Bay who didn't like anyone but Stub riding him. DL wore his military fatigues most every day, and Stubby never came out of the bunk house without a white shirt he'd ironed with a collared black tie and black pants he also pressed. After selling my rabbits for a little over $60, we went to the Saddlery where DL tried on Nocona boots but didn't buy them. Stubby bought a new rope, and they wanted a beer, so we walked down the street to the Bison Bar. At the end of the bar a poker game was on next to the side entrance door. I asked DL and Stub if I could play, and Stub said, "It's your money, kid. We've got a few hours. Do what you want."

They knew I could hold my own at the table with just about anyone, and after an hour or so, I was about $20 ahead. Then at five card stud, I got the two of Clubs in the hole and the Ace of Clubs up. I bet out with the Ace and a huge man called Haystack raised. He had a Queen up, so I put him on a pair or Ace-Queen. Another guy with a Jack-up called and so did I. I hit the four, five and three of Clubs, which gave me a straight flush, *The Steel Wheel*. Haystack pushed in all his chips, and Jacks and I called with all we had. Haystack flipped up a Queen for a full house, Jack Man showed his third Jack, and I rolled over the two.

Haystack complained that I was too young to be in there, yelling that he wanted his money back. The dealer told him to shut up because he had been willing to take my money, and he hadn't cared how old I was when I bought in. Haystack was cussing and yelling at the dealer for running an illegal game as he got up from the table and said he was calling the police. When he dropped a dime into the wall phone and lifted the receiver to his ear, DL was suddenly there from the bar, and he pushed down the receiver lever. I don't know what he said to Haystack, but he hung his head and walked out the side door, and the next thing I knew, Stubby put his hand on my shoulder, and said, "Cash in your chips, kid. We'll be going home now."

I think I won over $350 in that hand, which was a lot of money in 1964 for a kid.

But I had a good teacher. George Avalos had been a professional card player before he promised his wife he would never touch cards again. George worked for my uncle Wallace Lockie on occasion, and he'd sit next to me and tell me how to play my hands at a game for plastic chips with the hired hands. We never played for money, just the chips, and George would never touch the cards. He would sit behind me, look at my hole card and say, "Fold 'em, Mikey." Or "Bet 'em, Mikey." Or "Raise 'em, Mikey."

I can still hear his voice. He was a big man, and old timers have told me he made a striking scene when he got off the train with his wife Toni to play poker for a few days in Forsyth, Glendive, or Billings. He wore a three-piece suit, always with a silk cravat and a big diamond stickpin, they said. Toni, his petite wife, always dressed in beautiful black lace.

My aunt Eunice said he had come across the Mexico/US border with a younger brother when he was twelve. His father had sent them to sell a band of sheep. He gambled the money away, sent his brother back to tell his father what had happened, and learned to deal cards. A professional in Texas made him practice eight hours a day in front of a mirror, she said, until he could deal almost any card you wanted.

I verified that story with him when he was ninety-two, three years before he died. He still drank whiskey all day and never got drunk. He was one of those guys on whom alcohol had no effect. He was sitting in a recliner with a full water glass of Black Velvet the last time I saw him, and he told me about finally going back to Mexico with his niece to see his living relatives.

When I hear the debates about immigration, I think about George and feel saddened by our border problems with Mexico, the poverty there and our supply-and-demand drug infection. Why Americans are so unhappy that we resort to such epidemic addictions is beyond me, but I know that as long as we do, the supply chain will not stop. It is just too lucrative, and the violence, destruction and animosity on both sides continue to spread and become endemic. And I think we know we are beat, but we still won't act because we must see how bad it can get.

One of my junior broadcast students, Abbey Morales, reminded me so much of Toni Avalos that it was spooky. She radiated the same congenial energy, optimism, and humor from her 105 pound, five-foot-and a quarter-inch physique (*the quarter is important*, she said), that she was almost a clone of Toni. Her parents worked religiously to provide for their five daughters, and this ethic had been ingrained in Abbey, who was also extremely intelligent and Wyoming's Journalist of the Year.

She was in the editing corner of the studio one day with several students hovering and laughing around her, and I walked over to see what was going on. She had a spring-loaded knife she was showing them, a side-locking switchblade about six inches long.

"Abbey," I said. "What are you doing with that? You know you could get suspended for having it in school."

She laughed and flicked out the blade.

"I have to have it, Mr. Riley," she said, laughing even more. "I'm a Mexican."

I told her to put it away, to leave it in her car, and began calling her *Abbey the Blade*.

I wish we could all have her sense of humor about stereotypes, and I wish even more we could have her dedication to work. True to her nature, she helped three of my former students, Matt Hatton and the Reavis twin-brothers, tape graduation. We sold the DVDs at twenty dollars each for the Journalism Club, our best fund-raiser of the year except for the Quigley Buffalo Rifle Match. Envisioned after seeing the movie *Quigley Down Under* with Tom Selleck in 1990, Al Lee had started a long-range buffalo rifle match on his ranch, and it had grown from a few locals betting on their black powder skills to over 300 participants from all over the world. I had known Al since I was twelve, when he had been my hunter safety instructor, and he welcomed a small crew of my broadcast students to document the event. We sold over 200 DVDs at $20 each.

The crew wanted to go to the Lee Ranch again, so we did, and I would have loved to have them stay at the Bat House, but I rented motel rooms as I had the previous year because I knew the House would not be ready. When I tore down the east chimney and the one in the kitchen, I noticed guano in the soffit, so I needed to tear it off and replace it with one bats could not enter. I didn't want my students staying there before I ensured their safety, although my stepson Matt the virologist thought the guano from there would probably be harmless.

"It dries out in a day or two," he said. "The viruses' capsids, you know, the cells' protective sheaths, dry up and the virus dies."

He said bats have evolved as perfect repositories for viruses by developing immunities. They "shed" the virus through urine, feces, or saliva for reasons no one knows for sure — it could be stress from various factors, a weakened immune system, an infected pup population, or co-infection — and determining whether virus shedding occurs as episodic events or as transient epidemics is challenging. The more I learned about them, the more complicated they got.

Every year, Matt said, tens of thousands of people are treated after potential exposure to rabies by bats or other animals - post-exposure prophylaxis — and he told me the story of his sister-in-law's family that found a "wounded" bat by their cabin in southern Utah. They had four kids who picked it up, passing it around, petting it and keeping it for a few days before another sister-in-law came to the cabin and told them of the dangers. They sent it to Southern Utah University to be tested for rabies, and the results came back positive.

"Each shot costs thirteen hundred dollars," Matt said, "and you have to get three of them."

"That was an expensive learning experience," I said. "Five of them in the family, at thirty-nine hundred dollars per person."

"Yeah," Matt said. "They could have just taken a nine-hundred-dollar college course in basic animal diseases."

I couldn't help wishing that I had taken a $900 course in house renovation. The cash hemorrhaging didn't seem to end. Bo repaired the roof where the kitchen chimney came through and guaranteed no bats could get in there. H.R. said he would put up metal soffit so no bats could hang from it or get in.

I kept imagining the end of the repairs, when the Bat House would be comfortable, where I could offer the Quigley crew a free place to stay, and where I could bring my friends and relatives to the Yellowstone River to fish and hunt. My five-year-old grandson Alexander had been writing a letter a week and sending pictures he drew of fishing. He was addicted to fishing and loved to recite for people all the different fish he'd caught. The outdoor editor of the *Billings Gazette*, Brett French, published a picture of him with his first channel catfish, and after that, he not only told people he was a fisherman, he told them he was a *famous* fisherman.

Yoga

For about five years Theo had been raving about the benefits of yoga, coaxing me to try it, but I had resisted until I finally helped her finish her teacher training. She needed beginning students to come to a class she had to teach, so I rounded up the Reavis brothers, Matt Hatton, and a few other students. I had done some yoga in the sixties with Dr. Dean's dad, who had me standing on my head, lying on my belly and arching my back and sticking my tongue out like a lizard. Theo and I also took a class from a guy in the Marshall Islands who nearly killed me. I'd never been as sore as I was after one of his practices.

So, I was not too enthused, but beside wanting to help Theo get her certificate, I was reading a book on poker tells — physical reactions to cards that reveal what kind of hands players have. Heavy breathing, for example, might tell when they have a pair of Aces or when they are bluffing, or a tell might be as subtle as the way a player habitually handles chips. Tells are obviously subconscious, often uncontrollable, and sometimes calculated as false, which poker players often refer to as "Hollywooding." The author, a champion poker player, wrote that practicing yoga is the ultimate exercise in preparing oneself to read other players' hands and to control one's own tells. I was more than curious how that would work, and it probably motivated me as much as Theo's need for neophytes.

She had us sit on the floor with our legs folded like gurus on top of a mountain in a clichéd cartoon, and we began by lifting an arm, bending to one side, lifting the other arm, bending to the other side, and breathing. We lay on our backs, lifted one leg in the air, bent it at the knee, dropped it to the opposite side, lifted the other leg, bent it at the knee, dropped it to the other side, and breathe here.

This is about as ridiculous as it gets, I thought, *but I will get through this for her.*

After four years of calisthenics in high school football, where coaches screamed at me to do push-ups and sit-ups, to run a mile, then sprint a hundred yards four times, all in August heat with thirty pounds of pads weighing me down, this was sissy stuff from Na Na Land. I'd also played basketball and soccer in college, where I'd managed to break my nose, tear ligaments in my knees and ankles, and pop my Achilles tendon.

"Our motto at Here Yoga is 'No Pain'," Theo's teacher, Laura Vanderberg said.

Well, that makes sense, I thought, but then my back popped three times as Theo had us fold at the waist from what she called a "Sun Salutation." My knees were bent so that my thighs pressed into my lungs as my hands fruitlessly reached for the floor, and I was having difficulty breathing. In front of me, an upside-down girl in her twenties looked back at me, her head between her ankles and her arms wrapped around her calves.

Someone farted, and I looked at the Reavis twins who were doing all they could to keep from bursting into laughter. Hatton resembled a dead goose as we moved into "Reclining Pigeon" pose.

The practice began to change, ramping up, and soon I was streaming sweat and unable to breathe. I was bent over, my ass in the air, my head between my arms in "Down Dog," gasping like a carp tossed on the riverbank. My arms quivered and my legs felt like jelly.

A woman next to me had obviously done this before — she moved gracefully and effortlessly from one asana to the other, barely breathing as far as I could tell, as I huffed and puffed for oxygen through my mouth.

There must be some secret to this, I thought. *It's not right.*

I tried imitating her and the young girl in front of me, but my palms slipped in my sweat on the mat, and my hamstrings ached in an impossible stretch when I attempted to get my heels flat like they had them.

The practice began to unwind, thank the Buddha, and we ended by lying on our backs for savasana, where Theo and Laura put eye pillows on people who wanted them. I warily watched as they pressed little beanbag cushions across people's noses and over their eyes to the outer edge of their eye sockets.

No eye pillows for me, thank you very much. I just want this to be over.

But that night, when I sat on my bed to take off my shoes, I started to lift my right leg with my hand, and I did not need to as I usually did. There was no pain. I could lift the leg by itself without pain in my hip, and I realized that I had been lifting my leg with my hand to aid in the simplest movements, like pushing the brake in my VW van or crossing a foot over a knee to remove my shoes. It had become such routine that I had not even been aware of the accommodation.

After three or four more practices on the yoga mat, the pain all along my right side disappeared, from my knee to my hip, my wrist to my elbow, and my shoulder to my neck.

My friends couldn't believe I was practicing yoga, asking me questions like, "How can you let a woman tell you what to do? Is the teacher hot? How many women are in the class? How do you keep from getting a hard on?"

These idiots had no idea, and as I began learning to breathe, I decided not to reinvent myself as a Chip and Dale dancer with tattoos on my bum, but as a Yeti Yoga Man. I begin to study the "Yoga Sutra" of Patanjali, an Indian teacher who lived around 200 AD. I got the basics: Yama, my attitude toward things and people outside myself, and Niyama, how I relate to myself inwardly. I would not describe my study as cataclysmic awakening or hyperbolic spiritual rebirth, but I was aware of engaging observation.

Perhaps because of this yogic consciousness, or perhaps coincidentally, I became aware of several bizarre incidents, and I wondered if it wasn't the moon's influence on earth. I wondered at all of them, and looking back, I can only blame the moon. Laura said our bodies are eighty percent water, and the moon's pull affects us more than we might think. She had us do a folding practice to counteract the energizing influence.

I didn't know about all that, but I was not arguing with her, mainly because she had a PhD. in microbiology, and because of a few experiences I had that exhibited certain mysterious factors I could only explain as a new kind of awareness I believed yoga enhanced.

One occurred in Buff's Bar when I saw a man whisper in the ear of a woman from Florida who sat next to me at the poker table. I somehow knew she was going to win the hand and encouraged her to raise before the flop and after each two cards, which bewildered the dealer and owner of the bar, Curt Sample. When she won the pot on the last card with a full house by turning over pocket aces, Curt asked me why I had encouraged her to raise.

I told him I had seen the man in black whisper in her ear, and I just knew she would win.

"What man?" Curt asked. "Where is he?"

"I don't know," I said. "He disappeared."

I described what he looked like, and Curt told his son Steven to get a photo of the bar when it first opened in 1896. In it, various men stood on the sidewalk below an "All Nations Saloon" sign, and Curt asked me if the man I had seen was in the photo.

"Yes," I said. "Right there," and pointed to the man in black I had seen.

"Nels Anderson," Steven said, and he nodded to Curt. "He was the first owner. We often see him in here, usually when we are closing or opening and no one else is around."

Among several other odd experiences included an encounter with a bat that was hanging in the chimney corner under the soffit. I poked him with my iron rod to get him to fly away. He wouldn't budge, but chattered at me and squiggled around a bit like a teenager who doesn't want to get out of bed in the morning for school. I finally hooked the curved end of the rod under him and flipped him out of his slumber. He lit on the porch roof and looked up at me as if I had just killed his family and evicted him from the only home he knew. I probably had, but wondered if he was sick and couldn't fly.

"You had better find a new place to hang out, you rabid little hair ball," I said, "or I will mash your damned brain in."

He seemed to understand, for upon hearing this, he immediately flew up, circled my head in a flash and took off toward the river. I hoped he was the last one.

Seeing a ghost and communicating with a bat might not testify to a *raised* consciousness, I understood, and believing it did might inversely testify to *losing* one's consciousness. I'd had enough hallucinations and mystical epiphanies on magic mushrooms in Mexico, and on Maui Wowie, Thai Stick, sweats with Native Americans, cocaine, and whiskey to write an addendum to William James' book *The Varieties of Religious Experience*, and except for the Native American religious ceremonies, I might as well have been talking to a burro about the meaning of life as realizing any truths about myself or the universe.

Nevertheless, I was beginning to understand that awareness must be practiced in a conscious, disciplined effort, like practicing anything, say basketball or archery, but unlike those Zen routines of practicing for automatic responses, the more I practiced awareness, the more I was at least aware of things I could not explain.

Or maybe it was just the moon with bats flying around in its pale light.

Joy

During a full October moon, always weird and wonderful, my first night sleeping in the house mirrored it fitfully. Since starting the project, I'd either stayed at Red Rock Village in Miles City or the West Wind in Forsyth. I set up my old hunting camp cot, an extra-large, extra-firm, heavy-duty model I bought while cooking for an outfitter in the Scapegoat Wilderness and curled up in my ten-pound Hollofil bag. Leon had laid the sewer line running into the septic tank and tied in a sewage grinder. He installed a Rinnai hot water heater in the basement. The Insulator had foamed the walls and the Espinoza brothers had poured new concrete in the basement floor and stairway to the outside.

I set the thermostat at sixty, but was too hot, so I turned it down to fifty and was just right. I had a toilet but had to lift my feet high and set them down carefully on the rough fir floor or I got slivers. I had hot water and a shower, even though it smelled of sulfur. The walls were insulated but not sheet rocked. Theo and I had invested almost a quarter of a million dollars in the place, and I still had a long way to go before it would be finished, which affected my ability to relax and go to sleep.

Every sound was a bat crawling around above me, even a wrinkling sheet of plastic in the shower Leon left there, a piece of crumpled newspaper unfolding in the wastebasket, the crack of wood contracting. I used the northeast bedroom upstairs, Bill and Winnie's old room. It was my favorite. The geese coming off the river awakened me at sunrise as they cleared the cottonwoods along the lane and crossed the field to the east at the level of my window. They reminded me why I had bought the place, and I believed many more reasons would emerge. I was proud I'd made it this far and told myself that someday I'd sleep without hearing bats that weren't there. An important facet of the yoga sutra was gratitude, and I was beginning to learn that practicing it offered some peace of mind.

I realized how fortunate I'd been in all the driving I'd done — 200 miles each way with no accidents — and the next trip reinforced my gratitude. A bad storm hit eastern Montana just as I had returned from a Journalism Education Association convention in Kansas City. I shouldn't have left Cody because it was too cold to hunt and I didn't have a license, but I wanted to see the place in the cold. I started sliding on the ice around Custer and slowed to forty-five. Around noon I came upon a fatality by Hysham. The driver of a Dodge pickup must have tried to pass on the west bound highway and rolled it through the median, ending up in the east bound lane. Either that or he just slid sideways.

He'd been deer and antelope hunting from the looks of the wreckage — animal carcasses scattered among coolers and other gear. His wife had survived.

I must have been the third or fourth vehicle to arrive on the scene, and a few people were standing around in shock when I stopped. A guy said an ambulance for the wife was on its way from Forsyth. It was one of the saddest wrecks I'd seen. A western Montana guy and his wife going home after a successful antelope hunt in eastern Montana, probably full of good memories, looking forward to processing the meat, and suddenly he was dead.

I drove slowly the next forty miles to the house, and it was warm when I entered. H.R. had started sheet rocking the upstairs, and I was glad to see it. I decided to drive back to town, even though the road was slick, to go to the Roxy Theater. I didn't care what was playing. I just wanted to sit in the old theater I'd enjoyed so much in the early years of my life, eat popcorn, and drink a Coke. After watching *Harry Potter's Happy Valley*, I walked around in town and reveled in the beauty of ice crystals falling from the sky like jewels. I remembered how I used to walk around town in storms like that when I was a kid, slipping and falling because I never had good shoes. Now I was putting together a million-dollar home, and the joys of my past remained the same.

Before Theo and I married, she had come with me on Christmas Eve to see where I had grown up. While we walked around town, I told her about my high school years, of taking care of my invalid grandmother by myself, my mother in the hospital or home in bed, out of her mind on morphine. I was playing football and basketball, carrying a full load of the most difficult classes in school, and I had no money except my grandmother's Social Security checks. One of the most pleasurable escapes I had then, I said, was listening to Gordon Dean's dad late into the night as he told me stories about traveling the world, and then walking home under the stars at one or two in the morning. My sister was out of town that Christmas, so Theo and I stayed in her tiny rental with a rollout sofa, a little tree twinkling with lights at its foot, and we walked around the town during a brightly moonlit night of gently falling snow, the flakes as big as silver dollars. She'd said it was the best date she'd ever been on.

Then, as now, I realized, the money didn't matter for us to find joy.

As if I needed to be jarred out of romantic reminiscing, on my way back to the farm I hit a cow on the Carterville Road by Polich's, just a few miles from the Bat House. I was only going forty because it was a dark night, and the road was a solid sheet of ice. I saw something move ahead and hit the brakes carefully, but my Toyota Tundra couldn't do much. About nine angus cows were trying to get out of the way, but they were slipping on the ice too, and I could see no way between them. I broadsided one, and it felt like I'd run into the Federal Reserve Bank. She slammed into a cow behind her and knocked that cow down, but she stayed upright. The toppled cow got up, and they all ran into the field toward Polich's house. I walked out to see if any were down or limping, but they were fine. Their calves were being weaned in a corral across the highway, and they'd been trying to get to them.

The impact smashed my Tundra's grill and the left headlight. The hood was bent, and the driver's-side fender had caved back, crumpling into the door so I couldn't open it. I drove up to Polich's house, got out on the passenger side, and knocked on the door. Jim Polich had been my senior year football and basketball coach. He'd played for Eastern Montana College with my current principal, Dave Treick.

I respected him a lot, and feared for a moment, drilled into me by countless hours on the field and in the gym, that he would chew my ass out for hitting one of his cows, but then I thought I'd say, "Well, Coach, why were your cows on the highway?"

No one answered. He lived in Bozeman, his twin brother in Miles City, and his younger brother on Rosebud Creek. Both his parents were in long-term care. I thought it was no wonder his cows were on the highway and considered how the valley was changing. Most of the old timers were passing away, and their children were living lives of their own far away. I thought it was several years past due for wealthy Texans and Californians to have moved in, buying and changing my sense of place. Then I realized I sort of fit into that category, even though I was not that wealthy, and I had grown up there.

Rudy, Dr. Dean's older brother, and his friend Ron arrived from Arizona the next day to stay at the house and goose hunt. Rudy had been one of my best high school friends, and Ron was a former auto body mechanic who straightened out the Tundra so I could get the door open.

"Ron and I were talking about it, and we agree," Rudy said after staying at the place for a few days, "that you are doing a great job with this place, but whatever you do, keep the buffalo hunter's cabin. You should restore it so people can stay in it too. It is the epitome of this country and this place."

"Right," I said, "and both of you will help me pay for epitome."

I awoke in the morning to a frost that covered everything — hoar frost, a thick, hairy heavy frost. Hundreds of sharp tail grouse huddled in the cottonwoods and Russian olives around the house.

That, I thought, is the epitome of this place.

But Ron and Rudy had a point, of course. The cabin was a remnant of the history of white settlement in the Yellowstone Valley. Its presence represented the end of the Plains Indians' reign there. With the buffalo gone, their traditional culture was doomed. Things change though, and my priority had never been to renovate a piece of history. I was more concerned with how my own culture had changed, how we might be doomed with the loss of less tangible assets, like our sanity.

To illustrate, I was on lunchroom duty in the high school when a kid in one of the cafeteria's two lines cut ahead of about twenty-five other students and stood talking with his friend. I was in the other line and walked over to confront him.

"Are you in line to eat lunch?" I asked him.

He said yes, so I told him to go to the end of the line.

"Why should I listen to you?" he said. "Why should I respect you?

He was a tall, thin scraggly kid, unkempt, with a few hairs three inches long on his chin.

I explained that it was rude and arrogant to cut in front of people who are waiting in line for anything,

"I always do it," he said.

"Not while I'm on lunch duty," I said.

"I don't give a goddamn," he said.

"Well," I laughed. "Maybe you should start."

"Fuck off!" he yelled. Then, even louder, "Suck my dick!"

I'd never had a student say that to me in thirty-seven years of teaching. In the '70s, if a student had said that to me, I would have knocked him on his ass. No question. This was different. I would be on video as a perpetrator of violence against a poor kid, would lose my job, and would probably have to pay the kid a million dollars. But that isn't what stopped me. He appeared ludicrous to me. All those years of experiencing the joy of teaching, and my gratitude for it, just made me wonder about him.

I walked away to get the assistant principal, and he returned to the cafeteria with me, but the kid was gone. The cooks said he'd stolen food twice before this incident, and they were happy someone finally did something about him. He was eighteen, a "Special Ed" student, so not much could be legally done to him. The assistant principal suspended him for three days.

A teacher with a room next to mine had him two periods a day. She said she feared he was a predator on freshmen girls and was "a ticking time bomb." He lived with some woman who was not his mother. The woman had told her that she was "surprised" at this recent behavior because "he'd been doing so well lately."

Right. I wondered how surprised we all would be if this kid returned to school with a gun. For the last five or six years I'd sporadically imagined scenarios like this. Sitting alone in my office during a planning period, I found myself wondering what I would do if I heard gunfire. I looked at kids in the hallway during passing and asked myself, *Is that kid capable of walking through the doors with a gun and opening up on us? Or that one? How about him? Or him? Or her?*

Some argue that qualifying teachers should be allowed to carry guns in schools. Every school resource officer I'd talked with thought it was a bad idea, and so did I. I had not become a teacher to carry a gun to school.

Besides, if I'd had a gun in the cafeteria that week, I might have shot the student who swore at me. Finding balance in yoga, at that point in my life, seemed a far better solution for me.

Unsung Heroes

H. R. and his crew were hanging sheetrock, and I was beginning to see a light at the end of the tunnel: the rough work was getting done and only the porch windows, the flooring and essential appliances were left. It was ten degrees outside the week a trucker brought the windows, but the snow was so deep he couldn't back his truck to the porch door. I was gone so Wade Cole, my neighbor, helped him get them in the house.

I bought Wade in the next poker game for $80, and I won $260. Arvin Post busted my full house with quad 7's, and I lost about sixty-five dollars on that hand. Arvin told me after the game that he was bleeding internally — colon cancer. I didn't think he had a colon since he wore the colostomy bag, but he said the piece of intestine going into the bag was cancerous. He figured he only had two months left at best, but he was in good spirits after beating me with four 7's, and I degraded him for being such a lucky suck-out, but I was happy for him.

I've known a few guys in wheelchairs, and I don't understand how they remain so optimistic and cheerful. I almost see them as Panglossian, given their adversities. Arvin's life was pure hell, awaking every morning in his soiled bed sheets to a mother with dementia, but he continued to care for her with a love few healthy people have for their parents.

Derek McGuire, a former student and paraplegic who broke his back in a motorcycle accident his senior year, visited me at school, and I could not believe his attitude. His sharp wit, laugh and bright personality from high school had not changed. He demonstrated how he could climb stairs in his wheelchair and was excited about an all-terrain model he had just seen at an Outdoor Show. He had grown exponentially in his talent with music editing as well as in his pursuit to become a sommelier.

I am also amazed by Glen Kopitzke, a Miles City man my students interviewed for the Quigley Buffalo Match video, who was in a wheelchair because of an accident in his van. He dedicated himself in multiple ways to helping others in wheelchairs.

And I will always remember Levi Haugen, a former student with cerebral palsy, who brought the entire high school to tears in a television commentary he did at Christmas his senior year. He worked at the Buffalo Bill Center of the West after high school as security guard wearing a suit and tie, guiding tourists with his smile and heart as big as Wyoming.

I believe I would not have the will these guys had, or at least the cheery attitude they emanated. On the other hand, who knows? I can't forget the night at the poker table when Steven Sample, a hardy twenty-three-year-old, was complaining about a three-month run of bad cards and bad beats. He said it was enough to make him quit playing poker. He was so depressed, he said, he couldn't see how he was going to get through it.

"Well, Steven," Arvin said, looking at me with a sly grin, "you might be surprised at the adversity people can overcome."

A newspaper had featured me in a profile before this, and the writer had asked who my hero was. I responded with "Socrates" and still regret not mentioning these four guys in wheelchairs.

Ahimsa

One of the strangest headlines I'd ever seen appeared while I was back teaching in Cody: "Rooster kills California man in Cockfight."

A man apparently got stabbed in the leg with one of his rooster's blades and bled out before anybody could help him. Cockfighting was a misdemeanor in California, so he'd already paid $370 in fines and had pleaded no contest to owning and training an animal for fighting.

I could see why the fine wouldn't bother him much when I read that a bettors' pot had $10,000 in it at a cockfight south of Bakersfield.

And according to the *London Daily Mail*, in January a man in India died when a cock cut his throat.

All I could say was *How does it feel? Good for the roosters.*

On the other hand, I knew I should probably review the Ahimsa Yama, non-violence, before I went that route. The no harm Yama seemed to be the most troublesome for me. I couldn't help believing *my violence* would be *justifiable violence*. After all, I didn't see anything wrong with killing as many bats as I could.

Technology

The tools of teaching have undergone an obvious revolution, but using the tools effectively was slow to diffuse through the system. In April, I Skyped with Bart, Megan, Syd and Zan. In 1959, the "Weekly Reader" had a story about future telephones' potential for seeing the person on the other end of the line. I thought this was incredible and told my mother, who worked for the phone company, AT&T.

"Yes," she said. "That will probably happen in your lifetime."

Fifty-two years later, I had watched Zan play foosball and Syd play "I Got Rhythm" on the piano when it occurred to me that my Mass Communications class could Skype with a Cheyenne East graduate who co-directed *Saving Face*, the 2012 Academy Award winning documentary, so we set it up, and I realized how far behind I was in the possibilities of the technology.

Matt Hatton came to my home in Cody to hook up a wireless network so I could use my laptop anywhere, and I could order Netflix from the TV. I thought I might never leave the house.

But at the Bat House, where I had made enough progress to comfortably stay, I didn't have a TV and didn't plan to get one. It snowed ten inches there that weekend, and I snuggled in to read, listen to the radio, eat, and sleep. I imagined the Bat House as a refuge from too much technology, which seemed to make me work longer hours and not appreciate the natural world. But the pump kept running until I smelled it getting hot, and my retreat into serenity ended. When I shut the pump off, the connections down-line started leaking. I figured the joint compound had probably melted, so I tried to shut off the well valve outside in the culvert, but it was frozen. Jack lent me a milk-shed heater, which after two hours thawed the pipe out, and luckily the pipe did not break. Judd Fitzgerald helped me take the pipes out and re-tape them. It was finally working, and I had to admit I was grateful for the technology of the heater.

H.R., Bo, and Bryant almost had the sheetrock done — everything except the porch, and the wiring was done in the panel. Strangely, I felt closed in. The house had been open for so long that I didn't want the walls up, but I imagined Alexander Spencer, the old buffalo hunter, hunkering down in his cabin during a snowstorm and was grateful for my propane furnace and hot running water.

Private Histories

The countryside had begun to thaw when I attended Gale Youngbauer's funeral. He was a school friend's dad and my Scout leader with Bob Meredith. I always knew that he delivered Sanitary Dairy's milk out of Miles City, but he was so quiet about his World War II service that I knew little about it. Only at the funeral did I discover he'd been a Medic in the Bismarck Archipelago, the Philippines, New Guinea and Luzon. He was highly decorated with medals of all kinds, and I could not imagine what he had experienced. After spending two years in the Marshall Islands and diving the wrecks there, where I saw the terrible devastation of artillery's effect on ships, I at least came to a vague idea of what treating the burned and maimed of that war must have been like, but he never talked about it that I remembered. He was a happy man, ready to laugh at a good joke, a baseball coach, and always willing to teach me something. It was much too late to honor him, and I could only feel less ashamed of how I took him for granted when I realized I had to mature and learn something about history to appreciate him.

In Buff's Bar at poker, I won $370 playing mostly Omaha, and besides thinking I had the ghost of Nels Anderson whispering in my ear, I remembered the first time I sat at the polished wood bar with its embedded silver dollars to drink a glass of beer with Gale and Bob. I was twenty-one, and I thought I had passed into the Ultimate Zone of Manhood by perching myself on a stool, resting my elbows on the bar, and cradling a mug of cold Great Falls Select that bubbled in front of me. They made me feel like their equal there, with all my naiveté at that age, and only later did I realize how distant from their manhood I was. But then, they had accepted me and were sincerely interested in my life that far.

Cleaning up after H.R. and Bryant put in the windows on the porch of the Bat House, I realized how distant I was from them too, but I consciously practiced bridging the gap of our histories. H.R.'s knee was swelling and hurting from a fire-call injury, and he had to get back to Cody for a wedding, so they drove away in his Saab. They'd both been my students, and I'd taken them fishing since they were little, and just as Gale and Bob had histories obscured by the world's continual motion, mine was obscured to H.R and Bryant, and it did not seem important. What did matter, and probably the main reason I became a teacher was to discover from them what struggles they had in their lives and to offer whatever I could to move them along in a good direction, as Bob and Gale had done for me.

After they left, the sky opened with a steady, hard rain, and everything was mud, but I made it up the hill to the Rosebud Dump where a sandhill crane came right over my head, opened his long beak and "whirrrrr" ed at me. I wondered what it was trying to tell me. On returning to the House I discovered that the pump had no pressure — I called Frank Askin, and he told me to crack the gauge and turn it on again. It worked. I had water.

After stuffing openings in the porch with fiberglass before I left, hoping the bats would stay out as the weather warmed, I thought the sandhill crane might have also been trying to tell me something about learning as much as I could about people's histories, especially those closest to us. I was eager to be home with Theo.

The Flood

Because of the heavy snowpack and continuous rain, the Yellowstone River crested in May at its third highest level on record in Billings, Forsyth, and Miles City. The news was full of washed-out bridges, closed highways, and loss of livestock because of flooding in eastern and southern Montana. The town of Roundup seemed to have suffered the most. Drinking water, food and medicine were major concerns. Twenty miles of Interstate 90, from Livingston to Springdale, were closed. A state of emergency had been declared in a total of fifty-one Montana counties, cities, and Indian reservations.

Every basement in Forsyth was flooded. The town's antiquated sewage system could not handle the flow.

"I never realized how many people in Forsyth eat corn," Dr. Dean said, "until yesterday when I went into the basement."

My principal gave me permission to miss graduation and leave a few days early to find out what was happening with the Bat House. I called Jack to have him check on it, and he went into the basement as I listened for the bad news.

"The river is flowing over the field 50 yards to the south of you," he said, "but your basement is dry."

When I arrived, the house was nearly surrounded by water. The drain ditch had backed up a half mile and flooded the road, but the basement in the Bat House was dry. The only problem I had was Paul Wilkinson's texture on my drywall. The air was so humid that three de-humidifier pumps he had run into the showers and the basement drain could not dry the air fast enough for his mud to dry. The river was running over the field to the south of me, rolling huge cottonwood trees across it. The young man who leased it had planted corn, and he had lost all of it. It would be almost impossible to farm. *Someday the river will decide to cut across it,* I thought, *and the Bat House will have river frontage.*

On June 21, the river had begun to drop, and I managed the day, the longest of the year, on one hour of sleep. I was playing poker when the day started, and didn't get to sleep until 3 A.M. I put my cot in the usual east bedroom and was awakened at 4 A.M. by obnoxious robins. I couldn't sleep with the windows closed because it was too hot. The attic felt like a swamp, and the air conditioner was not hooked up yet. It sat in the grass under the apple tree like any logical air conditioner would.

The sun came up about five and blasted me through the un-curtained window. I moved the cot into the west bedroom. Wrestling the behemoth through the doorways without scratching any newly painted walls woke me up as much as I could be without coffee.

I dressed in fresh Levi's and shirt, had what coffee was left in my metal thermos and checked my bat traps, carefully stepping onto the porch, watching out for any pissed off cripples flopping around, and very slowly stepped around the chimney. There were two. One face down in the muck looked like he was close to the Great Bat God, or there already, and the other flapped with one wing, stretching his neck and showing his teeth at me, struggling and swinging with his whole six grams to get out of the goo.

I went downstairs and outside to find my old bat killer, the mop head on a weathered handle. It was lying in the weeds alongside the house by a mouse bait-station. I whacked him in the belly with the point of it, and blood poured out onto the deck, but he wasn't dead, so I whacked him in the head about four times. That did it. I just pushed the other guy's face deeper into the glue, and he pulled away, staring at me, as if he were begging for mercy. I pushed at his neck until blood rolled out his mouth.

"You little bastards," I said, "that'll teach you to shit on my deck."

I went down to the shed to find a crowbar or something to pull the staple in the glue trap and found an old iron rod about five feet long. It had a slight hook on one end and a circle on the other. I thanked Bill for his penchant for saving everything.

When I pulled them down, I inspected the flapper's wing barbs — they were at least a half inch, curved and wicked as a devil claw, but shiny and bony — much more dangerous, I thought, than the tiny teeth.

I started my chainsaw at six, an advantage to living in the country, and cut up the limbs of a silver leaf maple that had fallen. I imagined what my neighbors in Cody would think if I did that. Since the brush pile was much too big to burn, I hauled the limbs to the Rosebud Dump, then went to town and had breakfast with Paul Kanta and Harold McCaskie. Paul commented that my dad was "a helluva man with a chainsaw."

I said that could have been, but I'd never seen him get one to start, and Paul laughed. He said he remembered a time Dad was trying to start one and all it did was "putt-putt-putt", and he was swearing at it so hard he could hear him a half a mile away.

"That sounds like my experiences with him and chainsaws," I said. "One of the most important lessons I learned from him is to never swear at an inanimate thing. He had about five saws, and not a damned one would start no matter how much he cussed."

I had two McCulloughs," Harold said.

"I wouldn't expect anything else from an old Scot like you," I said.

"One lasted about two years, and the other one didn't last six months," he said.

"You were probably too stingy to put bar oil in it," I said.

"No, they were just too stingy to work very long," he said. "I finally bought a Homelite."

"How did that work?" I asked.

"Not worth a damn," he said. "I decided it was cheaper to hire someone to do the job."

I bought a Stihl," I said, "and I love it. My boy has one for his summer job with the Forest Service, and he recommended it."

"Where's it made?" Paul said. "China or some goddamn place?"

"Sounds German," Harold said. "Must be made in Germany."

"Summer job?" Paul said. "What does he do the rest of the year?"

"He's a school psychologist," I said. "A chip off his mother's block."

"The last psychologist I went to said I was fine," Harold said, "and I told him he was crazy."

Harold lived in Bob Hecht's old house, about a half block from my grandmother's house where I lived. Bob's son, Bob Jr., and I used to mow the grass on the roof of the old sod house they had converted to a one car garage in the alley. I would hand a push mower up to Bob, and we would take turns getting the blades to whirl at the roof's lawn, and Mr. Hecht would give us each a quarter for the job.

"Is the old soddy still in the alley?" I asked Harold.

"Why yes," he said, "and in fine condition. I water the roof once a week, but I can't get up there to mow it, so the grass is about a foot tall. My solution is that when I die, I'll just be buried inside the building, and they can fill it up with dirt."

"A sartorial sarcophagus of sod," I said.

"A magnificent mausoleum of mud," he said, laughing as his tongue danced around his four teeth.

After buying more glue traps, I returned to the Bat House and put them up. An adult weasel and its kit ran into the yard, not bothered by my standing ten feet away. The mother ran around the yard while the kit watched her. She finally loped up to my pickup, looked around, hopped under it and curled herself up. The kit followed and curled up next to her. I guessed she'd been harassed by an eagle, osprey, or hawk, and just needed refuge for a nap. I was glad I didn't have chickens. Every one of them would be dead with her around.

I mowed the lawn, and the weasels ran off into the field. At sunset, swarms of mosquitoes emerged. They hummed against the screens. I watched a fox trailing scent along the edge of the alfalfa. A rooster pheasant ran parallel to it about fifteen yards away. The fox paid it no mind, and suddenly disappeared into the grass. A hen flew up, and I thought the fox had found the nest or the chicks.

At dinner in Fitzgerald's, I ordered a rib steak and called Theo. The waitress had been a Toyota saleswoman and was going to college to be a pharmacist's assistant. She was the aunt of the girl the ghost whispered to at the poker table. She fulfilled my request to assemble a salad with tomato and bell pepper instead of the orthodox eastern Montana one: chopped iceberg lettuce with a few grated carrot slivers.

"Maybe we'll start a fad," I said, "if we could just get Rita to buy a cucumber, it might take off."

At the poker game, I found three ticks crawling on me.

Bats, ticks, mosquitoes, bedbugs, fox, and weasels, I thought. All blood suckers. Just like the House.

Lying on my cot at 1 A.M., I heard coon dogs not far away. I recognized their baying from when I was a kid, hunting at night on the Tongue River. I understood their calls, hot, confused, hot again, and finally treed. I heard the rifle crack. I fell asleep then and dreamed of hunting huge bats with my shotgun, but I could never hit them.

In the morning, I had four more bats in the traps. When I hit them with my old bat killer, they sounded like a cross between a snake's hissing and a kitten's cry. They also cackled and chittered — like witches in productions of Macbeth. I wondered at their natural enemies — snakes, cats, coyotes, but these could never get them unless they had access to high places — I remembered seeing a photo in Natural Geographic of a tree python catching a fruit bat in flight — no pythons around eastern Montana, I thought, just as well.

Bats are not as easy to kill as one might think. An equal force to a human would emphatically dispatch the human, but the brown bat collapses, then begins to twitch and jerk. I think it is "just nerves" as I have had the movement of dead fish, deer and pheasant described to me since I was four, and as I now explained to my grandchildren. What that meant, I was not entirely sure. I knew it had something to do with autonomic reflexes, but how that happened, I didn't know. I supposed the brain is not dead, but the heart and lungs are. One raised its eyes to me that morning, after I had punched it with the mop head at least six times, blood oozing from its belly, and looked at me as if desperately declaring, "Why? We were here first."

"Yes," I said, "but it's the last time you'll ever shit here."

I felt a bit like Stoker's Van Helsing must have when he drove the wooden stake into Dracula's heart — FINALLY! I had read that book as a senior in high school and got goose bumps during Study Hall in broad daylight when I read the passage where the Count scurries down the castle wall, his cape spread like a bat's wings, his head small and swiveling up at Harkins. Stoker's granting the vampire an eternal life, though cursed by sunlight and mankind, now presented itself as tribute to the bat, survivor of thousands of years of virus laden existence.

When I began to set up my glue traps again, I had an idea. Instead of stapling each trap into the soffit border and bending the glue pad, I realized if I screwed a teacup hook into the soffit, I could hang a clipboard with two glue pads snapped into it from the hook, so I made a trip to the dump and went to Clark Hardware.

Cal McConnel's store was a dump in its own universe. Betty and Ray Clark ran it for years, and it had not changed except for the antiques Cal bought. His most recent acquisition was a three-panel room divider, a sort of westernized shoji, with three different women who looked like soiled doves in first class bedrooms. Other than his penchant for buying objects of art like this, the store hadn't changed in fifty years.

It still smelled of leather, machine oil, and iron, an altogether pleasant and welcoming scent of sundry goods. Two customers meeting in the solitary aisle had to turn sideways to get by each other. Horse blankets and saddle pads rose in a corner almost to the ceiling. Snow sleds, weed trimmers, bridles, hackamores, lanterns, and fan belts hung along the walls. I had the feeling that anything I needed was somewhere in that store.

"Someday there'll be an avalanche in here," Cal said, "and I'll get buried."

It took him a few minutes to find them, but he had the teacup hooks in a drawer below seven rows of drawers full of ten-pound-and-up chain hooks.

"How many do you want?" he asked, holding a handful above the box.

"Four," I said, thinking one for each clipboard, each with two glue pads. I was getting serious.

"All that for just four?" he said.

"OK," I said. "Five. In case I drop one and can't find it. And I need some more glue pads."

"They're back, huh?"

"Yeah," I said, looking at a guy the size of a pro tackle who'd been waiting for Cal ever since the hunt for the hooks began. He smiled at me. He had no idea what to make of Cal's question.

"I also need a cooler," I said.

"What kind?"

"Just a cheap one."

"Styrofoam?"

"Yeah."

He walked toward the back room, and I followed him past his screen and window repair table. He had a two-foot path through all his merchandise, plumbing supplies, windows, pipe, rolls of screen and chicken wire, and maybe a few cadavers. He went to the far corner in the back, where he wrestled out a box the size of a coffin, ripped it open and handed me a lid first, then the cooler.

"How much is it?" I asked. "Nine hundred?"

"Buck ninety-five."

"Holy shit," I said.

The pro tackle laughed. "He should fill it with beer for that price," he said.

"What are you going to do?" Cal asked, "put the bats on ice?"

"Cookies," I said. "Chocolate chip. My wife made them for me for Father's Day. I don't want them to melt in the cab."

"She must have made a shitload," Cal said.

"I only have a baggie full, but they're precious," I said. "Precious."

With a ball point pen, Cal wrote what I bought on his hand, and I left to have dinner at Fitzgerald's. It was eighty-two degrees out when I went in, and I decided I would just have a salad. The waitress was very kind and made the same salad as the Florida woman had when I asked her, but she put it in a bigger bowl. I tipped her twenty-five percent.

After dinner, I drove to the diversion dam to check on the river's level, and Arvin sat in his wheelchair there amid a cloud of mosquitoes. He had bought some mosquito netting for his hat and said the netting allowed him to see long range through the cloud. He was trying to get people in Forsyth to build bat houses so they would eat the mosquitoes.

"They can eat twelve hundred of them in an hour," he said.

"Good idea," I said. "I hope they flap around your head to eat mosquitoes all night."

A New Shirt

At 2 A.M. I awoke to something banging around in metal. I couldn't tell where. I thought a bat was in the bathroom vent at first, but it came again, much louder, lumber rattling around too, so I decided it was a raccoon stepping on my ladder that lay on a stack of two-by-fours in the yard. But it kept occurring, and a coon would most likely be gone by then. I thought a bat was trapped in a metal tube. It could only be the vent, or perhaps the chimney. Maybe a squirrel. It was loud.

I never learned what it was, and in the morning, I went to Miles City early to meet with a roofing estimator. He had come out a few weeks earlier with his son to measure the roof and make an informal bid. He was a pleasant guy, and I liked his son, a ninth grader at Custer County High School. He was supposed to have a formal bid and samples of the product to go on the porch roof — something people can walk on, a combination deck and roof. I thought he should be coming to me, which most contractors do, but I needed a new work shirt anyway. All my shirts were mostly in tatters.

I was wearing a torn up one at a poker game a few days before, and as I raked in a pot, a player next to me said, "That's a damned good pot. Maybe you can afford to buy a new shirt now."

The roofing estimator had neither the bid nor the sample product. He told me about how he'd been in an accident and was on pain medication, and how his wife was too busy to type the estimate. I commiserated with him and suggested yoga for the headaches, which I suspected was just muscle tension in his shoulders. He broke down the cost for me on an index card, his printing neat and precise. It was $2,000 above the original estimate: $500 to put on a plastic railing and eight dollars a foot for the gutter instead of the original five.

"That's what my uncle told me," he said. "It's because the roof is so high, and it's out in the country. I just do this to help him out," he said. "I don't get paid for it." The total was $10,100.

I went to a lumberyard to check on egress window casements and talked with the owner about the quality of shingles and flat roof products. When I asked him about the reputation of the roofer's company, he shook his head.

"Fly by night," he said. They change names, states, and crews all the time. They're into me for about ten thousand dollars. And I don't think I'll ever see it."

He recommended Shugard's for a good work shirt. The sales lady who helped me there said she'd been selling boots in Miles City for forty-five years. I asked her where, and she said she started at the Miles City Saddlery.

"I used to go there when I was a kid," I said, "just to smell the leather and look at all the boots and hats and saddles I couldn't afford."

She said her husband's parents had run the Angela store and Post Office, which was all there was of Angela when I spent summers with my uncle and aunt at their Dog Creek ranch. Her married name was Holmlund.

"Tell him I probably owe him or his parents some money," I said, "for all the Crooks Cigars I used to steal when my aunt drove us there to buy groceries. I started smoking them when I was about nine. Still haven't kicked the habit."

She laughed, asked my name and found a Carhartt shirt that was perfect when I tried it on. As I was paying the cashier, she appeared at the exit and said her husband would like to meet me.

"Probably to collect for the cigars," I said.

We met at Gallagher's, and he seemed vaguely familiar. He began telling stories about my brother and him. One was about getting caught by my aunt Eunice as they were looking at a Playboy in the bunkhouse, and it shocked me a little to hear him call her by the nickname only the family used, "Noonie."

He remembered my uncle Wallace getting angry and throwing a wrench out into the field while trying to fix a tractor, and then realizing he needed it to fix the tractor. All three of them walked around in the field for an hour before finding it.

"He wasn't a good mechanic at all," he said. "He hated machinery."

"And cows," I said. "I learned to cuss by listening to him swear at cattle."

He laughed and said, "But he loved horses."

"Yes," I said, "he couldn't sit still at an auction if it had a good horse. He'd be popping up and down on his chair if there was a horse in the ring he liked."

"He knew horses," Keith said. "He had some of the best racehorses in the country."

"In the '80s I went with him to a simulcast at the Fair Grounds," I said. "I asked him which horse he thought would win and he said there was no question. Bet Your Ass would win by a mile. I had a $400 check I'd gotten that day for two weeks' work, so I put it on that horse. They came out of the gate, and Bet Your Ass took off, leaving the rest of the herd in the dust."

"Hell, I was thinking as Bet Your Ass headed down the home stretch at least five lengths ahead, there's nothing to this if you listen to Wallace. I'll double my money just like that."

"And then the horse stopped. He planted both front feet in the track and hung his head. Wallace said he blew a lung. I asked what that was. Wallace shrugged his shoulders, telling me the air sacs in his lung just burst."

"When I told him I just lost $400, he was more concerned about the horse than my money, telling me it was OK, he'd be all right in no time."

"'Maybe,' I said, 'but I won't.'

"I never bet on a horse race again," I told Keith. "But I've wanted to."

I paid the bill for lunch, assuaging my guilt a bit for stealing the cigars, and left them, sure we would visit more soon. I was driving down the highway toward Rosebud when I got a call from the roofer's nephew.

"We've got a problem," I said. "I will find another roofer."

"OK," he said, "Goodbye."

I called my cousin Leon about hooking up the air conditioner again, told him about the heat and humidity in the attic, and the roofers' opinions about venting it, and he said he'd stop in at an insulation business he trusted to find out what he could. He called back before I reached Rosebud.

"If the Insulator put at least seven inches of foam under the roof," he said, "you don't need to ventilate it. The heat and humidity are probably from taping, texturing, and painting in such humid weather. Just put a fan in the attic and on the upstairs floor to move the air out."

I drove to Forsyth to buy another fan and stopped at The Station to sign up for a free-roll poker tournament. $50 to the winner. Red Sorenson was sitting at the bar drinking coffee.

His son Duane was a good friend who had died in a plane crash a few years before. I didn't know many men who had drunk alcohol harder than Red. It seemed to me he'd been drunk his whole life. He was a short, slight man, almost a double for the Hollywood actor Red Buttons, and with a strong grip in his handshake. I could tell he didn't recognize me, so I told him who I was, yelling in his left ear, and then he remembered me.

"I'm ninety-two," he said with obvious pride.

"That's pretty damned good for all the shit you've been through," I said. "What island was it you caught the bullet? Leyte?"

"Yeah," he said, "that was a son-of-a-bitch."

"What other islands were you on? Kwajalein?"

"No," he said, "mostly the Philippines. There were so many of those small ones I don't remember their names. Hawaii. I got there the day after Pearl Harbor. But hell, that was all over."

"Where did you get hit?" I asked.

"Leyte," he said.

"No, I mean where did you get hit with the bullet?"

"Oh, in the neck," he said, feeling both sides of it. "I think there's a scar there somewhere," he said, stretching it and feeling both sides with his hands. "I don't remember which side, but it tore all the leaders in my shoulder here." He felt his right shoulder.

"Ligaments?" I said. "And tendons?"

"Yeah, the leaders."

"Did you go down when it hit you?" I asked." Or did you not realize what had happened?"

"You damned right I went down," he said.

"What was it like when you got hit?" I asked. "Like someone threw a helluva punch at your head?"

He grinned and said, "Yeah, a lot worse than that. I don't remember anything until I tried to pick up my rifle and couldn't. I knew my leaders was gone."

After promising Red I'd visit him at the assisted living center, I went back to the house and set up the fans, placed my bat traps, and fired up the weed eater. I cut down a ton of what looked like rhubarb, but which Pam told me was "dock," a weed she said grew big burrs that stuck to everything. I spent too much time chopping weeds, and I was covered with bits of green and sweat, so I called the Station to tell them I wouldn't make the free roll.

I showered and went in for the cash game. An Indian girl from

Arizona who was a welder at Colstrip had won the tournament. Her husband Billy and she sat next to me in the cash game, and she impressed me with her poker acumen. She slow played pocket Aces and took me for about a hundred dollars in one hand.

"Now I know you are one those sneaky Indians like in the movies," I said, and she got a big kick out of it, her depth of perception obviously more arcane than any of the tournament players had realized.

I told her she was too good for me and left while I was $80 ahead.

It was raining like hell when I came out of the bar. Lightening was flashing like tinsel strips in a black sky across the horizon from the south and north. I'd never seen anything like it. I stopped the pickup and watched it for about ten minutes — bolts straight down in constant lines for what looked like a hundred miles. I didn't think I would have any bats visiting me with that storm, but when I got to the house, the air was warm and still and full of flying insects. I tried to be optimistic.

I have a new shirt and eighty dollars toward the cost of a new roof, I thought, *and at least my leaders ain't gone.*

Anthony

I was home from the national journalism convention in Anaheim, where Anthony Prosceno did not win anything on his Huckleberry Finn story. It covered the "revised" edition of Huck Finn recently published by Twain scholar Allan Gribben at Auburn University. Gribben replaced the word *nigger* with *slave* 219 times, claiming he was "doing something constructive by simply eliminating a word that's a clear barrier for many people."

Anthony's story contained several opinions held by teachers and students, including one of the few black students at Cody High. One JEA judge objected to Anthony's sitting at a library table with several editions of Twain's book in front of him. He said it was "arrogant for a journalist to sit in a stand-up." The formal stand-up included a reporter *standing up* in front of the camera, often walking toward it or around in the scene being covered.

But Anthony's scene was a library, and I had the feeling the story was too candid for the judge, and it wouldn't have mattered if Anthony had been standing while wearing a tuxedo. He looked like a miniature Obama, which added to the emotional impact, and the story had balance, superb videography, and excellent pace in editing. I could not believe the judge's comments, especially since I had procured the judges and highly respected the one who made the comment, but like I told Anthony, "A judge is like a ref. Sometimes they just make bad calls."

He wasn't too bothered by it. Receiving the Al Neuharth

Freedom Forum Award and a scholarship to the Walter Cronkite School in Phoenix, Anthony would be an excellent journalist. He shook his head and moved on, just like Huck Finn.

Pittsburgh Boy

I had seven bats hanging in the glue pads when I woke up. Theo was leaving on a plane for Oklahoma at 5 P.M., so I got up at six, wanting to get home early to be with her for at least a few hours before she left. She would be driving back to Cody with our three grandkids and our daughter-in-law. From the tone of her voice, I didn't think it would make a difference if I spent the whole day or five minutes with her before she left. She was getting tired of my being gone. She was getting sick of the whole damn relationship, already suggesting that I just go to the Rosebud place to live by myself. She had no idea how this disheartened me, but I had kept it to myself, understanding how difficult it was for her to be alone for weeks at a time, and knowing that if I tried explaining how much work I was doing on the place, she would not be able to comprehend it. She only saw the money she was earning fly away with me to Montana.

It took me a couple hours to kill the bats, clean up and replace the traps. I only had two, so I put one each on a clipboard and hung them on both sides of the chimney. I closed most of the windows but left a few on the east side open a bit, turned the fans to medium and called Pam to see if she would come out to paint in the afternoon. It would be a week or more before I could get back again.

I ate a micro-waved Denver burrito, drank all the coffee I had and carefully folded the bats on the glue-traps and Gorilla tape into a plastic garbage bag. The most dangerous part of a bat, I decided, is the hook on its wing. And the piss that shoots out of them when they are dead. Or the blood. They hang upside down, and they tilt their stomachs so they don't shit on their head, but when they are dead, personal hygiene doesn't matter to them anymore, and a stream of urine can hit you in the face if you aren't careful. It can even if you are careful.

Their toes have rounded gecko-like pads, and each toe has a nasty claw with hair extending around the claw. Even while wearing thick leather gloves, I was extremely careful not to get stuck by one, and I sprayed my gloves with a Clorox and water solution. I often saw photos of live Little Browns being held in someone's hand, but I was not expert enough to do that. Afraid I'd pick up lice, fleas, or bat bugs, I didn't even want to hold a dead one.

All this careful cleanup took time, so I didn't get into Billings until about noon. I called Theo to tell her I needed to research roofing material and lighting, and she said she was not happy about it, but she could get a ride to the airport or take her own car and leave it there.

I was hungry, but I was also eager to talk with a guy who said the answer to my flat roof/deck was a product which I could paint on, so I looked in the phone book for the business address, and it was downtown on 4th Avenue. As I was managing the heavy traffic there, someone began honking a horn, and another man gave the honker the bird.

It occurred to me how angry people in America are about driving their cars. I had not experienced that high level of anger anywhere but in the U.S.

A few weeks earlier, I found myself behind an Idaho SUV crossing the railroad tracks in Forsyth. A locomotive sat idling fifty yards away as we started across, and the SUV was crawling. Nervous that the locomotive would start, and the semaphores would come down, I stayed right on the tail of the vehicle in front of me, all the time wondering why it was going so slowly. We got across the tracks, and the SUV swerved off to the right. As I passed by, the driver held up his arms in a "what was that all about" sign. Because several cars were behind me, I just looked at him and kept going.

When I pulled into the Town Pump to get coffee, the guy pulled up and honked his horn as I walked toward the door. I turned around and saw him give me the finger.

"Why were you on my ass back there at the crossing?" he said.

"I see you're from Idaho," I said, thinking I would explain that crossing to him. I had nearly been killed at it in 1966 when I was driving around town, a cigar in my mouth and my arm around my girlfriend, not paying attention to the oncoming engine.

"I'm from Pittsburgh, Pennsylvania," he said, like he was quite proud of that. I knew immediately he was part of the turn-over crew at Colstrip. He had flown to Billings from PA and rented the SUV with Idaho plates. The company was paying for everything, even his motel and meals. He would work at the Colstrip power plant for a month, and then move to his next job. I realized he was just as tired as I was, just as frustrated with his life, and probably a lot more fed up with eastern Montana.

"Well," I said, "there was an engine in the block there. I was afraid it would move forward. It would have thrown the switch, and the semaphores would have come down."

"Did it?" he yelled, and as I started to try telling him that was not the point, he yelled again, "Well, did it?"

I paused then, looking at him carefully. I thought I'd just drill him with a right punch to the nose. I figured I could break it easily from the angle I had through his window. I took a half step toward him and bent my neck to see his hands. I couldn't see his right hand. He might have a gun, a knife, or a club there. He moved his head back, as though anticipating my move.

If I'm the first to get violent here, I thought, I could lose everything I've worked nearly forty years for. My family, my reputation, my own sense of decency.

This all took about two seconds.

I looked directly at his eyes. They were alive and wide. I knew he had something in his hand. He was pushing me.

I turned around without saying anything and walked back toward the Town Pump door. As I approached my pickup, he yelled at me again.

"Fuck you, faggot," he said.

"Be careful," I said, shaking my head without turning around. "Be careful, boy." I had a chainsaw in the backseat of the pickup. It occurred to me to open the back door, get it out, fire it up, and walk back to his SUV. I could poke the running blade through his window to see if he wanted to continue.

"You fucking faggot," he said.

"Be careful, boy," I said again, and looked at him. He sat there by the gas pumps without moving his SUV.

"Fuck you, faggot," he said again.

Now I opened the door of the pickup and saw a can of fuel for the chainsaw. OK, I thought. I'll dump a little of this on you and flick my cigar lighter to get you started.

I opened the cap to the fuel and dug my lighter out of my pocket. When I turned around, he rolled up his window and drove away, still looking at me.

A high school boy stood in the parking lot watching and listening. I glanced at him as I put the fuel can back. He didn't say anything, but still stood looking at me. I thought of my grandkids and realized if I had done what I was going to do, I'd probably be in prison when they graduated from high school. I'd have given up everything for vanity. I was astounded at myself for seriously considering retaliating at an adolescent mix-up.

I could have just apologized for tailgating him, I thought. That might have defused it immediately. The Satya Yama: commitment to truth. Honest communication and action. On the other hand, we were only going five miles an hour. We weren't doing eighty down the Interstate.

I told Scooter about it later. He said I should have drilled him through the window. At least then, he said, even if I had gotten my ass kicked, I'd have retained my self-respect. He was half drunk when he said this. I didn't want to explain my self-respect had nothing to do with messed up people calling me names.

But I also came from the same place culturally as Scooter did. It was a code ingrained in us since childhood, and in the back of my brain, however deeply covered with education, a world of experience and sixty-one years of whatever wisdom I had garnered, it was still there, and it bothered me. "Yellow Belly," "Chickenshit," and "Spineless Coward" were monikers to be avoided at all costs, and whether Hollywood Westerns or schoolyard squabbles or alcoholic bar fights were the cause, I couldn't shake the haunting notion I had backed down from a fight, which I had never done.

When I told Dr. Dean how I had walked away from Mr. Pittsburgh, and that it was sort of troubling me, he said, "Ahh, you've just grown up. No matter what you had done, you could only have lost. It was just one of those situations."

Noise

When I came into Billings after a week at the Rosebud place, where mostly I had heard nothing but birds — no traffic sounds, airplanes, lawnmowers, snow mobiles, neighbors yelling, partying, car stereos blaring, dogs barking, or machinery of any kind except for occasional farm equipment — the noise was overwhelming.

The worst was motorcycles. A few riders are just obnoxious jerks, but most bikers think other people like the sound of their exhaust pipes. I'd had four bikes, so I knew the thrill of riding, but at a stoplight in 1968 in Madison, Wisconsin, on my way to the National Democratic Convention in Chicago, I popped the throttle as one is prone to do at a stoplight — just to hear it, I guess, or to draw attention to oneself probably — certainly not to keep it from dying, because any rider worth his salt will have it tuned to idle perfectly at a stoplight — a man crossing the street by the Capitol said, "Too loud," and I realized he was right.

I felt ashamed. Madison was quiet there. People were mostly walking. Quite a few bicyclists pedaled by, and I sat there getting my ego off by making noise, albeit a noise I had come to love from a variety of machines: Harleys, Moto Guzzis, BMWs, Nortons, Triumphs, Ducatis. They all had their own aural personalities, like rifles and pistols and canon. And I understood the advantage of having a bike loud enough a motorist can hear on the road. I'd nearly been killed six or seven times by unconscious drivers. But for some reason that day in 1968, perhaps because of the realizations the whole country was having, I knew that guy crossing the street was right. He was correct in telling me as politely as possible that I was a huge unnecessary annoyance to civilization.

I feel the problem of noise is epidemic. I remember and cherish the few places I've been in the world where it is quiet: the Grand Canyon, Greek fishing villages where the only sound is the sea and the murmur of conversation, deep in mountain ranges like the Thorofare southwest of Cody or the Scapegoat Wilderness in Montana, Prince William Sound in Alaska, and the Marshall Islands.

It's not just an annoyance. It's deadly. According to research by psychologists in Munich, children near an airport suffered from poor comprehension, memory, and attention skills; that is until the airport was moved, and then these skills improved, but the children by the new airport suffered from the same problems within six months. The researchers found much higher levels of adrenaline and cortisol (stress hormones) and higher blood pressures among the children next to the working airports. Similar research has been done on children in schools next to trains, like in New York City, with poorer reading skills as a result.

During my week at the Bat House, the only noises that stressed me were those I imagined had something to do with bats, and they all came as I lay in the dark on my cot. Maybe that was just as bad.

Gang Boy

In Billings on my way home, after negotiating the traffic, I pulled into a buffet style restaurant, where I had discovered I could eat all I wanted for six dollars and ninety-nine cents at the Early Bird Special, which started at 4 P.M. I sat down with a plate of salad. A girl who looked like Raquel Welch in a mini-skirt and a sleeveless, low-cut V-neck sat behind me. Her boyfriend was a skinny seventeen or eighteen-year-old wearing what I thought of as the gangland attire of L.A. — a blue and white, buttoned-at-the-neck checkered shirt hanging down over a pair of shin length shorts, Nike shoes and shaved head. He sat next to Raquel. Another young girl and an older woman I took to be his or Raquel's mother joined them.

Gang Boy was arguing with the mother about how he had not been out of line on some incident or other, how he had been "behaving," and his language was profane. Nobody at their table or at nearby ones challenged him. They were all quiet.

He finally shut up, and facing the buffet lanes, I thought it would be a great place to bring my grandkids if we didn't have to listen to someone like him. I believed *my* grandchildren would have impeccable manners and make healthy choices in filling their plates, and then quit kidding myself and realized they would probably dip their spinach in the chocolate fountain.

I leaned back in my chair to see the sign with kids' prices, and I offended Gang Boy's territorial imperative.

I didn't catch his exact words, but thought I heard something about putting his "fucking knuckles" against my skull. I realized I had probably leaned over into Raquel's airspace, possibly appearing like a pervert trying to peep at her cleavage.

"He wasn't doing anything wrong," I heard the mother say. "He was just leaning back to see the sign."

Gang Boy ranted about his near-death warrant on my soul. Every other word was "fuck." I wondered how they could live with this, and almost asked, but decided to keep my mouth shut.

Raquel and Gang Boy got up to get another plate, and he glared at me as he went by. I averted his stare.

A few minutes later, they came back, and he was swearing about something that happened during their foray at the buffet. They stood in front of me, holding their plates while he blabbered about what he should do to a man at the buffet. Raquel had a slight smile on her face, searching people's reactions to his profanity, as if she couldn't wait for an eruption.

A bottle of A-1 sauce, square and hard as gunstock, sat close to my plate, and I thought of asking Gang Boy if he'd please watch his mouth because it was ruining my meal. I imagined his movement, hitting him in the temporal lobe with the A-1 bottle, seeing him drop like a shot steer, and asking Raquel how she liked her Gang Boy now.

But I finished my salad and walked toward the exit, stopping when the hostess asked me how everything was. I told her I didn't appreciate Gang Boy's profanity. She asked me to identify him, said she was sorry and that she would tell the manager. I went to my pickup in the parking lot and waited to see them come out. I couldn't help but think of my old veteran friends like Bill, Red, Art, Gale, Bob, and old Ken Hill, a poker playing friend who had been knocked unconscious by a mortar round close to the Harley Davidson he rode as a courier at Anzio. He had awakened in England, and the first thing he'd said was, "Is the bike OK?"

What would they think of this kid? How would they feel about nearly losing their lives and seeing it come to this? I doubted they would care one whit about the little punk and concluded that they had probably experienced plenty like him in their lives. I reminded myself of most of my students who acted with courage, grace, and gratitude, like Anthony.

"I don't know anything about politics," I remembered Ken's saying, "but I can tell you this: she's worth fighting for." He was referring to the country, of course, and I supposed if he were alive, he would still feel that way, even if he could observe many Americans' behavior.

After ten minutes, I left, confident Gang Boy was making a scene Raquel loved after the manager asked him to clean up his language.

Nite Guards

I called Biff the Batman again to find the name of the company that made bat and bird repellant sound devices. He said several products successfully repel birds, like "Bird-B-Gone," "BirdAway," and others, but he didn't know if they worked on bats. I researched again on the internet. They wanted as much as $600 for some of the products in the bat category, and the reviews were less than encouraging.

Then I found "Nite Guard," a solar powered box the size of a cigarette pack that blinks a red light twice every second. "It is weatherproof, environmentally friendly," and "emits an LED 'Flash of Danger' seen by animals up to one-fourth mile away." If installed at the eye levels for various animals, it was supposed to repel deer, skunks, coyotes, foxes, raccoons, and other varmints that terrorize the night. I called the company and got a lady who said she had never had anyone try them on bats.

She assured me that if they didn't work, I could send them back, so I ordered two at $20 each. I still didn't have them on my next trip, when I got a call from Shale asking me if it was OK to hook up the air conditioner next week instead of that day. I said it was OK, and went to a roofing company, looked at a sample of Deck Rite, and asked about asphalt shingles. The secretary didn't have a sample and said her boss couldn't make it to estimate the roofing job because he was on the hospital roof taking care of some kind of emergency repair.

When I got to the house, I was standing in the driveway watching two spotted mule deer fawns hiding in the grass when a bat flew by my head. It was four o'clock and about eighty-seven degrees. I was trying to understand why it was flying around in the daytime, when a robin dive-bombed it, pecking it on the head. The bat circled a tree a few times where the robin had a nest, the robin on the bat's tail like a Messerschmitt, and then collapsed in the gravel road in front of me. The robin lit a few feet away, watching it and diving at it to slam it on the head. The bat lay there with its wings out and raised its head, baring its teeth when the robin attacked. After three or four of these skirmishes, the bat flew up, around the tree and off toward the northwest.

I was still wondering why the stupid thing was out in daylight when Theo called. I told her about what I had just seen, and she said, "Well, the robins are your friends."

About then the robin came from the east into the tree like a streak, and something brown fluttered to the ground. I walked over, searching the grass carefully until I saw it — a bat pup. It couldn't fly yet. It occurred to me then that the "wounded bat" victimized by the robin had been its mother. She had given birth to it in the same tree where the robin had her nest, and the robin would not have it. I figured the bat had faked being hurt to decoy the robin from her baby, just as I had seen killdeer, grouse, pheasants, curlews, and ducks do all my life, and I wondered how they learn that.

I walked to the house to get a two-by-four and returned, but I couldn't see the little bat. I soon found that it had crawled about five feet away in the thirty seconds it had taken me to get the two-by-four. I tapped it, and it raised its head, cackling at me before I killed it.

It wouldn't have made it anyway without its mother, I told myself. It was a mercy killing. Reverse Ahimsa.

I measured the egress window and the basement door for

ordering the window well and the steel outside door, cleaned up four bats, killing one on the chimney, reset traps, sprayed the area with Tempo, mowed the lawn, opened the entry to the attic and put a fan up there, and drove to Billings to pick up Matt. His wife, their three kids, and his brother were in Cody with his kids for the Fourth of July, and he had flown in at the last minute.

The next day, I took five-year-old Zan Man, and Sydney and Mason Eli, who were both seven, to the rodeo. They took turns looking through my binoculars at the clowns. I bought them kettle corn, root beer, hot dogs, and peanuts. They wanted cotton candy, but I told them it wasn't good for them.

A brother of one of my female students got his face slammed into the back of a bull's head, and he was knocked out. I saw her get up from the stands and run down to the arena. The crew carried him away on a stretcher to an ambulance.

"That is one mean bull," Mason said.

"He didn't mean any harm," I said. "He was just doing his job."

"Well, it looked to me like he was trying to kill the guy," Mason said.

"The guy got on his back," I said. "He was only trying to get rid of him."

"That wasn't good for him," Zan said. "He should have just had cotton candy."

I didn't understand why the robin got rid of the mother bat and her baby in my silver maple. It seemed they could have co-existed in the tree, but I didn't want to co-exist with bats in *my* house either, and I wondered at the creation of the comic book *Batman and Robin*. It didn't make biologic sense for Batman's sidekick to be "Robin, Boy Wonder."

Mason and Ollie

After the Fourth, Bart and his family had to return to Lyman, Wyoming, and I took Matt and his two boys, Mason Eli and Oliver, to the Bat House. Three bats were stuck to the glue pads, but their heads were curled under their bodies, not giving Mason Eli and Ollie a very good look at them.

"They're small," Mason Eli said, his big blue eyes studying them.

"Yeah," I said, "but they shit a ton."

Ollie cracked up at this. His eyes were brown and huge, and I thought he should be in Hollywood. His skin was the color of milk chocolate, his dark brown hair thick and long, while Mason Eli's was short and red, his skin as fair as mine. Their three-year old sister Melissa was a stunning beauty, with long auburn hair that was constantly falling across her blue eyes. I couldn't wait until I could take her fishing, but I was very glad she was not on this trip because she followed me around all day asking, "What are you doing?" in a sing song voice, with a stress on "DO."

I had the two "Nite Guard" solar powered lights the lady from Minnesota sent me, so I hung one from a tea hook, replacing one of the clipboards, and wondered how to do the same on the west side of the chimney, where it wouldn't get the solar rays it needed to recharge it.

"Set it down here on the concrete where it will aim up in the corner," Matt said, so I placed it there.

We loaded downed limbs, two garbage barrels, and scraps of construction materials into my trailer, and drove to the Rosebud dump, which consisted of two truck hauler dumpsters with iron mesh lids that cranked open and closed by using a windlass on the sides. Anybody who paid taxes could throw anything in them. The guy who hauled the dumpsters to Colstrip, forty miles away, had complained to the manager that I was dumping too much in there when I was gutting the house.

"I've seen just about everything except a human body in here," I told the boys, "and it wouldn't surprise me if one day I see that."

We drove the seven miles back to the house, and I put the boys inside the fences I'd built around the Haralson trees, Apple Tree Jail. I gave them each a bottle of water, gloves, and a hat and told them to pull weeds. They did a good job, so I took them to town for pizza and ice cream at Top That, then to the Roxy to watch "Cars 2."

The night was full of wind, lightning, and thunder. From the darkened bedroom, as I watched the lightning, Matt watched the storm on "Weather Bug", an application on his Blackberry.

"The worst of it is going north of us," he said, and later, after it had passed, he said, "Another one just popped up from the south and it's heading right for us."

I worried about hail. I had $23,000 in windows in the house. We walked around in the dark in our shorts, lightning occasionally brightening the room. The boys slept through the storm, even when a lightning bolt flashed white with a simultaneous canon-like boom.

A rotten muddy smell like that of dead tadpoles drifted through the windows. I remembered the stench from my childhood when I'd found dried mud puddles where the sperm cell shaped pollywogs had not made it to frog-hood. Matt could not sleep because of it, and neither could I, but the boys were like dead wood on their cots.

In the morning I took them to the Sand Creek bridge, which was washed out, so they could see the effects of water's power.

They stood at the edge of the road and looked down into the cut, about six feet deep and ten feet across.

"It's a good thing we didn't drive into this," Mason Eli said.

"Hey, a snake!" Ollie yelled, pointing at a three-foot water snake swimming across the creek.

Mason thought it might be a water moccasin, which he was used to in Oklahoma, and I explained they don't survive in Montana, like chiggers, possums, and armadillos. I wanted to add smart mouths from Pittsburgh, but I didn't.

He let me know about a time he was a hero at a birthday party by alerting everyone to a water moccasin's presence. He knew a lot about snakes, he said, and advised that if I ever ran into a rattlesnake, I should freeze. I was reminded of the story my mother used to tell of my trying to catch a huge rattler by the tail when I was in diapers. She said she looked out the window and I was hot on its trail, reaching down to grab it, each time inches away from getting its tail, but it just kept crawling away from me until it disappeared under the chicken coop.

Perhaps the magnanimity of that rattler had kept me from killing them during my life. I had always respected them for rattling to let me know they were close, and had only killed two, even though I had run into them by the score. I'd walked right over the top of them, reached down next to them to pick something up, and even stepped on them, but they'd never struck me.

The two I killed were both in the yard of a house we rented on Deep Creek out of Choteau, Montana, under the shadow of aptly named Rattlesnake Butte. I took Bart and Matt there when they were eight and ten. We just blew the snakes away with a 20-gauge shotgun without even thinking about it. A million gophers they could eat ran amuck just across the fence, and I drew the line of tolerance there.

I supposed I could have treated them with some "aversive behavior" therapy, like the grizzly bear specialist I traipsed around with along the eastern front by Choteau. I'd held the antenna as he crept through the brush trying to locate collared grizzlies. If they ran, everything was OK, but if they charged or hung around, he shot them with rubber slugs from a twelve gauge. He backed the rubber slugs up with lead ones, but he never had to use them. The idea was to keep them afraid of people.

I thought the more common theory, the "Three-S" rule as the locals referred to it, "Shoot, Shovel and Shut Up," was more effective concerning problem bears in that area, but I wanted to understand his reasoning, and one day I finally got it when we saw a huge rattlesnake in the middle of a gravel road out of Augusta. He got a long stick to tease it with until he grabbed its head, throwing it hard onto the road, then catching it twice more, each time thumping it down onto the road.

"He'll think twice now before hanging out in the road," he said as the snake crawled off into the prairie.

It was the first time, and the last, I'd ever seen anybody beat up a rattler for its own good.

Ollie wanted to shoot the water snake with my pellet pistol.

I told him he could shoot at a stick floating about ten yards away. He shot way over the stick, and the pellet skipped four times across the water before landing in the river. Then it became a competition between Mason Eli and him to get the most skips. A turtle popped its head up, and Ollie wanted to shoot it.

"He's just trying to make a living," I said. "And you wouldn't eat him anyway. There's no sense shooting something you're not going to eat unless it's threatening you."

"We could make turtle soup," he said, "like your dad did."

I couldn't believe he remembered that story. The last time I saw my dad, he had "a craving" for turtle soup. He often had "cravings" for weird food, I guess from having grown up through the Depression of the thirties when any kind of meat was considered golden: a jackrabbit, a raccoon, a beaver, even a skunk. Once he cooked a roast for my cousin Jimmy and me in his Monarch wood stove, having me slather the thing with gobs of lard for hours, and we thought it was the best meat we'd ever had. Then he told us it was coyote.

When I took Theo to meet him before we were married, a skinned raccoon hung from the cottonwood tree in the front yard as we pulled up to the Froze to Death ranch house, and just inside the porch, a pig's head sat staring up at us from inside a five-gallon plastic bucket. The house stunk like rotten sulfur.

"I'm making sauerkraut," he'd said, and showed us a twenty-gallon crock with a wood lid floating on a mass of chopped cabbage.

"What's the pig's head doing in the bucket?" I'd asked.

"Head cheese," he said. "Just haven't got around to it."

"And the coon?"

"Dinner," he said. "You'll love it."

Four days before he died, we threw out setlines, each with six number-two hooks baited with mice he had in his refrigerator, into a slough where he scooted on his rump down the bank to take a bath. He refused my help and said at my suggestion that he get a cane, "A cane is just a damned crutch."

In the morning we had three good sized turtles on the lines, which he dumped in his rain barrel "to purge for a few days."

After he died, I went to his house in Vananda to go through the things vandals had left. I peered into the rain barrel expecting to see the turtles, but they were not there. Evidently, he had satiated his "craving for turtle."

So about thirty-five years later, I told Ollie on the washed-out Sand Creek bridge we'd need more than that little one for soup. A fish jumped between the bridge and the river. He and Mason Eli got excited and wanted to wet a line. I had no Montana license, but I said OK, what the hell, if a warden wanted to bust me for letting my grandkids catch trash fish in the flooded creek, I'd pay the fine.

They were jumping up and down as I got the rods out of the pickup bed.

"I think it was a rainbow trout," Mason Eli cried.

"No trout in here," I said.

"Can we catch a catfish?" Ollie asked.

"Maybe," I said, "but more likely Goldeyes."

"What's a Goldeye?"

"A shad. Kind of a flat fish with real silvery scales. They're good fighters, and a lot of people can them."

"Can them. What's that?"

"Like canned tuna fish," I said. "Ever had that?"

I realized the kids probably didn't even know where chicken strips come from when they ate at McDonalds. I also realized I was becoming an old fart. I remembered the old Germans coming around when we butchered a steer and collecting the blood in a pan as the steer was freshly hung to gut and skin. They made blood sausage and blood pudding, and always relished the sweet breads, the white lumpish glands in the neck.

I baited the number eight hooks with worms on a slip bobber rig, and in about one minute Ollie had a fish on. He tried to lift it onto the bridge, but it flipped off before he could. He became depressed.

Mason Eli caught three in a row, bringing them to the bank at the end of the bridge to land them, and Ollie started to cry.

I asked him what was wrong, and Mason Eli said he was sad because he was not catching any fish.

"You'll catch one, Ollie," I said," and besides, you shouldn't feel bad that Mason Eli is catching them. Good fishing partners are happy when their buddies catch fish."

I could hear my wife telling me not to tell kids they shouldn't feel a certain way.

"There's nothing wrong with feeling that way," she would say.

"You'll catch one. Guaranteed," I said.

And he did. In about three minutes. Then he caught four more. "Way to go, Ollie!" Mason Eli yelled.

We traveled up over the Beartooth Mountain plateau from Red Lodge the same day. Long Lake, the one I'd intended fishing, was still covered with ice. A storm watch came over the radio, and I tried to beat it, stopping only to let the boys have a snowball fight where the snow was still thirty feet high on each side of the road, and to let Ollie climb some granite. He was a talented climber, scaling the most difficult routes in rock gyms where people applauded him, and reaching the top of a 110 feet grain silo in Oklahoma with little effort. I explained the elements of granite: plagioclase, orthoclase, quartz, feldspar, mica, and told him it was the favorite of professional rock climbers because it didn't flake. He reveled in the feel of it as he crawled up a thirty feet boulder while I stood beneath him.

"It feels beautiful," he said, and I couldn't help the shivers in my spine.

His father Matt used the same word when he was ten, while hunting ducks with me on New Year's Eve on the Marias River south of Chester, Montana. In 40 below zero weather, I carried him on my back as I waded across a shallow riffle to an island, where I set out a dozen floating decoys, and we hid in the brush. The ducks came in by the thousands, like bees, to this only open stretch of water for fifty miles, just before sunset.

As we watched them in the golden red light, Matt said, "It's beautiful, isn't it?"

That made my entire year one of the best of my life. We didn't need to be hunting. It was just that we were out there, the only people wild enough, or perhaps crazy enough, as many might justifiably think, to be on the river in that kind of cold.

The ducks lit in our decoys by the hundreds, flying past our heads within two feet, and I finally told him to stand, wait for them to fly, and shoot.

He stood. The ducks paddled about for a minute, ten yards away, cocking their heads at him quizzically, and finally flew. He brought the gun to his shoulder, aimed, and popped the single shot Harrington and Richardson .410 open, ejecting the shell that flew past his cheek, over his shoulder, and into a snowbank behind him.

"Why the hell did you do that?" I asked, expecting him to say something like he didn't want to kill them.

"I got mixed up," he said. "I thought this lever was the safety."

I wish I could say I responded with something like, "It happens to the best of us," but Matt now swears I cussed him out.

A few minutes later, he shot his first duck, a mallard drake. My dog Crow made the short retrieve, dropped the duck, and began biting the ice where it had formed between his toes.

Coming out of the Beartooths, we got ahead of the storm through Sunlight Basin, stopping at Chief Joseph look-out, and I told them the story of the Nez Perce, one of the most heartbreaking episodes in American history.

"Why didn't they just stay in Oregon?" Mason Eli asked.

"They were trying to walk away from a fight," I said, and thought of Pittsburgh Boy. "But the United States government wouldn't let them."

A Hot Jetta and Hot Nights

After the Okies left, my sister Lynette rode with me from Cody to Billings to drive a 2009 Turbo VW Jetta back while I went on to Rosebud. I bought it from the editor of *Magic Magazine* at the *Billings Gazette* to replace Theo's 2000 Jetta that had 120,000 miles.

She had all the maintenance history, extended warranty information, and even the original sticker. I thought she must be a very good editor with this meticulous attention to detail, and we talked about possible stories I might write for her magazine before Lynette got in the car and took off. When I got to Rosebud, I couldn't believe that the Nite Guards might have worked. There was no bat shit under the corners of the chimney, and no bats were stuck in the traps I left hanging by them. It's too good to be true, I told myself. Maybe it's just been too stormy, windy, and rainy, and the bats haven't been out.

But as I stood in the yard that evening, insects hummed like a violin above me, and the air was still. I saw a few bats flying around, and thought I'd have guano on the deck and bats stuck in the glue traps come morning.

Shale showed up from Billings, loaded the air conditioner with Freon, and was about to wire it to test it when I heard him say, "Oh noooo." HR had not wired it correctly, he said. "It should have twelve-two wire out here with a shut-off," he said.

I called HR, and he talked with Shale. It was not a big problem, he said. He just needed to run a different wire.

My anticipation of sleeping comfortably disappeared. I didn't know when he'd ever arrive to do that. And the roof over the porch had puddled the rainwater. HR said it had a six-inch slope from the house to the edge, but it was not running off.

No roofer in Billings would even answer my phone calls. They were so busy with the previous year's tornado damage and this year's hail damage they were booked until next spring, so I called a guy in Sheridan, Wyoming, almost 200 miles away, who did flat roofs and would come estimate the house roof while he was at it. He used a product called Deck Tek that he assured me was a great system.

It was ninety-three degrees at 9:30 P.M. I had three fans running at top speed, but I still couldn't sleep until about 3:30 A.M.

Pam showed up at 6 A.M. to stain windows while it was cool. I got up and mowed the yard again, the old Jacobsen billowing white smoke and using a quart of oil just to get through it. Anyone driving by might have thought the whole place was on fire. I realized half-way through the job I had not checked the bat traps and shut the old mower off.

No sign of them. Clean as a proverbial whistle. Again, I couldn't believe it. The Nite Guards might be working.

I played poker that night and was so tired I lost $180. Bill, a helicopter pilot in the Army, got quad deuces in Omaha, and I asked Dr. Dean if he had Ace — Deuce for low.

"If he had a deuce, we should change decks," Bill said. "You should just go home, Mike." Of course, he was right.

After about four hours sleep, I called Bob Hecht, the eighty-four-year-old electrician, to see if he could help me out with the air conditioner. He was in Miles City. His sister was dying. He didn't think she'd make it through the week. She was eighty-nine.

"I'll stop there on my way back," he said, "to see what we need to do."

He showed up a little before the roofer from Sheridan. Bob said he could fix it without too much trouble, and the roofer said he'd send me a bid through e-mail as soon as he got back.

No bats.

I played poker that night and won over $400. I figured it was enough to pay Bob, and even though it was late, I called Theo to find out how she liked the Turbo Jetta.

"It's hot," she said. "Just the way I like it."

"You talk big," I said. "I wish I were there."

"I was dreaming about you," she said.

"Are you sure it was me?" I said. "Or somebody from your shadow side?"

"We were in a field of mountain wildflowers," she said. "Why don't you hang up so I can get back to it?"

I wasn't sure if she wanted to get back to the wildflowers, me, or both. Not many people knew it, but she used to have two Porsches and race them before we were married. I preferred to think she wanted to get back to the wildflowers and me.

Babysitting

Bart brought Alexander and Sydney from Lyman to stay with us for a week while he worked in the Uintas for the Forest Service and his wife took a week-long class in Laramie. With all the work needing to be done at the Bat House, I was reluctant to agree to babysitting that long, especially since Theo had to work at her office most of the week. I felt edgy about taking on the responsibility by myself, but right off, Zander made me pinky promise to take him fishing. I had never heard of "pinky promise," but it felt like a sacred commitment when we hooked little fingers.

I dug out Charlie Chaplin's *Gold Rush* and *Modern Times*. He was still a hit, especially during the scenes in *Gold Rush* when Big Jim thinks Charlie is a chicken, and in *Modern Times* when Charlie's assembly line numbed brain causes him to attack women with large buttons on their chests and rears. When we ate corn on the cob, Zander imitated the automatic feeding machine they strap Charlie into in *Modern Times*, even mimicking the fizz, pop, crackle of the electronics gone haywire. Not to be upstaged, Sydney slapped her face with the napkin as if she were Charlie being beaten by the infernally malfunctioning machine.

I took them to a sculptor friend's workshop where they could see him chisel away at his newest creation, an osprey half underwater to catch a trout. And I took them miniature golfing, where Zander whacked the ball as if he were in the rough at St. Andrews in Scotland, saying, "That one doesn't count, OK?"

I set up a plastic wading pool in the backyard, gave them the garden hose, and watched the mayhem. Zander quickly realized that if he kinked the hose, he controlled the water flow with which his sister was drowning him. They squealed and screamed, hid and ran, splashed and soaked, snot running out of their noses, their little bodies tanned and muscled, until they were exhausted. I brought out a bowl of cherries and we had a pit-spitting contest.

Somewhere in the week, I realized I had forgotten about the Bat House. Their energy and intelligence overwhelmed me, and I was enjoying their company as much as I had enjoyed their dad when he was their age. Theo and I had started with very little money, but we had discovered happiness in the joy of living and discovery with our boys.

I lit a cigar as I watched them play, and Sydney told me I shouldn't smoke "those awful smelling things."

"Smells like fishing," Zander said.

"I do yoga," I said. "It clears my lungs."

"Yoga, schmoga," Syd said. "They're still bad for you."

"You're right, Syd," I said. "I'm trying to quit."

"You should try harder," she said, and I could see she would never be a co-dependent.

I packed them in the pickup to go fishing at Sunshine Reservoir south of Meeteetse, forty miles away. Sydney said her dad gave her permission to buy a pocketknife, an eight dollar one at Ace Hardware.

"I don't think it's a good idea," I said. "I'll bet you five dollars in five days you either lose it or cut yourself, or both."

"Oh no," she said, "I learned how to whittle. I always cut away from myself."

"Why do you need one?" I asked.

"To lend to my friend Mitchell," she said.

"Let him buy his own pocketknife," I said, feeling like a wise hard-headed grandpa, and immediately countered the thought with a softened idea that she would always be a good friend to people. I had been accused of being generous to a fault, of being a people pleaser to gain acceptance, and I suppose that's from where the comment had come. I knew I had been guilty of that, but I also understood to give unreservedly was in my nature from having grown up poor. I'd never had expectations of people to return my generosity or been angry if they didn't. I'd been taught by my grandmother to share whatever bounty we had, no matter how insignificant.

She'd had me take Thanksgiving and Christmas dinners on plates wrapped in foil to an old herder who lived in his sheep wagon by the river. My friends were afraid of him, belittled him and even threw rocks at him when they saw him pulling a little wagon filled with whatever he had scrounged from the grocery stores' dumpsters. I felt sorry for him, and when I climbed the few wooden steps to knock on his sheep wagon door, he'd open it, take the plates in his greasy, filthy hands, say thanks and smile at me. My grandmother told me that at one time, he'd been one of the biggest sheep men in the world, the richest man in the county, shipping more wool and sheep out of Sumatra, Montana, than any place in the world except Australia. She had cooked for his lambing and shearing crews, and he had paid her more than she'd ever made in her life. He'd lost it all to drought, gambling, and the Depression.

She also had me take bunches of dill, or bags of tomatoes, cucumbers, peas, or carrots, to several of her old friends around town. I would sit and visit with them, amazed at their stories of homesteading and growing up in places I found exotic, like Oklahoma with its tornados, or Florida with its alligators and sharks. If someone died, I carried casseroles and pots of stew to the families' homes. It was simply a way of life. They were grateful, and nothing else was expected.

Believing this was also Sydney's nature, I gave into her and took her to K-Mart, where I convinced her a two-dollar knife in a leather case with a belt attachment would suffice.

She was ecstatic she still had six dollars of the eight Theo had paid her for picking up pinecones at five cents a cone. Zander decided to keep the five he'd earned until he saw something special. I wanted to lecture them on Thoreau's essay "Economy" but decided my own investment in the Bat House had completely ignored anything I'd gleaned from it.

At the reservoir, Sydney asked me if I had any anti-itch cream. She had a mosquito bite on her ankle that was a constant irritant. I made a paste of Bufferin and water, and when I applied it, she said it immediately relieved the itching. We used slip bobbers and worms again at the reservoir, and Zan caught the first fish, a fat seventeen-inch cutthroat, but it got off the hook as he was hugging it to his chest and it flipped out and off the rocks back into the water.

"I should have put my thumb through his gills, huh Granpa?" he said.

"Yeah," I said, "I should have gotten over there to help you."

"He was a beauty," Zan said, looking disconsolately at the water.

"You'll get another one," I said. "There's a lot of fish in this lake."

I looked for Syd's bobber, but it had disappeared.

"I think you have a fish on," I told her, and she looked up from her whittling.

"Oh," she said, as if she'd found a penny on the sidewalk. She carefully folded her knife, put it in her case at her side, slowly got up, brushed off her bottom, picked her way over the rocks toward her rod, and began reeling in a mile of slack line, stopping to brush her hair back several times. When she finally got to the tension of the fish's weight, she cranked on the reel like a mad woman.

"Loosen the drag," I said, "or you'll break the line."

"What's a drag?" she asked and kept cranking away.

I'd shown them a million times how to adjust the drag, but it was useless. Somehow the line held, and she brought another fat cutthroat flopping onto the rocks.

I put it on a stringer, and they caught three more. I was helping Zan untangle his line when I heard Sydney.

"Well, Grandpa, you were right," she said. "I cut myself."

She had nicked the end of her index finger, and it was bleeding all over the tie-dyed shirt she had made herself.

"It'll be all right," she said, sucking on the tip of her finger.

"Don't do that," I said. "I have stuff in the truck to take care of it."

She was crying as I poured hydrogen peroxide over it and swabbed it with a cotton ball. I taped a piece of cotton over it, and she decided to stay in the truck. She said she felt like she would throw up.

I told her not to do it in the pickup and went back to Zan at the bottom of the rock dam. He was sitting on a rock next to his rod, staring at his bobber with the intensity of a rattlesnake about to strike.

"We shouldn't bring Sydney fishing, Granpa," he said without breaking his concentration on the bobber. "She doesn't even like fishing."

She kept coming to the edge of road above us, asking if we could leave, and I finally gave in. On the way to Meeteetse, she wanted me to throw her knife away.

"Why? You've just learned how not to use it," I said. "Besides, you might want to lend it to Mitchell."

We stopped at the Meeteetse Chocolatier, and she felt much better. We got Meeteetse Mud for Grandma and chocolate covered pretzels and macaroons for the trip home, where I gutted, chunked, and brined the fish, then smoked them the next day. What Zan and Syd didn't eat with cheese and crackers, I took to our teachers' Thursday night poker game in Coach McDougall's wood shop, where they were promptly inhaled. I won $63.

Theo took the kids to the Park County Fair that night, and they got to sit on a George Farm dairy cow. They rode on the "Tornado." Syd said Zan combed his hair straight up to make the qualifying height line, and Theo had to go with them.

Zan bought a machine gun with his $5. It ratcheted a high-pitched automatic firing noise with a red light blazing at the muzzle. He laughed while he shot me in the butt, and I told him he had bad aim.

Friday morning, I got them packed for their trip home, and then took them to the Firearms Museum at the Buffalo Bill Historical Center, where I showed them the purse guns, Gatling guns and buffalo guns. Zander pointed out that the taxidermy grizzly bear standing on his hind legs was a boy and asked if he was real.

"Guns, guns, and guns and bears," Sydney said before he could answer, obviously fed up with the machismo. "Where is the fancy Indian dress you said you'd show me?"

I took them through the Center's Plains Indian Museum and explained how hunters would get the two ivory teeth from each elk to sew on their daughters' dresses. It showed their prowess as hunters and made the girl more desirable to have a dress decorated with something so valuable.

They were familiar with elk ivories from their dad's elk. He had shot four monster bulls in the last four seasons, packing into the back country with horses twenty miles to get away from the crowds of hunters in the low country.

We found a red deer hide dress just Sydney's size covered with ivories. I counted eleven rows of ten teeth on the front, and at least the same number on the back. The shoulders and sleeves were covered too.

"That's at least two hundred elk the father of this little girl shot to make this dress," I said.

"Wow," Zan Man said, his eyes big with wonder.

"I better tell my dad to get busy," Sydney quipped.

They ran all over the place in the Draper Museum, an environmental, hands-on museum for kids that portrays four ecosystems from alpine to low riparian. I knew Nancy Draper, the woman who donated the money for the museum. I knew that if she could see my grandkids feeling skins, wood, feathers, horns and antlers, and following tracks on the floor to find beaver dens they could enter, buffalo they could open by compartments to see how the Indians used various parts, and pushing buttons to hear wolves, elk, birds, and varmints, she would know she had done a great thing.

They came to the gift shop, where Sydney went buttery cuckoo over a stuffed raccoon, and Zan squeezed an owl. I bought the stuffed animals, plus a combination chert arrowhead/Indian nickel package for Sydney and an obsidian arrowhead/Indian penny for Zan.

I carried all the loot in a plastic bag with the receipt as we walked toward the museum's exit when Alexander grabbed my hand and pulled on it, stopping me in the hallway. A look of panic filled his eyes.

"Thank you, Granpa," he said, "for buying me this stuff." His eyes were wide, as if he were in shock. "I just didn't have any money."

He waved his hands out and around, showing me the emptiness.

"I didn't know what to do," he said. "I didn't have any money at all. Thank you, Granpa."

"It's OK, Zan," I told him. "Just don't shoot me in the butt with your machine gun anymore."

He took my hand, and we walked out into the sunlight.

Reunions

Theo drove to Laramie in her Turbo Jetta to attend her fiftieth-class reunion. I did not want to go for various reasons, but mostly because I'd been driving too much. Other than that, I didn't care much for reunions of any kind. I had wanted to attend the Cody High School class of '81s congregation at the Elks Club during the Fourth, but the kitchen sink clogged, and while everyone in the family went to Theo's sister's for dinner, I rented a fifty-foot snake and got the damned thing flowing again. It was too late by the time I finished to shower and make an appearance.

I especially wanted to see if a boy who was blind was there. He was a good musician and one of the happiest people I'd ever known. He had three beautiful sisters, and they all exuded a caring and love for each other that was phenomenal. I thought about trying to find him on Facebook, but I imagined he would not have an account there, and several states had passed insane laws (even though well-meaning enough) concerning teachers' communicating with their students on social networks. Many journalism teachers around the country used it to clarify assignments, stay current with production schedules, and to store data, but I wouldn't even touch it. I risked plenty in the classroom by being human without having to defend myself to parents or administrators about some joke I would likely make, or an "inappropriate" comment I might write. Expectations of teachers had turned so many of us into robotic, emotionless automatons that I opted for keeping everything in the classroom where I had witnesses to verify the context and purposes of my antics.

I was reminded how fortunate I'd been when I ran into a former student at the grocery store who told me the best lesson he had learned in high school was in my class when he did not provide the editor with anchor footage for a twenty-seven-minute television production.

Not remembering the incident, I said, "I imagine I was a little upset."

"A little?" he said. "You threw an eraser at me and cussed me up and down. And you made me get the anchors in the studio at six in the morning just to get a zero. You said if I didn't have the footage by eight, you'd deduct sixty points from my grade."

He is in the military now, and he said he takes his responsibilities seriously, which he never did before that. It changed his life, he said.

If he had complained to someone, no doubt I would have been written up for child abuse, rather than a realistic lesson about classroom management.

Another one of my former students said, "You were the best teacher I had in high school because you were real."

I was baffled by that comment. "I can't imagine not being real," I said. "What were your other teachers like that you didn't consider them real?"

"Phony," he said. "They acted like they knew everything and treated students like idiots."

"You are idiots," I said.

He laughed and said, "That's exactly what I mean."

The class of '76 had a reunion that summer, but I didn't get an invitation. I would have really enjoyed seeing those kids because I was young when I taught them, and they were a wild bunch, effected, I believe, by the oil boom in town those years. They came to class drunk, high on pot and LSD. They had fistfights in the halls almost every day and sex like rabbits at night. Of course, I loved them, but after teaching for thirty years, my tolerance for those behaviors had slimmed considerably. As I looked at their group picture in the paper, I was amazed at how old they looked. Only two or three seemed to be in shape, and I wondered if those few did yoga.

After Theo left for Laramie and her reunion, I wished I had gone with her. She had been looking forward to the event for at least nine months. She had told me several stories of her classmates, but they only meant something to me because of their connection to her, yet I regretted not being with her to appreciate her from a different perspective. I would have gone with her if she'd really wanted me to, but she'd had an ambivalent attitude about it, so I thought I might be in the way more than anything. But shallow as it was, in the back of my mind, I thought that she would probably be in the best shape of anyone there, and I felt like I had missed an opportunity to walk around as her husband among all the poor schmucks who'd been in love with her.

The Electrician

I went to Rosebud when Theo left, arriving as another lightning storm closed in, and found Bob Hecht in the basement, working on the air conditioner's wiring.

His sister had died, and she didn't want any kind of service, true to her lifelong personality, he said, never wanting any attention brought on her, the opposite of his other sister, who continually searched the limelight. She was 83, and his other sister was still living at 93. Bob was an extremely slow talker, with long silences I just waited out, and as we sat in what would become the dining room, the lights began to flicker. He explained why that happened during a lightning storm, and said before the advent of automatic relays, he had to go climb poles during storms to throw a switch. I said I imagined that was about as hairy as it got.

"Oh, yeah," he said. Long, long, long pause. "The worst part was if it was raining."

We talked about men like George Avalos, the old Mexican who taught me how to play poker, and how he drank a fifth of whiskey a day until he died at ninety-three, as well as one of Bill Lloyd's cousins who lived a few miles up Sand Creek in a little shack all his life. His brother would go to town every day to get the mail, and he would bring him a fifth of Teachers whiskey, two on Saturdays.

"I went up there once to work on a pump," Bob said, "and his shack was just old boards cobbled together. No tar paper or anything, even on the roof. He didn't even have an outhouse all those years."

"Anyway," Bob finally said after about a minute, "he told me he was going to put a new roof on his shack that day, but he said he must have drunk too much the day before, because he felt awfully hung over."

"Well," Bob said, "I guess that's why he never got a roof put on. He drank the same amount every day."

Just as Bob was backing his truck away from the Bat House, a rooster pheasant popped up out of the corn next to him and lit in the yard, followed by a hen, and then a spotted fawn. All three of them stood there for a few seconds looking at him, and then walked into the grass by the fence. About thirty seconds later, a doe jumped out of the brush and flew into the corn, ready to beat the hell out of a fox, I figured.

Bob looked at me, smiled, and said, "You've done a great job here, Mike."

I walked around the fairgrounds with Dr. Dean that night, and visited with Henry, a retired electrician Dr. Dean's age who had taken on the job of Fairgrounds supervisor, and he sang Bob Hecht's praises at how he had set up all the juice necessary to run everything during the Rosebud County Fair.

"He's an amazing man," Henry said. "Eighty-four, still working every day, and he just has a slight limp in his right leg."

Bob's son and I had been close childhood friends, so close that when we were about ten or eleven, I wondered out loud with him why I lied so much. I used to embellish all kinds of stories or completely make them up to aggrandize myself one way or the other, and he knew it as well as I did. He didn't denigrate me for it. We just didn't know why I did it, so he asked his dad, and he told me his dad said, "Security. He lacks security in his life."

I wondered how much of my buying the Bat House and restoring it had to do with that. I was proud that he approved of my accomplishment there, and I thought perhaps I believed not only his, but everybody else's approval would offer me the security I'd needed. But I didn't take it too seriously. I thought it was more a desire to own a choice piece of property close to the Yellowstone River. It had most everything I loved about the place. I'd just never counted on bats.

Road Rage

On my way to Cody, I waited in the Coffee Company parking lot in Laurel for the light to turn green so I could pull out into traffic. A little Ford pickup was first at the light, and when it turned green, the driver sat chatting with a kid on a motorcycle who had pulled up next to his window.

A woman with a Red Lodge plate honked her horn once, and the driver sat there talking to motorcycle boy for a few more seconds, then ripped through the light into a left turn, getting his torso out the window so he could flip her off and yell the corresponding profanity at her. As she pulled out in the same direction, he whipped his little pickup over to the right, waited until she was alongside him, and then hung half his body out the window as he sped up next to her, still waving his middle finger at her and screaming even more profanity. He sped up and cut in front of her then, missing her front fender by inches, hit his brakes to force her to slam on hers, continued waving his finger out the window at her as he crawled along, and then took off toward the south when she turned left onto the Interstate. He was going at least seventy miles per hour in a forty-five zone.

I punched my Tundra and caught up with him just across the Yellowstone bridge. He had slowed to the speed limit. I repeated his license plate number to myself aloud as I pulled up next to him in the right lane. He looked at me with an arrogant, self-satisfied smirk on his face as I stared at him. He was about eighteen, dark skin and hair, cut short, with one of those faces that could be part Indian, Mexican, Italian, or even Turkish. In good shape. No shirt. Around five-eight.

"What's the matter with you?" I said at him, emphasizing the enunciation, and he looked away at the road, then back at me. I had a cigar in my mouth, so I doubted he understood what I'd said.

I wanted to swerve the Tundra into his little Ford and send him flying off the road, but he suddenly pulled left off the highway onto a dirt road before the bend that takes the highway under the railroad bridge. I drove a bit farther until I had room to pull over, turned on my flashers, and called the Laurel police department.

A woman answered, and I briefly explained what I'd witnessed, giving her the kid's license plate number and telling her I knew it was probably a small matter in the course of her day, but that all this road rage I'd been seeing this summer was getting to me in a bad way, and it was time I did something.

She asked me if I'd like to file a complaint, and I said sure, I would do that, so she got my phone number and was getting my address when she put me on hold. I waited for about ten minutes before she returned. She apologized, saying they had suddenly been inundated with a flurry of incidents, and finished getting my address.

"I know this is crazy," she said, "but there is no law against gesturing. We can't do anything about that."

"So what if I track him down and beat the shit out him?" I asked, images of popping the punk across the back of his head with Bill's old prison sap flitting through my brain.

"No, no, no," she said. "You don't want to do that. We can do something about the profanity and the reckless driving, but gestures are not illegal."

"The lady with the County Ten plate didn't deserve that," I said. "She just beeped her horn at him once, and he was holding up about fifteen cars."

"You're not listening to me," she said. "There is no law against gesturing."

"I understand that," I said, "but he could have caused an accident by the way he was driving at her."

"So he didn't do this to you? You just saw this?"

You're not listening, I wanted to say, but I understood that the last few minutes had been hectic for her.

"Right," I said.

She said she'd turn it over to an officer, and I pulled out onto the highway. About five miles down the road, I saw police car lights flashing, and when I went by, I saw that a van had hit a whitetail doe, crumpling the hood and smashing the windshield. The doe lay bloody and bent about thirty yards behind the van, where a woman stood looking at the damage with a Laurel sheriff.

Must have been why I was on hold for ten minutes, I thought. About forty miles away from where I'd made the phone call to the Laurel police, an officer called me to tell me he was going to track the kid down.

"He needs a good talking to," I told him. "There was no reason to get that angry at the woman for just a little touch on her horn. He was holding up traffic, and he could have just waved and driven on instead of cursing at her."

"And possibly causing an accident," he said.

"I'm just sick of it," I said. "Maybe I'm just getting old, but I see more and more of that kind of behavior and think it needs to be stopped."

"Believe me," he said, "I know."

"I teach high school, and I know how to talk to kids," I said, "but I'm afraid in this case it would have escalated. It's better if you talk to him."

When I told Theo how I'd handled the incident, she said, "Good for you. It's the yoga."

Flooring

I practiced on my yoga mat every day for a week. I felt better than I had in years when I arrived at the Bat House after picking up $385 worth of window molding and a box of three-quarter inch Brazilian Cherry flooring on loan from Rick at A & H Turf so I could lay it out to see how it looked. He said he was stuck with 10,000 feet of it and would give it to me for $5.10 a foot. I talked with a Lumber Liquidators rep in Denver, and they wanted close to $10. It rates 2350 on the Janka Hardness scale. Guayacan, Patagonian Rosewood, and Brazilian Ebony are at the top three spots, at 4500, 3840 and 3692, respectively. Basswood, Eastern White Pine, and Balsa are at the bottom at 410, 380 and 100.

I asked every flooring installer I knew if they thought engineered wood was as good as or better than solid. They all preferred engineered wood except one, a former student who had lain the oak and tile in our Cody house. He had mixed feelings. It was easy to lay, he said, having less expansion and contraction, with a finish baked on about seven times. But if solid wood is installed right, he said, and if it has a good finish, he liked it better. On my way to Rosebud, I took some sample pieces to him in Powell, where he scratched it with a knife and said it looked good.

"It's kind of a gamble," he said. "You don't know until it's installed and you have lived with it for a while. You might want to go with engineered, but I would go with this if the guy will replace any twisted pieces."

Rick said he would when I asked him, and he gave me the box to lay out. It looked beautiful when I did, and was ready to call him, but decided to wait and do more research. I wasn't able to afford it yet anyway, given the roof expense.

When I drove back to Cody, I called Theo who was on her way to Eureka, Montana in her black Jetta to attend a week-long yoga retreat toward the next level of her instructor certification. I told her to go through Powell to avoid road construction. It was only about ten miles farther and about an hour quicker. With the use of our cell phones, we met on the highway outside Frannie. We hugged and kissed and said we'd keep in touch.

I thought she had never looked so beautiful. She wore brown, heart shaped jade earrings, amber sunglasses and a tan shirt with grey pants and brown leather sandals. Her hair was short, salt and pepper, and I ruffled it as I kissed her. She planned to make it as far as Bozeman to spend the night, and then drive up through Kalispell and north almost to Canada on Saturday. I hated to see her go, but knew she deserved the break, and understood it would be relaxing for her.

When she drove away, I realized how schizophrenic my life had become. It became even more dramatic to me when I was driving in Cody the next day and saw an eleven Wyoming license plate on the car in front of me and thought, "Hmm, a car from Cody," not realizing that I *was* in Cody.

Although Theo had wanted me to go with her, I felt I had too much responsibility at the Bat House, and I also had to begin a week of "professional development" on Monday.

As I watched her Jetta go up the highway, I was hit with a heavy emptiness. I loved her more than anything, and we were not together enough.

A Dream Deck with No Bats

I hired Dirk Moos to finish the flat roof/deck over the porch, the framing, and the windows. In the basement bathroom, he laid part of the tile Dr. Dean traded me for $50 worth of cigars. He also installed the egress window in the basement bedroom and leveled the main room down there, getting it ready for tile. I knew his mother, Rosie, who was probably about ten years older than I, and she was always kind to me when I was a kid. Dirk started working building construction right out of high school, went to Steamboat Springs and California, where he worked on expensive, exclusive homes, and returned to Forsyth because of some murky relationship with a wealthy woman.

"Long story," he said.

The woman called him constantly, so he left his cell phone in his truck and checked it at noon. He was fast and extremely organized and hated wasting material, taking back to the lumber yard every nut and bolt and screw and square foot of lumber he did not use. His work was well worth the money I paid him. He was precise, on the job early in the morning, and he was built like a tank and strong as a gorilla. He had fixed the mess on the porch roof, cutting out about three feet of plywood that had swollen from being wet, and asked when I got there why I had used OSB plywood.

I didn't know, but assumed it was OK, since HR had done it.

"I'm not disrespecting his work," he said, "but I would have used CDX. If your roofer puts glue down for the DuraDek, it'll be cancerous to the OSB."

I called Frank, the roofer in Spearfish I'd been talking to about DuraDek, and he said he wouldn't lay it unless it was on CDX.

"The chemical in the glue will turn the OSB to mush," he said. "You could put a piece of half inch CDX on top of it, though."

"If you lay a half inch piece of CDX on top of the OSB," Dirk said, "you'll be higher than the doorjamb coming out from the bedroom."

The roofer looked at the digital pictures I'd sent him and said, "Yeah, that would be a problem. And you'll get ambient moisture into the OSB eventually. The best thing to do is rip up the OSB."

"Damn," Dirk said. "I knew it. I should have called you."

Frank e-mailed me his bid the next day: $4,700 if Dirk replaced the OSB and countersank the screws into three quarter inch CDX only on the supporting beams. And Frank wanted half the money up front.

It would take him a day, at least, Dirk said, to get it ready. I'd pay him at least $300, plus the cost of the CDX. Over $5,000 for a flat roof ten feet wide by thirty long! And then there was the railing. I wondered if it was worth it. I could see the Yellowstone River from up there and imagined sitting with Theo at a little table as the sun rose, enjoying strong black coffee and a cigar, watching the deer and wild turkeys walk below us, the geese and ducks flying by, and listening to all the songbirds.

On Monday I mailed Frank a check for $2,350 and hoped it would become that dream. A dream without a bat story, I told myself.

Almost everybody has a bat story, but two stories that summer made national news. In July, "a flying animal" was flapping back and forth along the aisle in an airplane bound for Georgia from Madison, Wisconsin. A passenger used a phone to get video of its flight up and down the cabin, before it was trapped in the bathroom. The plane had to return to Madison, where a Delta employee "coaxed the bat from the washroom and set it free." It looked to be a large brown bat from the video, but in comments to the story, several respondents didn't believe it was a bat.

"Mel" wrote, "If you watch the video closely it is clearly a bird with wings. Bats do not have wings! Their power of flight comes from a membrane stretched between their four legs."

"Manuel," whose photo showed two people in the military, wrote in Spanish and English, "Este es un Vampiro que tenía que viajar a Atlanta y no quería pagar extra por el sarcófago. Ellos también deben sacrificarse en esta economía." This is a vampire who had to travel to Atlanta and did not want to pay extra for the sarcophagus. They also must be sacrificed in this economy."

And "Smile" wrote, "I love bats. They won't hurt you and yet people freak out! One thing that really pisses me off is when people try to kill things and it's doing no harm to anyone."

In the video clip, one guy tried knocking it down with his hand, but missed it. I wondered at the lawsuit that might have ensued had it bitten him.

The other story in March concerned a bat flying around in the AT&T Center during a San Antonio Spurs/Sacramento Kings NBA game. According to various blogs and news stories, it scared the hell out of some players until a Spurs player, Manu Ginobili, knocked it down with his hand, picked it up, and carried it off the court. Manu is a better man than I am, I thought.

Duradek Tattoos

Frank and his wife Jo put on the DuraDek, and I wished I had not chosen "granite" for a pattern. It looked hideous next to red brick. Jo had a piece of brown DuraDek they had chosen for their roof, and it would have been great. Theo chose the pattern from DuraDek's website, and I seriously could not understand why she liked it.

Frank and Jo were in their early thirties, very fit and strong, friendly, fast workers who shared a cigarette or a beer when they took a break. Frank lived in Cody for two years, but he didn't have enough work as a flooring installer in the winter to make a decent living, so he moved to Spearfish. Jo looked like she could be Indian, or Russian, but when I asked her, she said she was German, that her natural hair color was auburn, but she had dyed it black.

I had never thought about dying my hair, even though I knew women did it all the time. It was kind of like getting a tattoo. Except for the purely decorative tattoos, scrollwork and waves and bands I saw on Pacific Islanders, most of the tats I saw were undecipherable. They look like smeared blue mud. The bride at a wedding I had recently attended had verses on her shoulder blade. I stood directly behind her but couldn't read any word in the three lines. I understood it was for her, not me, and I tried to imagine what words I would have tattooed on my shoulder blade.

Perhaps, "At death, disregard this notice."

Or "This page intentionally left blank."

I thought maybe I should have a bat tattooed across my forehead, its wings, excuse me, "Mel", its *membrane* spread, and its teeth bared.

Before school started that year, during our week of professional development, a young female teacher wore cutoffs and a tee shirt that exposed her midriff. Below her belly button, which had a ring in it, a tattooed duck sat looking at me in silhouette, like a carnival target at the top of her pubic bone.

"That's a mallard drake," I said, pointing at it. "Any particular reason you chose that?"

"Oh," she said, looking down, "is it? No, I just liked it."

"It should be a diver," I said.

"What?"

"A merganser, or a loon," I said. "They're diving ducks."

She looked at me then with fear, as though I was the crazy one, and obviously did not get the joke, and I realized that if she had, I probably would have been reported for sexual harassment, so I pressed on.

"Or better yet, a Fairy Tern, its wings folded and headed straight down for the kill."

She knew I was crazy then, and nervously laughed and walked away, looking over her shoulder at me as I stood there in the hall.

The Dam

I was so tired and hungry while Frank and Jo worked on the deck that I went into town, bought a pizza and drove to the dam, where I parked under the cottonwoods and watched the river flow over it. The dam was built in the 1930s to divert water for Carterville District irrigation. The north side of the river, where the Bat House stands, benefits from the big ditch that feeds its irrigated ground. Without it, Jack said, all the wells over there would dry up.

Plans were underway to restructure the dam so fish can migrate past it to the west. The pallid sturgeon is endangered now. When their eggs hatch, the fry often drift 300 miles to Lake Sakakawea, where they are devoured by bigger fish or smothered in the stagnant water. Jack was on the Irrigation Board and said it would be a big improvement for the country. He'd worked with the Army Corps of Engineers, the U.S. Fish and Wildlife, and Applied Geomorphology, Inc. out of Bozeman to get it started. It would be completed in about five years, he said.

I hoped so, as I sat watching the muddy water flow smoothly over it, then down two or three feet. It doesn't look bad, as far as rapids go. It looks like just a gentle curl over a low rock and concrete ledge that breaks below into violent waves, but they are not normal rapids. The river drops so suddenly over the six feet ledge it creates a backwash, an undertow with tons of pressure. I'd seen cottonwood trees go over the dam, get sucked into the undertow, and bob around for hours before floating away.

When he was in high school, Rudy Dean, went over it in an inner-tube and was caught. He'd pushed off the rocks below him as hard as he could four times, just getting his head above water so he could take a breath before being sucked under again, until he pushed clear of the powerful curl.

He'd kept his cool. Plus, he had thighs like Nureyev. He said his last push was his last. He'd had no more in him. "This is your last push," he'd told himself. "Give it all you've got."

The constant wash plays tricks with your eyes. If you try to follow the current, your eyes stop soon after the water drops, hung up on the splash and leap of froth, but if you try to focus and hold on a particular point in the current, your eyes will drift into the churn, and you begin to believe you see fish trying to rise and swim over the dam.

When I was nine or ten, I saw paddlefish, the prehistoric, platypus-billed monsters of 40 to a hundred and twenty pounds, wiggling and tailing up and over the dam, but I used to fish and watch the water for hours, mesmerized by the flow and roar of the river here. I imagine some still do swim over the dam, but no one sees them. At least I like to think so. Now they are closely monitored, the limit of fish strictly imposed, mostly at Intake Dam near Glendive, 200 miles down river, where men line the bank to snag them with weighted treble hooks thrown with surf casting rods.

I remembered reading a feature column in the Wall Street Journal, about a guy who ran up and down dirt roads in his '57 Chevy station wagon somewhere in Tennessee, I think, collecting the roe from paddlefish fishermen and perfecting a caviar recipe. He took pounds of it to New York City where he invited the caviar connoisseurs to a tasting party, and the head honcho caviar critic declared it every bit as good as Beluga, which I had seen in St. Petersburg, Russia selling at $500 an ounce. Fishermen now give the roe to processors, and they sell the caviar in Glendive at twenty dollars an ounce.

I only caught one in all the time I fished at the dam. It was at night, and as I sat by my fire under a full moon, the bell at the end of my rod clinked a few times. I took the rod out of its holder and waited, but nothing happened, so I eased the rod back, and there was a tug, so I yanked up and back as hard as I could to set the hook, but then all I felt was steady pressure. Nothing moved. I thought I was snagged on a log or a rock, and I began backing up the bank to break or bend the hook.

I would never break the line because as a young boy I used an old bait casting reel with about a ten-thousand-pound test, braided line, and as I backed up, with the line wrapped around a piece of driftwood so it wouldn't cut my hand, the snag began to move. I thought I had dislodged a heavy piece of wood, a limb, or a sunken piece of trash, but then it began to jerk and run, and I knew it was a fish, a big sturgeon, I thought. I fought it for a good hour, running down river and wading to an island before landing it, and I was terrified when I saw it in the moonlight against the gravel shore. Its eye glistening there reminded me of Quasimodo's in the old black and white movie with Charles Laughton, *The Hunchback of Notre Dame.*

It was a small one, as paddlefish go, probably twenty pounds or so, and I had no idea what to do with it, so I cut the line just above the fin where I had hooked it and pushed it back into the river. I remember standing there in the June moonlight wondering why I had done that with no witness. I never told anyone about it, though, not because I was afraid they wouldn't believe me, but probably because they would know how afraid I was of a fish.

Sitting at the dam, eating my pizza fifty years later, I realized the fish was just too much for me. It was like pulling in an alien. The river always had surprises — I never knew if I'd catch a catfish, a carp, a goldeye, a ling, sturgeon, or sauger — but sometimes the surprises took on the macabre, like the time I had watched three grown men go over the dam.

I was working on my tree house one Saturday in 1964 about a half mile upriver from the dam when I saw them floating on what appeared to be two or three rubber rafts lashed together by a wooden deck. A little motor putted away at the rear, and they sat on the deck in lawn chairs. It was a chilly day, grey with the promise of rain. I could hear them talking and laughing. I watched them for a minute before climbing out of my tree and running to the bank.

"There's a dam down there," I yelled, pointing east with the hammer in my hand.

They looked at me but did not respond.

"There's a dam down there," I yelled again, louder this time. "And you shouldn't go over it." I was positive they heard me.

They talked to each other, and I caught a few words, but they didn't acknowledge me.

"There's a dam down there," I yelled again, cupping my hands around my mouth, yelling much louder than before. "You can pull out at the slough."

"We know," one of them said, in a tone that meant, *Go away, you irritating little shit*. They didn't change course. They stayed in the middle of the river.

They kept talking and laughing, slowly moving about, stashing things here and there.

I didn't believe they intended to go over the dam, and they would have to begin angling soon to get to the bank, because the current was swift, but they were not making any move to get out of it. I had to see what they were planning, so I rode my bicycle to the dam along a path through the brush and arrived as they floated toward it about a hundred yards away.

"There it is," one of them said, standing at the back of the raft and pointing down river.

They were past the mouth of the slough, and when they hauled up their motor, I knew they were going over the dam. They were quiet then for about a minute. They did not laugh or talk, and this made the waiting electrically numb, where all power and control is released for the next few moments to something already set in motion, and you are stuck there, unable to change anything, understanding this was your decision and action, but you are afraid, and you are perhaps more alive than you have ever been, incapable of anything but acquiescing to forward energy.

I stood in full expectation of doom, even though these were grown men who knew and understood much more than a thirteen-year-old boy. I could hardly breathe.

The front of their raft went straight down, throwing the man at the rear clear of the undertow. I saw the other two come up and go under several times, and pieces of boards and coolers and red life jackets rose and fell and churned in the waves. And then that was it. A few pieces of the wrecked raft floated by, but the two men had disappeared.

The man who had been thrown clear drifted to the island below, crawled on his hands and knees on the gravel and stood up. A seat cushion hung from his left hand as he turned and looked back at the dam. Nothing. Nothing but the smooth water like silky melted chocolate before it roared over the rocks and frothed and foamed. It began to rain, and he just stood there.

Finally, he looked at me. He was a huge man, close to three hundred pounds.

"Go get help," he said, and even with the constant roar of the river going over the dam, I could hear him easily.

I rode my bicycle to the Standard Gas Station, where I told Clyde Brumfield what had happened. He made some calls, and they brought a boat down, went out and picked the man up, and brought him back to shore. He was shivering, I remember, and I looked directly in his eyes, but he didn't seem to recognize me. Later they told me he was in shock, the first I'd ever heard of it.

About eight boats set out dragging the river, past Rosebud, but they didn't' find the two drowned men until three weeks later, one by Miles City and the other almost at Glendive, a hundred and twenty miles downstream.

They were agate hunters from Minnesota. I felt sorry for them until Scooter Strong told me that the survivor had asked in the Elks Café why that kid on the bank hadn't swum out and saved his friends. And he told the Sheriff that he had tried to help one of his friends before floating down to the island.

I thought he was the stupidest man I'd ever heard of then, but as I sat there at the dam, eating pizza, and getting ready to take a nap, I realized he must have still been in shock. Who knows what might go through your mind if that happened to you?

At the end of my nap, two boys and two girls rode up on their bicycles. The boys were fishermen. They cast Rapalas into the river close to a tree that had come over the dam and stayed thirty feet from shore. They both got snagged. One of them walked along the bank jerking his rod like an expert. He was used to this, I could tell. The Rapala came loose, and he reeled in a little fish.

I got out of the pickup and walked over to him. The two little girls came over too, looking at the fish.

"That was lucky," I said.

"Yeah," he grinned. "Maybe he hit it and got me unsnagged."

"Maybe," I say. "Or maybe you got unsnagged and he came out from under the tree. Is it a walleye or sauger?"

"Sauger," he said, and I was impressed. It's not easy to tell the difference for a casual fisherman.

"Going to keep it?"

"Nah," he said. "Too little."

He struggled to get all the hooks out, squeezing the fish too hard.

"Don't want to hurt him," I said, and helped him release the Rapala. He flipped the fish into the water.

"Thanks," he said.

He reminded me of H.R. when he was a kid. The first fish he ever caught was on the North Fork of the Shoshone. I had stood with him on the bank, showing him how to cast, and flipped a bobber rigged with a worm and split shot into the river.

"Now watch the bobber," I said, "and when it goes under the water," and the bobber disappeared exactly then, "set the hook," which I did, and handed him the rod. He landed a two-pound rainbow.

He was recently married, the wedding gargantuan: a rehearsal dinner for at least 200 people outdoors twenty miles up the South Fork on the Big Hat Ranch and a dinner at the Cody Convention Center afterwards.

After coaxing him a bit, he drove up in his Saab to work on the wiring. He arrived about a half hour after I got to the Bat House and immediately went to work, hanging fans, wiring switches and receptacles, setting sconce lights, and mounting the chandelier in the dining room. He said he spent about $7,000 on the wedding bash, his father-in-law $15,000, and his dad and mom — who knew how much? It was a good time, I admit, visiting with people I had not seen in twenty or thirty years, but damn, that seemed like a lot of money for a wedding.

Theo and I spent twenty dollars on ours. We bought the license, and the next day we walked down an alley in Logan, Utah, through a side door into an office where a Justice of the Peace warned Theo about burning my toast, and me about not telling her I loved her every day, and that was pretty much it. Bart and Matt threw rice at us. We had dinner at a bad restaurant, went to a bad movie called *The Hunter* starring Steve McQueen, and went home to bed where I read Stephen King's *The Stand*, and Theo read some psychology text.

These days, she didn't toast the bread enough, so I just toasted it a bit more, and I told her I loved her about once or twice a week. We didn't go to bad restaurants because I could cook better than most chefs, and only I watched bad movies because I watched almost any movie. She read before going to sleep, and I did crossword puzzles.

"Doing my puzzles," I told her, "guarantees we won't have any bad words between us in bed."

"Yuck, yuck," she said.

Guilt

I walked out on the porch roof on a Saturday morning to check for any sign of bats, and there on the east side of the chimney, between it and the Red Eye flasher, a bat hung sleeping.

I got the two-gallon pump sprayer, mixed Tempo Ultra SC as hot as I dared, and let him have it with a straight stream. I expected him to fly away, but he hung on, moved to the corner, and cackled at me. I kept spraying him until he slipped down the brick, then fell with a splat to the porch roof. I got a broom and whacked him, breaking the plastic head of the broom off the wooden handle.

I thought he was dead until I rolled him over and he fluttered, lifting his head, so I pressed the wooden handle of the broom into his head. I felt horrible.

"Why did you decide to sleep there," I asked, "of all the places you could have gone. Were you born in this attic? Was that your pup stuck in the rat glue-trap? Were you sick, cast out, fallen from grace, by the colony?"

Perhaps it came there after the sun rose when the red light was not blinking. I hoped so. If they were not afraid of the Red Eye, I was back to square one, and I didn't think I could stand killing them anymore.

A Paradox

Toward the end of October, my frustration came to a new low. I was scheduled to give a presentation in Missoula for the Montana Education Association on starting a broadcast program, and driving ninety miles an hour to make it on time, I was picked up by a highway patrolman who fined me $100. I missed my presentation slot by half an hour. On my way back from Missoula, I stopped at Lowes to pick up my kitchen tile and delivered it to the Bat House, then played poker and lost about $120 before calling it quits at eleven.

In the morning I met with a mason from Miles City, who was going to lay the stone around the fireplace, but he said the stove had to be raised about two inches to be done right. I had driven almost a thousand miles in two days and was very depressed about the trip, the House and all the money I'd put into it. The lights in the bathroom didn't work because of a short H.R. said he could fix, but I wondered when. I called Shale, and he said he would raise the stove within the week, and Dirk Moos would tear out the plywood framework so he could get at it.

I took Theo to the House a few days later, and she was impressed with the work I had done. That helped my spirits a bit since she seemed to enjoy herself there. She helped trim several apple trees being taken over by grapevines, and we hauled the vines and branches to the dump, her pleasure clearly apparent at the physical work. That night, after she crawled into her sleeping bag on one of the cots, I had a cigar outside where the stars were brilliant, and the coyotes set up their howling from the river to the hills in the sparkling light.

In the morning, my rooster pheasant appeared on the road as we were leaving. He flew over to the ditch at the edge of the field and disappeared in the tall grass, then poked his head out to watch us drive by. He had survived. It was good to see him. I could never shoot him. I had bought the place to have a place to hunt, but now that I owned it, I didn't want to shoot anything. Not the deer, the coons, the fox, or coyotes. Not the squirrels. I even felt bad for the bats.

Gratitude

I finished giving finals at 11:30 and took off for Rosebud, even though I was not feeling well. It was like a return of the flu or something that had kept me out of school for three days two weeks before, and it was characterized by urinary problems. The temperature was about 29 degrees when I got to the Bat House, and I peed in the snow as soon as I got out of the truck, let Mac out to run around, fed him, hauled the grout I had bought, my gun and clothes inside, and went to bed at 8 o'clock. I had a fever, chills, and I peed all night in small dribbles every hour, but finally slept from about three to six without getting up.

I let Mac run around the property for about a half hour and then drove to the Sand Creek Bridge where I had taken Ollie and Mason Eli fishing in July. I'd read in the *Billings Gazette* that four young guys drove their car into the creek early Monday morning. Three were killed and one was flown to Billings.

Signs saying, "Road Closed" and "Road Construction" stood in the middle of the road. A mass of re-bar, a work trailer, piles of bridge planks, and heavy equipment lined the road up to where the bridge was out. The workers had built a temporary bridge from planks, and I stood there wondering what could have happened. The guys would have had to drive around all the signs, beginning at my lane, and around a dragline, if it had been there Monday morning, and missed the plank bridge. Not much water was in the creek. It was mostly mud. A small patch of ice had a pool of red under it, and I wondered if it was blood.

It didn't make any sense. How they could have driven off the cut in the road was beyond me, especially when I considered all the equipment, construction material and signs along the way. They must have been drunker than hell, I thought. Or drunk and stoned too. There was no other explanation.

I understood it, though. I understood it too well. About twenty-five years before, I had been drunk and stoned, and I nearly killed three construction workers on the highway between Lincoln and Great Falls. I was going about eighty. I blew past three huge yellow caution signs, forced a guy holding a stop sign and waving a red light to dive into the ditch, missed a guy by inches who rolled onto the hood of his car, and slammed head-on into a pilot car.

I know how this happened, I thought. I was just lucky. These boys weren't.

Standing alone on the road, looking down into the Creek and listening to the geese on the river, I felt horrible for the boys and their families. I didn't know any of them, but I knew their invincible attitude, the absence of mindfulness and its self-destructive inevitability. It's bad enough if a deer jumps out in front of you, I thought. You don't have to drive into the creek where the bridge is washed out. But that's consequences. You don't think about losing your legs until they're gone.

The quiet, except for the geese, was like iron around me. Hardly anyone knows this spot, when you think about the whole world, this one Sand Creek among ten thousand Sand Creeks, and the world will not notice these deaths more than in a few newspaper articles, perhaps a fifteen second television story, and these deaths will largely be forgotten, their loss senseless.

I walked back to the truck, turned it around and drove toward Cody. It was about 7 A.M., and Jack was loading feed with his tractor for his cows, so I stopped, and his son Mike waved and gave me a big hello. He lived in Three Forks, working at the mine there. He was a big man now, 6 feet-8 inches, and he slipped a glove off his huge hand to shake mine.

"Are you up goose hunting?" he asked.

I told him I had planned to, but I was feeling sick and decided to get home.

I asked about his son, Neeko, whom I had taken on his first goose hunt the previous year, although he sat in the blind with me for two years before he got to shoot his twenty gauge.

"Yes he is," Mike said, "and he's been asking if you're coming."

"Tell him I'll try to get back after Christmas," I said. "Maybe after the first. Right now, I just want to get home and go to bed."

I asked them about the boys who drove into the creek, and Jack said one of the kids on the school bus first saw them at about seven in the morning, and he called his dad from school in Rosebud.

"His dad said it looked like the car launched over the creek, hit the bank on the other side, and fell backward on its top," Jack told me. "He said he yelled down there to find out if anyone was in the car, and he heard someone yell back, 'Yes. Help me'."

So he got a couple more guys and they rolled the car over before the ambulance and fire department got there to cut him out.

"He's twenty-four," Jack said, "and he's in the hospital in Billings, but the other three are dead."

"How in the hell did he miss all that construction equipment and go into the creek?" I asked.

"They must have been traveling pretty fast to go clear across the creek and have the car land on its top," Mike said.

"They had to have been pretty drunk," Jack said.

"I believe he'll be looking at twenty years in prison," Mike said.

I was shaking from the cold, even though it was only about thirty degrees out.

I told them I'd see them after Christmas, got in the truck, and wished I had a cigar as I started the drive back to Cody. It would have taken my mind off the pain.

Sometimes I think God must have failed Creationism 101. When you have eternity at your fingertips, why would you install a gland that fails after about sixty years in a man, and worse, cultivates cancer? It's like designing a $10,000 engine that depends on a fifty-cent plastic valve. My urinary problems turned out to be prostatitis, inflammation of the prostate, a condition I do not wish on any man, but without going into the morbid details, suffice it to say it was not prostate cancer, or so we hoped. My PSA was 9.3, and after huge doses of Herculean penicillin for a month, and shingles and hives and dizziness from a sulfa allergy I didn't know I had, it went down to 2.1.

My urologist from Billings said, "Good job."

"I didn't do a damn thing," I said. "The penicillin did." He looked at me as though I had spurned him in some way.

The condition improved remarkably in early January when Theo and I enjoyed a week of yoga, good food, beautiful ocean, pleasant people and Tamsulosin (AKA Flomax) in Puerto Morelos, Mexico. I peed with ease and didn't get up in the middle of the night three times. Between Cancun and Cozumel, the reef at Puerto Morelos is a national park, where commercial fishing is illegal.

Theo and I were awakened every morning by a loud rhythmical chorus of chachalacas, large birds with long tails that peep, whistle, and cackle as they glide and hop around in the brush. I only saw one, but we could hear them clearly. Yucatan parrots, cardinals, scarlet tanagers, and blue grosbeaks were all over the place. A small boa slithered across the road in front of us as we were walking back to our Villa one night, and I had the best rib dinner I'd ever eaten at an Argentinian restaurant. It consisted of one rib as big as a sombrero.

I labored hard at reading for hours in a hammock, and we snorkeled, fished, and did yoga twice a day in a screened studio.

Laura Vanderberg, our yoga teacher, had put the trip together. She had us work not so much on asanas as learning the other six "limbs" of yoga — better breath control, awareness, and meditation skills — yama, niyama, pranayama, pratyahara, dharana and samadhi.

I wondered how in the hell I would ever remember all of it, but I finally felt good again, and I comforted myself in the realization that I was lucky to be alive, that I was at least trying to live with mindfulness, and that I had Theo in my life.

The Bakken

I was finally enjoying the Bat House. Sitting on the roof-deck of the porch one evening as the sun went down, I listened to the birds and watched them catch moths. No mosquitoes. A slight cool breeze from the east. Coyotes very close to the house by the drain ditch began to howl, and a whitetail doe perked up, then continued feeding. I imagined her fawn was safe but thought it must be unnerving to have predators like that so close. I had seen does drive single coyotes away, striking with their sharp hooves, standing their ground, and chasing them, but I imagined a pack after a fawn would be a different thing, though I'd never seen them get one.

It was the second time since buying the place that I had finally enjoyed just sitting, relaxed, listening, and watching. A whitetail came out of the brush and walked directly under me toward the ditch. It was dark, and I'd seen one bat. One had been hanging from the east side soffit by the chimney, despite the Red Eyes, one of which had a weak battery I would have to replace.

I had been timing the silence — the longest that evening without a train or car on the highway to the north of the house was thirty minutes. I was hoping it would be longer than that as I spent more time there, but the old road increased with more traffic all the time. Perhaps the Bakken oil fields in North Dakota and Eastern Montana had something to do with it, as they certainly did on the Interstate.

Obviously, the Bakken had brought all kinds of vice and criminal behavior to the area. In January, two men kidnapped and killed a math teacher from Sidney as she was out for a morning jog. They'd been on drugs for several days, and they grabbed her, threw her in the back of their vehicle, raped her, choked her to death, and buried her next to a wind row. One of the men, named Spell, could not read. He told a girl in Colorado about his crime, and the FBI caught them.

I wondered how long this kind of activity would continue, if it would change the country by the Bat House forever, or once the infrastructure of the Bakken was completed, if it would die with the exodus of workers. And I couldn't help but wonder what generations a hundred or a thousand years in the future would think of our lives.

It occurred to me in a sort of waggish thought when I had a contractor dig around the basement entrance on the north side of the house so I could patch the concrete where I'd found termites in a chunk of wood. Paul Wilkinson, who was sheet rocking and taping the porch, stayed around an extra half day to help me wrap the concrete steps from the footing to the top with a rubber liner. We glued it to the ten-foot deep and eight-foot-long structure, the crazy stuff in a big roll that stuck to itself and us as we tried to manipulate it onto the concrete while we stood in the trench.

I told him we were lucky we didn't get stuck together down there, wrapped tightly facing each other in the black goo, an archaeological find in the far future. I could imagine their theories revolving around a homosexual suicide ritual, termites and diets of beef, potatoes, and iceberg lettuce, the orthodox eastern Montana salad.

Ishvarapranidhana

A former student, Preston Randolph, won the Wyoming Short Film Festival with a film called *The Summer of '81*, about a teacher's aide at Cody High School. He got $25,000 to use for his next film, and he wanted to do a feature. When he asked me for ideas, I suggested three stories: the drought, a sex offender, and Barry Beach. I was trying to make sense of these.

Montana held the infamous record for acreage on fire that summer — 250,000 at last count — the Ashland fire was the largest at 110,00. People had to evacuate, and their homes burned to the ground, their livestock untended. The previous summer a flood hit the Crow Reservation horribly on the Big Horn, and this summer, a fire had devastated the Cheyenne. If this were the east coast, I thought, federal agencies would be crawling up our yahzoo, but as best I could see, no one in eastern Montana was getting help from anyone but themselves. This neglect of western ranchers and Native Americans needed illumination.

In September of 2011 law enforcement arrested a fifty-nine-year-old man I'd played poker with a few times and charged him with five counts of sexual contact without consent on victims under the age of sixteen. Felony Sexual Assault.

He pleaded not guilty, then changed his plea to "No Contest." His wife ran a childcare facility, where two incidents allegedly occurred, and another on a swimming trip to Spotted Eagle Reservoir in Custer County. The judge withdrew his bond of

$100,000, released him under his own recognizance and placed him under house arrest. Counts III and IV were dropped as part of the plea agreement. He had been looking at life in prison.

I never did like him. I had played poker with him, and if he won a tournament, he wouldn't stay for the following cash game. Anyone who won't stay for a cash game after winning the tournament has no courage, no spine, no love of the game. He complained in a passive aggressive manner whenever I busted him out, and I never said anything to him. I always just let it go, not worth the breath.

He was an obese man, and I typically didn't care much for obese people, unless they were my students, and then I went the opposite direction, showering them with positive comments as much as I could, probably from a feeling they hadn't yet had enough time to work on the problem, and they were not at fault. I was extremely sensitive toward them, and my wife told me my whole attitude was messed up.

"Everyone has their addictions," she said in reprimand.

OK. Let it be. But then the guy got sentenced on June 18, 2012: an eighteen-year suspended sentence! He was designated as a "Level 1" offender and prohibited from entering a bar or casino, but he requested and received a change so that he was allowed to enter a "bar-restaurant if the two are combined." That pretty much described every bar in Montana. I didn't know of one where you couldn't buy a pickled pig's foot or a bowl of chili.

I didn't know how he could show his face in public in that small town. And I didn't know how the parents of the children he assaulted could keep from killing him. I knew I would kill him if they were my grandchildren. I didn't think I could play in a poker tournament with him. To say I was not very forgiving of him was an understatement, and I knew how important forgiveness was, but I couldn't even think of him at the same poker table with me.

"No judgments," Laura always said. I knew I should

probably learn more about that, and the Ishvarapranidhana Niyama — Surrendering your will to a greater intelligence in the universe. It was not easy for me because I usually thought I was the greatest intelligence in the universe. Anyway, I thought his story should be brought to light.

The other idea for a story I suggested to Preston was a documentary on the imprisonment of Barry Beach, a convicted murderer in Deer Lodge's Montana State Prison since 1984. In Florida, he confessed to the 1979 killing of a seventeen-year-old girl on the Fort Peck Indian Reservation. In his trial, he claimed Florida detectives coerced his confession, never allowed him legal representation during interrogation, and threatened him with prosecution for other murders in Florida. He pleaded not guilty, and they sentenced him to a hundred years without the possibility of parole.

The year before, a District Judge released him on his own recognizance after ordering another trial because of new evidence linking the girl's death to a fight among a group of teenage girls, some with relatives on the police force. He was living and working in Billings, waiting for the new trial, and for several reasons, I believed he was innocent of killing the girl.

In 1973 and 1974, when I taught writing classes in Montana State Prison, the cons had a standing joke about how everyone in there was innocent. "I didn't do it" could have been written on every wall with pink flowers dotting the "i's." I could easily see through their veils, especially after working with them on personal narratives they wrote that revealed more between the lines than they knew.

Although I'd never met him, this guy Beach struck me differently. Everything I'd read about the case nudged me toward believing him. In poker games around the state, I had met people from the area where the murder took place, and when I asked what they believed, they immediately and unequivocally said Beach was innocent. They told me that evidence had disappeared, and they believed law enforcement officers destroyed it to protect their own relatives. They said people were too afraid to come forward with what they knew because of reprisals.

And a particular quotation in the *Billings Gazette* pushed me further to believe he never killed the girl, even though on the surface it had the same ring as the old "I didn't do it" joke.

"I had to truly accept my life as it was," Beach said. "Then, amidst the chaos, I accepted my situation and God, then found a calmness within me."

That is how I understood the Ishvarapranidhana Niyama. They are all innocent in prison, and they all find God, but the "found a calmness within me" phrase spoke to something else. I could have been wrong, but I thought it spoke to innocence. Anyway, it was not for me to judge. I just thought it would be an interesting documentary, and Preston began to work on it.

The Help

I was staining hemlock for the window and door trim. While waiting for the stain to dry, I rode to town to get a few things, and ended up in the basement of the courthouse to look at the history of ownership on the Bat House. The legal records were in shelves with brass rollers under them, and the books weighed about sixty pounds each. They were water stained from the flood the year before, but in the oldest one, dated 1917–1923, I found the place: Township 6, Section 6, Range 43.

I nearly dropped the book when I read the first name: W.B. Dean (Gdn). Dr. Dean's grandfather. He had 423 acres, and it was taxed at $100. The next year, 1918, he sold it to the Schleuter Brothers, and the value went up to $1,500. I figured they built the house. They were the ones in the picture Cal McConnel showed me of a whole lot of people sitting and standing on an oil derrick. They owned it until 1923, when they sold it to Gertie Western. It looked like Gertie owned it by herself until 1928, after which she and Marjorie Carpenter owned it together for the next forty years. And in 1948, Marjorie's name appears in the book as the sole owner, until 1952 when she sold it to Frank and Joe Barley. They were Bill Lloyd's uncles. Bill and Winifred bought it in 1962.

I couldn't find anyone who remembered Gertie Western or Marjorie Carpenter, and I couldn't help wondering what their relationship had been from 1928 to 1948. Because the Milwaukee Railroad came to Miles City in 1907 and extended northwest to the Judith Basin by 1910, I wondered if they hadn't run a boarding house for the crews, or perhaps for the passengers who might have been relocating here. The old Monarch cook stove in the basement, with the servants' window at the head of the stairs, might have testified to that.

"The help," one old timer told me, "was not to be seen in those days," which might have explained the window I tore out in the main floor bathroom, perhaps a pantry then where the host, maybe Gertie and Marjorie, received the prepared food from the cooks and served it at the dining table. It was a hazy assumption, but the Monarch might have been the main source of heat for the house too, the coal chute on the north side sliding down in the same room as the stove. I assumed another stove vented through the same chimney in the kitchen because a vent was blocked there, but the mysteries of the house were locked in the graves of those who worked and lived here.

A Squirrel with Pam

One thing I would bet on was that Gertie and Marjorie didn't have any squirrels around then because we never had them west of Miles City until the '70s. I shot my first one at the Bat House for stealing apples. Pam was going outside to have a smoke after staining the trim and applying polyurethane when she asked me if I were training the squirrels to peel the apples. Just out the north French door one was tearing away at an apple to get the seeds.

"That's unacceptable behavior," I said, and went upstairs to get the .17 caliber rifle I had for raccoons and skunks.

"There are plenty of seeds bigger than apple seeds out here," I said.

He ran off toward the big cottonwood to the northwest and sat there like an arrogant taunting thief when we came outside and sat on the steps. I set the scope to thirty yards. He was in focus, standing up now and staring at us as if to ask how we had the temerity to try to punish him, and the shot put him in squirrel heaven.

"I've worked too hard on my little apple trees to have him tearing them to pieces," I said.

"Well, he won't eat no more apples now," Pam said.

She had a classic West Virginia hillbilly sense of humor. When she was five, she was helping her dad repair broken windows and replace bad caulking for people. She cleaned semi-trucks in high school, poured and floated concrete when she got married, and took care of twenty-one coon dogs, nine children, and one alcoholic husband.

When her husband got out all the guns after beating her up the third time and swore it was going to be another Ruby Ridge before she left him, she called the police. They gave her enough time to load the kids in a station wagon pulling a trailer with all the possessions she could fit and drove west. She was answering an ad in a magazine for a female ranch employee in Montana. The rancher turned out to be Dick Ferguson, Jack's older brother, who helped her become established in Montana.

I had been in the mountains with Dick about fifty years before on a Boy Scout backpacking trip. The last night we were there, we were out of food, so that evening I caught a huge mess of Brook Trout to feed the troop breakfast before we walked out. I put them on several stringers and threw them into the water. Early the next morning I heard screaming and cursing and looked out my tent to see Dick in his shorts, a hatchet raised high, chasing a black bear out of camp. The bear had eaten every fish, maybe sixty or seventy of them, leaving us only the heads of the Brookies on the stringers, which lay stretched neatly on the shore of the lake like weird Christmas lights.

I asked him what he would have done if the bear had stopped and turned on him.

"I would have killed the son-of-a-bitch," he said, and I thought he was a lunatic then, but there I was, shooting a squirrel for stealing an apple.

Misperception

I'd been practicing yoga for about three years, and I knew it had been good for me — all my stiff neck, shoulder, elbow, hip, and wrist problems had disappeared. That was enough to continue practicing at least three times a week. Also, once, toward the end of summer, I had a feeling that life was perfect in that moment, and for a few hours, I felt a contentment I'd never experienced.

It occurred not as a sudden realization or epiphany of any kind — it was more just a feeling of warmth and contentment with life, maybe just my own life, but not my entire life, just the fact of being in a perfect time. I was breathing and stretching, nothing strenuous, just sitting, a slight twist, and my eyes were open, and life was perfect just the way it was.

"Perfect" is probably not the right word here. With perfection, I suppose we could expect exaltation or immense joy, bliss, or tremendous sensory exuberance. None of that. Contented acceptance might be better. Perhaps a feeling that the way things exist are the way they are supposed to be, and the way they are supposed to be is perfect might be close.

There was no need to change anything. I was not overjoyed with that notion, nor did I question it. I did later, because nothing seems perfect in this world, but it did then. My life was perfect, and I asked Laura, my yoga teacher, after practice if she ever got the feeling that "life was perfect" while practicing yoga, and she smiled and said, "Yes."

I tried telling her how I felt, but I couldn't find the words.

"I am so happy for you," she said. "Did it occur while you were sitting just before savasana, because I noticed your face being very red?"

I wasn't sure. "It was a calmness," I said.

The closest description I could find to the feeling was in Yoga Sutra 1.33: "By cultivating a friendly attitude toward the happy, compassion toward the unhappy, delight in the virtuous and equanimity toward the non-virtuous, the mind-stuff retains its undisturbed calmness."

I didn't believe I had cultivated such attitudes, but I began to understand more when the first thing one morning as I walked through the school doors, I heard a student yell, "Fuck you!" to a girl who was walking away from him.

"What did you say?" I asked him.

"Fuck you," he said.

Equanimity, I told myself, feeling my blood pressure rise.

"I can't believe you would yell that here in the foyer, in the open, in front of the main office," I said.

"Why?" he said. "You hear it all the time in the halls."

"That doesn't make it a virtuous thing to yell at someone," I said. "You might want to check your hole card."

"What?"

"Do you play poker?" I asked.

"No."

"OK, never mind then," I said. "I could take you into the office and fill out an inappropriate behavior form for an administrator, and you would be disciplined with a day of In-School-Suspension, or worse, depending on your attitude."

"At least I'm honest," he said.

"I'll give you that," I said, "but perhaps you need to change something."

"Like watch my mouth," he said.

"Well, yes," I said. "That would be good, but I was thinking of something else."

"Like what?"

"Like checking in with how you treat people. Like how your mind is working toward others. Do you understand?"

"Yeah," he said. "I think so."

"OK," I said. "Maybe the next time you feel angry like that, you can pause and check yourself. Will you let me know how it goes?"

"You teach Broadcast Journalism, right?"

"Yeah," I said. "And English and Mass Comm."

"OK," he said.

"OK," what?"

"I'll let you know how it goes."

It surprised me how I hadn't reacted as usual; in the old days I would have grabbed him by the throat. I let it go quickly. I saw him in a class fourth block and planned to check in on him. I couldn't help thinking I needed to check in on myself too. It was a change I didn't quite understand, but it felt good.

Laura had offered as explanation of the feeling I'd experienced that day in her practice as Samadhi, a state of meditative absorption. It is attained, according to Patanjali, by the practice of Dharana (focused attention) and Dhyana (effortless meditation) when the True Essential Nature is known, without the distortion of the mind. It can be thought of as the culmination of meditation process. That all seemed beyond my understanding then, but I was happy to hear it.

The first time I saw Laura, she was running across Main Street on a November night with her arms hugging her torso minutes before the Outdoor Film Festival was to begin. The orange, red and yellow lights from the marquee glistened in the wet street.

She wore a fleece vest, and she was smiling as she ran, as though she were happy with running in the cold, as though that was the only thing in the world right then, to be running across

Main Street in the cold, perhaps late for the films or perhaps not, or perhaps to grab a forgotten coat from the car, or maybe to get some other place, but not at that moment.

I could still see her running, her head down, both feet off the pavement, suspended with a smile before her extended foot landed on earth. That smile was her seminal characteristic — it emanated from her like the brightest star in a constellation. I'd never seen anyone quite like her.

"Who the hell is that?" I asked Theo.

Theo said, "I think she's a yoga teacher."

"She's crazy," I said.

"What makes you say that?" Theo asked.

"Her smile in the rain," I said. "She reminds me of Don Lockwood."

"Who's he?"

"Gene Kelly in *Singin' in the Rain*."

I was talking about the kind of crazy Kelly exhibits in the musical spoof when he splashes around in the downpour and swings from the lamp post, the cop staring at him with concerned bewilderment, not the wind-in-the-willows kind of crazy.

I had learned that yoga is the ability to direct the mind exclusively toward an object and sustain that direction without any distractions. The mind is the activities that occupy it. It cannot be perceived except in terms of five activities: comprehension, misperception, imagination, deep sleep, and memory.

According to the Sutra, misperception is the foremost problem, but it could be humorous too, and I chose to focus more on that slice of misperception. It was more heartening, like Theo was on a morning just before Christmas.

"What's this?" she asked more to herself than to me. She laughed as she said it. In her pajamas and robe, she was reading the daily paper as we ate breakfast.

"Jerky lovers find good recipes for cure." By the end of reading the headline, she was laughing uncontrollably.

"What about it?" I asked.

"Oh no, I'm not awake," she said. "I thought it meant, you know, jerky *lovers*."

I shot a mouthful of egg across the table and choked on a bite of toast.

She was laughing now with her head in her hands.

I finally got my breath and started cleaning up the mess I'd made. "Your job is getting to you," I said.

"I guess," she said. "I was wondering if they were researching new rhythms or something."

"I think it might be a problem in my neck," I said, jerking my head around uncontrollably for a few seconds, "and I'd like to try the recipes for the cure."

"That's enough," she said, still laughing as she folded the paper on the table. "Oh dear, I have to get dressed."

And I found heartening misperception again when Bart and Megan brought Syd and Alexander to Cody a few days later for Christmas. Zan and I were up at first light to go ice fishing while everyone else stayed snuggled in their beds.

When we arrived at Newton Lake, three groups of fishermen were already on the ice. No one was catching anything, and they had not had a bite. They stood like wooden posts, silent and enduring. I drilled four holes and Zan had a fish on before I could get my rods ready. He pulled out a seventeen-inch cutthroat, and everybody on the lake came over to look at it and ask him what he was using.

"You are an awfully lucky guy," a man said.

"No," Zan said. "I'm a professional fisherman."

After Christmas, he came with me to the Bat House to goose hunt, and even though he was only six, he stayed in the blind with Mac and me until I had my limit of five. It didn't take long, but I admired how happy he was to be out there in the cold, fascinated with every detail of the geese, which were as big as he was.

He wanted to know if I felt bad about shooting them because they were so beautiful.

I said, "No. We will eat them, and we are not hurting the population by harvesting a few."

"Thanks to God," he said. "He gave them to us."

"Well, not entirely," I said. "We had to get our butts out of our warm beds, set up these decoys and aim right."

"Thank you, God," he said, wagging his head and looking up at the sky with his arms outstretched, "for Granpa's aiming right."

I thought, *You are your own yogi, Zan Man.*

Onychonycteris

On the Fourth of July Matt brought his family to Cody from Oklahoma where he'd taken a job at a lab. I took the boys fishing almost every day, and they were content every day to go to the dock at New Cody Lake and catch a million perch and crawdads. Melissa asserted quite bluntly one day that she couldn't see any reason why she couldn't go fishing with the boys, so we took her along, and she caught her first fish, a perch about a millimeter long, but she was ecstatic, jumping around, waving her arms and screaming.

Melissa had no problem telling you what was on her mind, even though she could not fully pronounce her r's. She was out walking with Theo when she looked up to seriously study her.

"Gwandma, youaw ooold," she said.

Theo laughed. "No, I'm not," she said. "I'm not old."

"Why ahh you laughing?" Melissa said. "Have you looked at yowself in the miwah?"

She wanted to know about bats, so I showed her an article about a twenty-year old Rocky Mountain College student, Zachery Farrand, who was researching bats in the Beartooth Mountains. Farrand recorded bats' echolocation frequencies with his sensors to identify the species of bats in the area. He was hiking into the mountains, carrying his audio equipment in his backpack, to log twenty-four nights of bat calls, and he had identified "seven of Montana's fifteen known species."

According to *Bats of the World*, a Golden Guide from St. Martin's Press, "most species use signals between 20 and 80 kHz." I bought this fascinating little book at Fossil Butte National Monument where I learned Bonnie Finney found Onychonycteris fossils in the Green River Formation in 2003. The Finney bat lived about 52 million years ago, as old as, if not older than, Icaronycteris, the most primitive species known until her find.

Scientists still debate if it used echolocation, but the book says modern bats target insects by varying the rates of pulses, from ten per second to locate them, from twenty-five to fifty to home in on them, and up to 200 pulses per second just before nailing them. Distance to the target, size of the target, and direction of the target's movement all get processed in the flying bat's brain.

That is extremely high-tech instrumentation going on in milliseconds. It's taken humans thousands of years to develop that capability in electronic gadgetry, and bats developed it somewhere around 50 million years ago. No wonder Farrand could not catch any in his "12-foot-high mist nets" when the wind caused them to flap and billow.

I knew they communicate with each other by using high frequency pulses. I'd watched them land on the sealed roof by their old chimney entrance as others flitted around, then suddenly take off all at once, as if one of them said, "Guess what, boys? It's closed."

I just wished I understood how to communicate with them so I could explain that I could not live with their shit dropping on my head.

Birds of Different Feathers

My not knowing everything had become more obvious to me the older I got, but my experiences with the Bat House had at least fortified my resolve to be at peace with that realization.

Several of my neighbors around Rosebud laughed at me for sticking transparent plastic decals on my large black windows, but I didn't care. The decals reflected ultraviolet sunlight that birds can see, but people can't, so after a while, I didn't even notice them. They had stopped birds from flying into my windows, which reflected the trees and sky like black mirrors, whereas without them, I was finding two or three dead birds every day.

"You're crazy," a friend said when I told him I pay about $1.50 for each decal. "There are plenty of birds in the world."

"Not enough," I said. "And we're killing them by the millions. I put three decals on each of twenty windows, so every six months I replace them at a cost of a hundred and eighty dollars a year. That's cheap," I told him. "Get it? Cheep, cheep?"

My friend was born in a dugout sod cabin, and he had just about every tool, truck, backhoe, skidder, tractor, loader, and lifter you could imagine. He was one of the most self-reliant men I'd known, and he'd been extremely generous in helping me with various problems, but he didn't see the need to worry about songbirds hitting my windows.

I told him that according to *National Geographic* articles I'd read over the past five years, Americans alone are killing billions of birds every year with wind turbines, night lights, insecticides, skyscrapers, pet cats, coal plants, communication towers, destruction of habitat, and windows.

$180 a year was much less than paying a fine for every bird my windows killed. Duke Energy would have to pay about a million dollars in fines for violating the Migratory Bird Treaty Act, and the Bald and Golden Eagle Protection Act on their Wyoming wind projects. According to American Bird Conservancy, Duke's 176 wind turbines had killed fourteen golden eagles and 149 other protected birds since 2009, including hawks, blackbirds, larks, wrens, and sparrows.

The previous year a scientist named Smallwood estimated that the wind-energy industry kills about 500,000 birds a year and warned that the total will grow exponentially with the Department of Energy's plan to increase wind-generation twelve-fold by 2030. Wind turbines also kill over 500,000 bats a year, according to a Colorado researcher. They are either looking for a "tree" to roost in when they hit the blades spinning at 170 mph, or their lungs explode from barotrauma, much like a scuba diver's will if external pressure drops too quickly.

In Wyoming, three species of bats migrate: the hoary, the eastern red, and the silver haired. They are Wyoming's only tree roosting species, and they must migrate to survive the winters here. As energy companies build more wind farms, I thought we'd better know the bats' paths, or we'd wipe them out. Or maybe, I wondered, if we could make sure the bats know the turbines are not trees.

Geomyces destructans

Matt had taken a job with Lawrence Livermore Labs in California, and while he was looking for a place for them to live, Kristin and the kids drove up from Ponca City, Oklahoma for spring break. While I was grilling ribs in the back yard, six-year-old Melissa asked me why I killed bats.

"Who told you that?" I asked.

"Mason and Ollie," she said. "You showed them one and it was dead. Deadah than a doah nail. You killed it."

"I don't kill all bats," I said, "just the ones in my house."

"But why don't you just set them fwee?" she said, shrugging her shoulders and holding her forearms out. "They eat mosquitos, you know!"

She put her hands on her hips and stood in front of me, shook her head, swiped her hair to the side and rolled her eyes up at me.

"And theah noses get all white and they can't bweathe! And then we have too many mosquitos!"

"I kill them because they keep coming back," I said, "and pooping on my deck."

"Oh yuck!" she said. "That is gwose! I wouldn't want to clean that up!" She skipped away on the sidewalk to the garage to get her jump rope.

But she had me thinking with her forthright accusation. She'd obviously been taught by her dad, or Mason, or in her first grade Oklahoma class about "white nose syndrome," Geomyces destructans, "the destroying fungus."

She had part of it right, anyway. According to several articles I'd read, the fungus does not asphyxiate the bats, but irritates their wings, keeping them too active during hibernation. They burn up their fat reserves, and if they do not die during the winter, when they emerge with infected wings, they cannot fly well enough to provide adequate lactation for their pups.

Although the fungus was first discovered in 2006 in New York among little browns (Myotis lucifigus), my bats, it had spread through six species and many southern states, including Oklahoma, where someone had taught Missa about it. But it also spread north into Canada, and some scientists predicted the little browns' extinction in the Northeast by 2025. Tom Kunz, an ecologist at Boston University, estimated the cost to farmers, if the fungus spread to corn and cotton states, at somewhere between four and fifty-three billion dollars in pesticides alone.

He sees "roost modules," baffled boxes for bats to rest in during the summer, as the only glimmer of hope. Little bat houses, the type Batman Biff had recommended to me five years before, provide a warm place where the fungus cannot survive above sixty-eight degrees. Missa had me thinking I should make some.

Retirement

When I decided to retire from teaching, I began cleaning forty years-worth of educational material out my classroom and my Broadcast Journalism Studio office. I was not systematic about it at all. I walked around mumbling, looking through file cabinets, wondering what I should leave for my replacement, Erika, one of my former students, and what I should trash. I threw material into boxes with some kind of fuzzy idea this should go with that, read old *National Geographic* magazines, sifted through piles of DVDs, attacked cork boards pinned with photos and news articles, and opened cabinets I had forgotten held stacks of texts, novels, and handouts. I was happy to find things I had lost.

When I took down all the posters that had been hanging for years, my students told me how sad it was to see the walls bare. They were shocked when they noticed the discolored rectangles on the corkboards where my pictures had been tacked. I took down a newspaper photo of Mr. Halberstam at his desk just before he was killed in a car accident and told a girl who was watching me that I didn't feel so slovenly when I looked at this photo. His office held ten times the clutter of mine. I gave her a bamboo Japanese folding-fan pinned there from some obscure Prom I chaperoned maybe twenty-five years before.

I gave a little stuffed fish with a safety pin on the back to a blonde boy who pinned it on his shirt, smiled, puffed out his chest and turned in circles so everyone could see it.

I draped a lanyard with a whistle on it over a girl who just happened to be dressed in a police uniform for a video skit. She immediately walked around the studio piercing the air with it and pointing her finger at people.

I tossed a deflated volleyball with *THIS THURSDAY* (our old logo for the student TV production) to Abbey the Blade, the current news director. She hugged it to her chest and rocked back and forth as if it were a baby.

I handed a pink Barbie paper plate to a love forlorn junior boy.

"Put a piece of cake on it and give it to a girl you like," I told him.

I thought for a moment as I dangled a velvet rope tied into a hangman's noose in front of Tawni, a very proper, extremely kindhearted, dark-haired girl who only dressed in black and white and had a black belt in Tae Kwon Do, then dropped it on her lap.

"That's offensive," she said.

"If anybody can deal with it, you can," I told her, and gave her a block of wood with a swaddled baby Jesus on a pile of straw with a star on a pipe cleaner over him.

She wanted me to sign it.

I found a whole stack of pink Barbie plates on the top shelf above my desk and handed them to Gabriella, an Italian princess with hair to the middle of her back. She had been chief anchor for two years.

"Ohhh," she cooed, "that is soooo sweet."

I read an unsigned note with no date written in pencil on a half-page of spiral notebook paper that I had found on my desk at the end of some forgotten year.

Mr. Riley, Good Bye. Out of all my teechurs I probable remember you the most! Thank you. have a good summer.

I folded it up, put it in my shirt pocket, and thought I would like to be buried with it.

Then I was down to the stuff my current students had absolutely no idea about and that I carefully considered for a few minutes before throwing away.

There were three newspaper articles with photos. The first was of a graduation-robed girl in line to receive her college diploma. She had raised twin boys by herself since high school and was now an English teacher.

The second was of a girl in a thin red blouse at a radio microphone with a wild grin and raised arm. I once stopped her from beating the snot out of a sophomore boy who had a habit of sexually harassing and molesting girls in the hallways. She was a six-foot-two state champion volleyball player, and she had the guy lifted off the floor against a locker, one hand gripped around his throat, the other balled into a fist ready to smash his face in, when I talked her into letting him go. I saw her at the rodeo about ten years ago, and she ran up to me and gave me a bear hug, all lean mean muscle, and kissed my cheek with a smack like the pop of a rope. She was home from San Diego, where she was a highly respected, popular DJ.

I also had a small picture of Jake, a uniformed Navy man above a thin newspaper column describing his accomplishments in Iraq. He had wanted to be a SEAL more than I have ever known anybody to want anything. He trained like a man possessed in high school, on the swim and football teams, rock climbing, rafting the river at night, running, lifting weights, and he was surprisingly strong, given his easy quiet way with a sardonic grin.

I wasn't sure why he didn't make it, but he told me he blew out his knee in San Diego. He was a hospital corpsman in Iraq in 2003 and a Cody police officer in 2005. He came to visit me often then, and we watched old *This Thursday* episodes with another student and him as "Gino and Francisco," hosts of a satirical cooking show who were shirtless under full aprons. With weird Russian-Italian accents, they demonstrated how to cook delicacies like chocolate covered dog biscuits and roasted kitty-cat while barely surviving accidents like exploding barbeque grills. They danced in a circle, clapped hands, and sang nonsensical syllables like "OIY!"

He told me on one visit to the school that he was having trouble adjusting to civilian life, that he was "emotionally unsettled." He left the police force shortly after that and moved to Portland, Oregon, where he flew helicopters.

And that was the worst part of packing it up: the deaths of students. I was sitting alone in the teachers' lounge two days after throwing Jake's photo and thin column into the trash when I opened the local newspaper to the same photo of him on the obituary page. He was 34. Suicide.

When I began teaching in 1974, the teachers' lounge was elbow to elbow at lunch. Most teachers packed their own in little brown paper bags. They smoked cigarettes, pipes, and cigars until the room was a cloud. They argued incessantly about politics, bitched and moaned about students, delighted in students, and they helped each other in every way possible. It changed in the '90s, with the advent of the internet. They began sitting at their desks while they ate their lunches and surfed the net. For the last three years, I had usually been the only one at the four large tables, except occasionally for the choir teacher and his wife, who prepared his lunch for him at home and met him there.

But on that day, I was alone, and I couldn't help crying. I hadn't even known Jake was back in town. I sat there overwhelmed, my head in my hands, wondering why I hadn't seen the danger. He was such a beautiful, determined kid, full of piss and vinegar and always with that little smile.

I will always remember the uneasy regretful feeling when I decided to crumple that newspaper clipping in my hand and toss it in the garbage. I didn't know what to do with it, just as I didn't know what to do with the Tom Jolley Memorial Award, a big heart shaped plaque with photography students' names engraved from 1981 until 1999. It sat on top of my closet cabinet, hardly ever noticed now. One of the best photographers we ever had, he was killed in a car accident just a few months before he would have graduated in 1980. He carried his camera around his neck constantly, his baseball cap backwards so it didn't interfere with a quick shot. Trying to get a winning image, he was kicked off the football field three times in one game before the refs told him they would have the police escort him off the premises if he did it again.

Skidding around a corner, Tom hit a pickup truck head-on in his iconic VW Bug. He was like a little brother to me — I took him fishing, ate dinners at his home, and let him use my four-wheel drive when he needed a truck.

Another photo was still on the corkboard in the Broadcast office. It was of a student named Kurt playing guitar with a friend. A quirky, creative kid, he might have been a filmmaker, a poet, or an actor. He made an excellent short film his senior year about becoming a werewolf. He never drank booze or used drugs, but if you didn't know him, you would have thought he was always stoned. A kid set his hair on fire in my class when he was a sophomore, and when I asked the kid why he had done it, he said Kurt had told him to. I asked Kurt if he had, and he'd said yes, but that he'd been joking. Kurt had been the boyfriend of Erika, the former student who was replacing me. He was killed in a car wreck just months after graduation. One minute I thought I'd let Erika decide what to do with the picture, and the next I thought I should crumple it up and throw it away too.

It had been thirteen years since the attack on the twin towers in New York City. I remembered the girl in my tenth grade English class who said, as we watched the news on television, "Why would anyone want to do that? They'd kill themselves."

And the boy who laid his head on his folded arms at his desk.

"It just makes me tired," he said as he went to sleep.

I was sobered by the girls' naiveté and angered by what I saw as the boy's apathy and indifference, but I didn't say anything.

When I told Theo about his reaction, she said, "That makes sense to me."

He died a few years later of a rare heart condition.

I had to take a break from this somber reverie and returned to the school on a rainy Sunday. With a new sense of direct practicality and unsentimental verve, I began throwing almost everything in the trash. Jake's memorial service on Saturday had torn me up, but somehow it gave me relief. Scott Richard, another one of my former students and one of Jake's best friends, expressed the qualities of their friendship and Jake's personality in a speech that just amazed me. I realized how far Scott had come, how mature he was, how articulate, honest, true, and thoughtful. When I was leaving the church, he was standing in the foyer, and I shook his hand.

"Good job, Scottie," I said. He pulled me to him, laid his head on my shoulder and cried, hugging me close.

The hug was what I needed most to pack it up.

Having Scott there, alive with a wife and child, released me from the need to hold on to the clippings, photos, and mementos. I had many, many former students who were living and well, and they mattered most. I needed to pay attention to them, listen closely to where they were now, and help them if I could. The rest was just a bunch of stuff.

Except, of course, for the anonymous, undated note.

Cancer and Blaze

In September, Theo was home from breast cancer surgery, and someone's escaped parrot was living in our crab apple tree. Theo's tumor was .6 millimeters, on the line of Stage 2, so we were optimistic, but I had been optimistic after my mother's and my aunt's first surgeries too. I was afraid I had not been much support during the decision process. I sat passively through the discussions with her doctors, asking only a few questions and trying to suppress my pessimism and mistrust. I wanted Theo to be as positive as she could, knowing I would let her make the decisions and help with whatever she needed.

She worried about the bills, and I told her not to. Insurance would cover it. I believed in having a lot of insurance. She did not trust insurance companies, and neither did I, which is why I called them a lot and read the fine print.

Trying to catch the parrot broke my obsessing on her cancer. I first tried a fishing net, but the bird did not even let me get close. I opened the upstairs bedroom window, where I could get a good shot at him with it, but it was a ridiculous effort. He did not fly far each time, just to the neighbor's ponderosas, and returned after a few hours to slice into the apples with his sharp beak.

About a foot long including the tail, he was crazily colored and patterned, as if he had flown through a hurricane in a paint store. He had a crimson head and white cheeks. The upper breast was red, with bright yellow and mottled black feathers above the wings, and the belly gradient to pale green before it slammed against another patch of bright red at the base of the tail. The rest of the tail was dark green, except for the lateral feathers, which were blue like parts of his wings.

I knew he was in the tree when I heard his sbonk. It was a metallic, underwater sound, like I used to make by banging a brass D-ring on my scuba tank when I needed other divers' attention. It was getting colder at night, and I thought he would die by morning, but then I heard his sbonk about 10 o'clock.

The City's Animal Control officer arrived with a live-trap baited with various types of birdseed, and we set it on the ground below the apple tree. It rained a cold drizzle that night, and I didn't hear a sbonk for two days. I thought he'd frozen. Then I saw him happily munching on crabapples a few feet above the trap, and I realized he had no interest in birdseed.

I called Susan Ahalt, known in Cody as "The Bird Lady," an eccentric, self-appointed Florence Nightingale of ornithology who drives about eight million miles a week trying to rescue all sorts of birds in all sorts of dire straits.

Although most of the birds she rescued were owls, hawks and eagles in Wyoming, and she'd handled hundreds of each, people did bring her the occasional bat.

In July a family in Douglas who had just purchased an old house that had been vacant for two years called her because they'd found "a bunch of baby bats on the floor under the chimney opening" in the basement. The pups had evidently fallen three stories, and only six were still alive. The mother of the family, who was breast feeding a four-month-old daughter, pumped her own milk to feed them, and Susan picked them up after a five-hour drive. Two died, even though Susan fed them every six hours using a sponge soaked in a baby bat formula.

Susan did not have a stellar success rate with bats. She had been given Little and Big Browns, mostly, but she had also cared for a Western Pipistrelle, or canyon bat, the smallest bat in the

United States, and extremely rare in Wyoming. She fell in love with a Big Brown pup she named Yoda, and it died at about six weeks old, close to Susan's release date for it. She was heartbroken and felt sorry she'd failed it.

In 1987, Susan started Ironside Bird Rescue, Inc., "a non-profit corporation for the rehabilitation of wild injured and orphaned birds." She enlisted an army of veterinarians, game wardens, dentists, doctors, optometrists, and citizens like me in her missions, and she approached each case as if she were squad leader of a Delta Team.

"This is what we're going to do," she said. "You will spray the parrot with water from your garden hose. You must stay right on it. Keep spraying it as it goes down, even after it hits the ground. I will throw a towel over it as fast as I can."

Sure, I thought, this is a tropical bird whose feathers will not be ruffled in the least by water unless it's a blast from a fire hose. But I gave her the benefit of the doubt and opened the nozzle on the poor guy, who immediately streaked to the safety of the ponderosas.

What Susan lacked in results, she more than made up for in kinetic enthusiasm and perseverance. She had found the owner and said the bird's name was Blaze. He was an Eastern Rosella, native to Australia. She said he distrusts men. Perhaps he had been abused by one.

And you wanted me to spray him with the hose, I thought.

She brought his cage from the owner's home, and we set it as high as we could on the deck under the tree. Placing his favorite food and toys inside, she left a gate open on the top. I put a few apples in for good measure.

"When he goes in," she said, "you'll have to sneak up on him from under the tree and throw a towel over the gate."

After several attempts, it finally worked. Blaze was a prisoner again. The Bird Lady wrapped a towel around him and had me hold him while she clipped his wings.

"I don't understand why people don't do this in the first place," she said.

I couldn't help but think how happy he was in that apple tree, sbonking away, free to fly to the ponderosas or down to the river, but I knew that with his flamboyant colors, he'd be an easy target for a hawk or cat, and in just a few weeks he'd probably starve or freeze.

Theo was happy I caught him. She was dressed in one of her favorite blouses to do volunteer work for the Art Show at the Buffalo Bill Center of the West, and when I looked at her, saw her determination, the optimism in her smile, and her soul emanating from her eyes, I believed she would never have any more trouble with cancer.

Since beginning our research on cancer-fighting foods, our meals had changed, including much more "organic" produce and less use of the microwave. I tried to cook as many of the recommended foods as I could: Brussels sprouts, walnuts, broccoli, pomegranates, lentils, blueberries, salmon, spinach, eggs, rye bread, buckwheat groats and kale, and I was always looking for better recipes.

I couldn't believe Brussels sprouts, those bitter miniature cabbages that grow on sticks like green warts, had ever been anyone's favorite, but I tossed them with olive oil, red pepper flakes and Kosher salt, then baked them at 400 degrees for about thirty minutes until they were crispy and burned and then ate them like popcorn. Delicious.

Theo threw spinach in everything, and I grilled salmon on cedar planks.

She had always loved lentils, but I had not discovered how to prepare them without suffering the sulfurous side effects of her Scottish industry that awakened me and drove me out of bed to open a window.

D.C.

Because the fall JEA convention was in Washington D.C., Theo and I decided to take Sydney and stay for a week, thinking that at eleven, she was of the impressionable age where experiencing the nation's capital would be a milestone. While I judged student work, attended my Mentor workshop, and presented sessions, Theo guided her through a list she had made from several books she had read about D.C.

Sydney believed she would like nothing more than to become a Supreme Court Justice, so she toured that building and danced on its steps, as well as spent a day in the House and Senate, arranged through Mike Enzi's office. I brought her into the convention to listen to Bob Woodward, the keynote speaker, and tried to explain Watergate before he spoke, boiling it down to President Nixon tried to lie his way out of a bunch of other lies he'd told, and Woodward exposed him. I also took her to Mount Vernon, where she was quite shocked to learn that Washington had slaves. Theo and she bicycled around the parks, and I bought tickets to *The Little Dancer* at the Kennedy Center for Performing Arts.

I enjoyed the ballet depicting what might have happened to Degas' model immensely, but I enjoyed watching Sydney's rapt attention more. At intermission, I asked her what she thought of the performance so far.

"My eyes are dried up," she said.

"What?"

"I was afraid I'd miss something, so I didn't blink," she said, "and my eyes are like the Sahara."

Every evening, she did her homework so she would be abreast of her classes when she returned to Wyoming, and because it was a warm November, I took her outside to see if we could see any bats emerge from caves and bridges, but we saw very few. I told her that the Big Brown Bat was the official state mammal of D.C., that the area was home to seven species of bats, and two were endangered. I told her the fungal disease White Nose Syndrome had presented itself there heavily in recent years, and it was spreading rapidly to other parts of the country. I explained that it disturbed their hibernation and birth cycles, causing them to weaken and die, and characteristically of Syd, she felt sad for them and wondered what could be done to save them. I didn't tell her how I had treated them at the farm.

Every morning, as tired as she was from her long days, she got up early so she could join me for breakfast at the Omni Shoreham's elaborate, all-you-can-eat buffet.

On the plane home, I asked her what her favorite part of the trip had been, expecting her to say the Supreme Court building, hearing Bob Woodward speak, or seeing *The Little Dancer*.

"Unlimited bacon," she said. "I ate about a pound of it every morning."

Jamming and Smelling

Theo and I were enjoying the Bat House as often as we could. I often heard her say, "Every window I look through has a beautiful painting."

And there were a lot of windows. In the kitchen, we could watch the sun come up to the east behind old apple trees, and upstairs, we saw it rise over alfalfa and corn fields. We watched it go down from the big windows of the dining room or the living room, or from the upstairs master bedroom. One upstairs bathroom window opened to cottonwood trees along the river and the hills on its south side, and the other to the eastern fields and the lane's row of huge cottonwoods I had remembered from driving there with my mother. Plum trees and chokecherry bushes lined the foreground to the north and east. Early mornings and late evenings always revealed wild geese, raccoons, pheasants, deer, turkeys, coyotes, or fox close to the house. We often sat on the upstairs deck off our bedroom to watch the stars appear, and some mornings we had our coffee there. Bats flew close to us, but none hung from the metal soffit or the chimney corners.

One evening we listened to CBC radio's *Quirks and Quarks*, on which Dr. William Conner from North Carolina explained his research on one bat's jamming another bat's echolocation signals to confuse it so the jamming bat can swoop in and nab the prey. They are Mexican free-tailed bats, like those in Austin and Carlsbad Caverns that we used to watch thunder out in the millions. Competition for food is fierce, so the bat listening to another's pulses on a target sends out a siren-like pulse that disorients the first bat, then swoops in to whack the moth.

He was studying a sonar-jamming moth in southern Arizona, one that "makes forty-five hundred clicks per second," that confuses hunting bats, when a higher altitude signal "like the vibrato of an opera singer" caught his attention. He identified it as a jamming bat signal and set up high-speed cameras and high-frequency microphones.

"It's a bit like warfare," he said. "It becomes a complex aerial dogfight, where bat number two will jam bat number one, and vice versa, and they go back and forth, jamming each other back and forth until one of them finally wins."

All this "happens in a fraction of a second," he said, and explained that they catch insects in their tails, "like a catcher's mitt," and eat them mid-flight.

I had no idea they have sonar systems as sophisticated as the world's best navies and air forces, including defensive military strategies, as another researcher, Danilo Russo, recently found in Italy where greater mouse-eared bats mimic the buzz of hornets to keep owls from attacking them.

I knew from my experiences on the island of Kosrae in Micronesia that some bats do not use echolocation. Theo and I were in an outrigger canoe when we saw a huge black bat fly out of the mountain jungle and cross the ocean in front of us high in the sky. It looked prehistoric, as if it had been animated against the gray clouds in the 1933 film *King Kong*.

I thought it might be a vulture or some sort of hawk, but our guide Kato said it was a fruit bat (one I realized later as a Gigantic Flying Fox). Frugivorous bats locate over-ripe fruit by smelling it, and they pollinate many of the fruit trees on the islands and disperse seeds for new growth. Kato said they make an excellent meal, but he had stopped hunting them because their population had declined so radically in his lifetime.

"What happened to them?" I asked.

"Market hunters," he said. "There used to be thousands of them."

Basketball, Voles, and Bees

With Theo's blessing, I went to the State B Girls basketball tournament in Great Falls.

"Have a good time," she said. "I'd love to go with you, but I have a full load of clients."

After several barn burning games I wished Theo could have seen, I won enough in a poker game to make a down payment on a jet boat, and when I pulled it to the farm, the first thing I noticed was how my apple trees were leaning over onto the deer fences around them. They looked as though they were pushed over by a big windstorm, but as I examined them, I saw that the bark had been chewed away at their bases, and the roots had been chewed through.

Voles had killed my apple trees. Voles. They burrowed beneath the deep snow in winter and ate the bark off at the ground. I wondered how many other pests there were in the world that I knew nothing about, but which invariably found their way to the Bat House.

It was May, and while the plum, chokecherry and apple trees were in full bloom, which made me imagine a giant woman, perhaps the Jolly Green's wife, had spilled her bottle of Clive Christian's Imperial Majesty perfume, only a few bees worked at the blossoms. From the house's east deck, I only counted about ten on the old apple tree, and they created nothing like the constant, deep viola hum of two years before.

Montana honeybee colonies had declined by forty to fifty percent in the last year, according to the Department of Agriculture.

"I lost about thirty percent," an apiarist who lived down the lane told me. He said mites, viruses, and herbicides were all factors. American Foulbrood, a serious disease caused by bacteria, he said, was also on the rise.

I asked him about neonicotinoids, an insecticide Bayer Crop Science produced and if he thought it had harmed his colonies. Crop seed is treated with neonicotinoids, and according to some beekeepers, it transfers to the bee's winter bank of pollen and kills young bees.

I also asked him if perhaps the major problem is big agriculture's raising only one crop, mostly corn, that doesn't offer bees high quality nutrition, but instead gives them the toxic chemicals that go along with it. But the apiarist told me African bees brought the mites, which are the most serious problem, not the African bees themselves.

About the only thing I could see that was winning in the world was a lucky poker game, and because of it and Theo, I had a new fishing boat.

Otto

Otto Bendewald died June 13th at ninety-years old. When I was in high school, Otto gave me a job at his Standard Service Station on the south side, next to the old highway before the Interstate was built. I learned to pump gas, wash windshields, check oil, run a cash register, charge credit cards, and fix flat tires, but I remember the people I met there best.

Otto was born in Vananda in 1924, and his brother Mervin, who owned an antique store and furniture restoration business in New York City, hired me one summer to help him scour the countryside around Forsyth for antiques he could take back to his shop in Greenwich Village. One day in the sagebrush on Red Killen's grazing land, he picked up a sun-bleached cow pelvis in perfect shape, and you would have thought he'd found the Lost Dutchman Mine.

"I'll set a fern in this," he said, holding it up and turning it, "and hang it from the ceiling of my store. I should get $250 for it."

I knew then New Yorkers had to be crazy. On a hitchhiking trip in 1970, I found his store, and in the front as I walked in, I saw a juke box I had helped him buy for $300 from Dr. Dean's mother. When you dropped a nickel in it, a curtain opened at the top, and a miniature band played as your seventy-eight record was selected and dropped onto the turnstile. He had a "Not for Sale" sign on it.

Working for Otto opened my eyes to the world in many ways,

but perhaps the most poignant awakening occurred late one hot July night when two black men in a beautiful '65 Cadillac convertible with Louisiana plates rolled up to the pump. I filled it with gas as one man went inside and the other got out to stretch and walk around a bit. Both were tall and thin, and they wore shiny silk shirts and pants and sleek leather shoes. I had only seen two African Americans in my life, the Proctor sisters, whose father had been a slave and had homesteaded near my grandmother's place, so these two men fascinated me. I was excited to talk with them and welcomed hearing their story. They were as exotic to me as two Masai hunters returning from the Serengeti.

Just as I was checking their oil, the man outside started jabbering so fast I could not understand him, and he spun around several times, glancing and dancing about as he pointed up at the hill where the Lutheran Church had erected a cross lit with white incandescent bulbs.

"Hey man," he was saying, "you got a KKK here?"

I had no idea what he was asking. He said it so fast that it did not register with me. I thought he had a stutter, and he did not give me a chance to reply.

He was yelling at his friend who was inside to hurry up and pay me, pointing up at the cross and saying that they needed *to get out of here now!* I did not know what was wrong, but the man inside came running out, handed me a $20 bill, jumped into the Cadillac without opening the door, and took off.

They only owed me about $10 for gas, and as I stood there, I figured out what had happened, but it was too late. They were probably half-way to Miles City the way they tore out of town.

When I told Otto about it in the morning, he told me to keep the change from the twenty. I had never seen grown men that afraid before, and I regretted not being able to explain to them about the cross. I had never connected it to the Ku Klux Klan, but seeing men live with that kind of fear made a lasting impression.

"It is too bad," I told Otto, "that I never got to talk with them. I wonder who they were."

"They come from a different world," Otto said. "And you're right. It is too bad."

Otto was Chairman at the Lutheran Church, so he felt as bad as I did about their misinterpreting the cross he had supported putting on the hill.

I don't think he ever missed one of my home basketball or football games. He was always positive afterwards, encouraging me with his humor, even if we had taken a beating.

I ate with him at the Chinese restaurant a few years after hitting the Montana Cash lottery, and when we finished our dinner, I told him I believed in fortune cookies.

"Two weeks before I won the lottery," I said, "my fortune cookie said I would soon come into a large amount of money. And another one predicted I would be honored for my work just before Arch Coal gave me $3500 for their Outstanding Teacher award."

"Damn," Otto said. "Sounds to me like you ought to buy them by the box."

Harold McCaskie had died in January. Paul Kanta died in Miles City at the VA Care Center a month after Otto, and I felt a huge loss with them gone. An entire piece of the north country around Sumatra, Ingomar and Vananda had vaporized, as well as the antidotal sense of humor that helped them survive it.

Restitution

I was writing at my desk in the screened-in porch at 8 P.M., the August air still and cool, when I got a call from Casey Nichols in Sacramento telling me the Journalism Education Association decided to give me their Lifetime Achievement Award. I told him I felt honored, and knowing his wife Sarah whose workshops I had attended, I invited them to the farm if they ever got to Montana. It felt good to be comfortable enough with the place to extend the invitation.

Theo was going on a four-day, twenty-five-mile hike in the Tetons the next day with her brother and sister, our niece, and Matt, who had driven from California. We talked on the phone for a while about her reminders when I got home — to feed her fish, water her flowers and make my doctor's appointment on Wednesday. She'd been training the last four months for this hike. I asked her if she had a fresh can of bear spray. She didn't but said maybe her brother would. I told her to go to the sporting goods store to buy one. She said she would.

"I'm going to put up some bat houses around here," I said.

"Why?" she asked. "I thought you didn't want them around."

"I want them around," I said. "I just don't want them in the house. I haven't seen any this summer, and I'm worried about them. I think I might have wiped out a whole maternal colony. I feel guilty about it."

"Well, put them far away from the house then," she said.

"I've picked out two cottonwoods," I said, "the old gnarly one to the west by the drain ditch and the other one by the old well to the north."

"Oh yes," she said. "That should be good."

"I haven't seen any," I said. "Usually there are at least three or four flying around, and I don't know what happened to that poor little devil I found on the concrete a few weeks ago. I miss them."

We said, "Goodbye. I love you," and I listened to the approaching night. Coyotes yipped and howled for a few minutes. Crickets and frogs had taken over with their constant cadence, an owl hooted, a goose squawked on the river, and the moon was half full in a clear sky. Perfect, I thought. Life here at this moment is perfect. It is everything I've wished for.

Then I saw them in the last of daylight outside the screens. They were diving at insects attracted to my computer light. I got up and stood close to a screened window so I could watch their acrobatics. Most were small, but several were big. They were splendid, superlative flyers.

One suddenly flared at the screen, hovering in front of me, its outspread silhouette perfect against the moonlight. The slowness of its wings surprised me. It was as though it recognized me, and I could not breathe for three or four seconds as it hung there, undulating inches from my face.

What are you going to do next?

"Welcome back," I said. "I'll build you a house of your own," and it flew away.

Stage 4

We enjoyed the Bat House for two years, from 2014 to 2016, while Theo worked at her private practice, and I took a yoga teacher training class to get a 200-Hour certificate. I brought boxes of apples from the farm for my fellow students, and they brought jam, garden vegetables, herbs, and canned sauces. We grew close, and being the only male in the group, I often could not resist offering a masculine sense of humor to the mix, like demonstrating the rooster asana I had created.

I taught a weekly class called Yoga for Grumpy Old Men, which included men from oil field workers to doctors, teachers, lawyers, and a foundry owner, who all had at least one physical ailment. They had pins and screws in almost every joint in their bodies, and I found it a challenge to keep track of them when designing practices. I also substituted in established yoga classes for another teacher while she was at the Wyoming Legislature and for Laura when she was out of town, so my schedule was full, and I learned a tremendous amount in a short amount of time.

Then I got a call from my old principal at the High School who asked if I'd be interested in coming back to work for a year to revive the journalism program. Erika, my former student, was doing a great job with Broadcast, but the student newspaper and the yearbook classes were struggling, and their teacher was leaving. I interviewed, got the job, and enjoyed two years of being back in the classroom. I rebuilt the journalism program strongly enough that a few of my students got under the skin of several Cody residents and school board members who didn't appreciate their views on gun control. The students were invited to *Speak Your Piece* on local radio, where they defended their positions admirably, even though they were blindsided by callers who quizzed them on the Constitution and lectured the specifics of semi-automatic weapons. They also caused a running letter-to-the-editor battle in the local newspaper. They turned out to be much more intelligent than the adults who attacked them thought they were. I felt I had done my job well.

During those two years, Theo and I traveled to a yoga retreat in Costa Rica, where Theo renewed her surfing skills from her lessons in Hawaii, and I fished with my old pal, Laura's husband Steve. We took the whole family in the summer to a Canadian fishing lodge, where Missa caught the biggest walleye of the trip and learned to help the staffs at the filleting table as well as the cooks at the dining table. We all celebrated Theo's seventy-third birthday in December by hiking in the Valley of Fire State Park in Nevada.

Theo chaperoned a group of my students in Seattle at a JEA Convention, and we bought a yellow British Lab that Theo named Belle to replace Mac, whom we'd had to put down two years earlier. Theo was against getting another dog, but once she sat on the grass among the litter of puppies crawling all over her, it was a done deal. Belle became her dog, not mine, and she closely watched when I trained Belle to hunt and retrieve birds, scolding me if she thought I was being too hard on her.

I held my fiftieth high school reunion at the Bat House, where everyone who came seemed to love the place. They sat to eat, drink, and visit at the big dining room table, the east deck Stan had built, and the porch roof deck Dirk Moos had built solidly enough to land a helicopter on. We had lost nine of our class, five from the effects of Vietnam.

We rented the Bat House to a family of goose hunters from Gardiner, Montana who cleaned the place better than I did, and to a group of competitors in Al Lee's Quigley Buffalo Shoot. I was hesitant to rent to six welders from Georgia who were working turn-around at Colstrip, but they proved to be perfect southern gentlemen who helped me with several heavy projects I could not accomplish alone. They were all huge, well-muscled men who called me Sir, and they paid us $7,500 for two weeks, less than what they would have paid for a motel without cooking facilities.

Theo had always wanted to ice skate at Rockefeller Center, so I arranged a week at the Lotte Hotel in New York City during Christmas. On the morning of her seventy-fourth birthday, it was ten degrees, but she put on her skates and after a few minutes of getting her feet under her, she was sailing around the ice like a pro, her smile as bright as the lights of Times Square. We dined at Club 21, where we always ate when the owner, Pete Kriendler, was alive. The maître d told me I was the only one he knew who had ever eaten there free and wanted to know my relationship to Pete.

I told him I had been his fishing guide when he came to Wyoming, and he said, "Oh, that is why. Fishing was sacred to Mr. Pete."

I was amazed that he remembered me, and he gave us our usual table where Pete said he had informed J. Edgar Hoover in 1941 that Pearl Harbor had been bombed. Theo loved the service and the food and seeing me dressed up in a tie. We felt like we were in high school again, but with Pete's absence, when I looked at the bill, I asked the maître d' if the waiter hadn't misplaced a decimal. I was thankful the Georgia welders had paid us so well for renting the Bat House.

I retired again in 2018, and Theo thought she would, but she still volunteered to work as a therapist for Critical Incident Stress Management, where she provided help to first responders to alleviate post-traumatic stress. She also worked for the school district and Wyoming Workforce Services "because there is such a need," she told me. She had been president of the Wyoming Psychological Association, a board member of Children's Resource Center and Heart Mountain Free Clinic. She was on the Buffalo Bill Art Show Committee and taught Ministering to Others at the LDS Church. All this was hard for her to let go.

She was an Honoree of the Cody Medical Foundation in August of 2018, where she said, "Volunteering gives a purpose across a lifespan. It helps us to be resilient, takes the knocks off life, makes social connections, and creates a routine. I've learned a lot by being affiliated with different groups of people. I've learned to take the other person's perspective. I've always felt fortunate to have my education. I like sharing it."

I talked her into travelling to Ireland in June and to South Carolina and Georgia in October. She was a serious student of the Civil War, having widely read about it and visited several famous battle sites, and she wanted to see Charleston, South Carolina, and Atlanta. While driving to Andersonville, the infamous Confederate prison camp, she began complaining about a pain in her side, and I tried getting her to go into a medical clinic for an X-ray, but she believed it was a pulled muscle from coughing too hard as the result of a cold. I stopped several times in front of clinics, but she refused to go in.

When we returned to Cody, the pain persisted, and she tried several therapies that did nothing to help her. In February of 2019, she was diagnosed with Stage Four, incurable bone cancer. The breast cancer had metastasized into her spine, pelvis, and ribs. The oncologist in Billings gave her two to five years to live. All they could do was offer palliative care, a term I had never heard that meant making her as comfortable as possible until she died.

We were stunned, of course, and so was everyone who knew her. Several gave us well-meant advice, none of which Theo would take. She agreed to go to Huntsman Cancer Institute in Salt Lake

City, and their incredible team saw the current diagnosis and treatment as the same as what they would offer. Theo accepted her fate as "the draw of the cards."

She endured chemotherapy and some radiation that targeted specific areas but was relegated to an infusion a week within a month, and I managed a host of pills for her to keep her pain low and her internal organs as regular as possible. It was a balancing act we could not win, and seeing her lose her hair, her weight, and her strength began to take its toll on me too, though her attitude remained optimistic and cheerful. She gave me several books on how to deal with the stress of caretaking, and the best I could do was walk Belle after doing yoga in the morning and doing another calming practice at night. I quit teaching my yoga classes and started to think about selling the farm. I couldn't manage it with the care it needed as well as giving Theo the care she needed. I didn't want to leave her side. Time with her was the most precious thing in my life.

The boys arrived with their families during the Fourth of July, and Theo baked pies and took walks with the grandkids, her energy seeming to rebound, which astounded me. She planned for us to drive to Lake Tahoe in October to stay in a condo with Matt's family, and I told her if she wanted to do it, I would buy a new vehicle more comfortable than our old Tundra. I found a new Tundra she could ride in without pain in her side and back, and we made the trip. I chartered a boat to take the kids fishing on the Lake, and Theo took them shopping. She only became sick to her stomach twice on the entire trip.

I sold the Bat House farm in November of 2019. I waffled on the decision as long as I could, but finally gave in. The stress was too much for me. Art Schiffer's grandson, Billy, and his wife bought it, and Theo said she was happy they would be neighboring Billy's dad, who lived at Art's place, because their kids would be close to their grandfather.

After it was done, I thought I would regret it, but I didn't. I just felt relieved.

Theo began to take walks with Belle and me, her energy seeming to rebound again and her joy of being outdoors fulfilled, even in freezing weather on the ice edged shore of Buffalo Bill Reservoir. The last week of February, she said she would like to go the Mountain States Basketball Tournament in Las Vegas, which started March 4. I didn't think I could get us tickets considering the late date, but Wyoming was not expected to win any games, so I managed to get us premium seats and a room at the Bellagio, where the poker room was one of my favorites. Wyoming won their first two games in last second barn burners, and Utah State, where Theo received her Ph.D., won theirs. She cheered for both teams and anxiously followed every second of the close action. People from all over Wyoming came to our seats to say hello to Theo, Coach Strannigan's daughter, and she lit up conversations with all of them. In the championship game, a player from Utah State held the ball in a dribble until the last second when he made an NBA three pointer to win. She was ecstatic, and I loved seeing her so happy.

In April of 2020, she began walking with Belle and Linda, a neighbor and sorority sister from their days at UW. Linda had lost her husband in an accident, and Theo renewed their friendship. She walked along the Reservoir and by the river daily, and in June, a year before she died, all the grandkids showed up to be with her. In July, I surprised her by taking her to a mechanic's shop in Billings where I'd left a red 1952 MGTD I'd found in a barn in Huntley. She jumped in, started it, and couldn't wait for the mechanic to get it roadworthy. Unfortunately, I had to haul it to Colorado after she died to get the engine rebuilt, so she never got to drive it.

All summer she began going through my books. I had hundreds of them, many of them valuable first editions, some signed by the authors. After looking up their values and setting some aside, she put them in boxes and told me to pull out any I wanted before hauling them to the library. I told her I felt like she was giving away my old friends. She had no idea how often I went in the basement to find one passage from some old book I hadn't read in forty years, but she needed something to do, and it gave her great satisfaction to clean up the house of what she deemed as clutter, so I left her to it.

By September, she was struggling to walk up the 130 steps of the stairway from the river below our house, but she would stop for breathers and smile at me. We spent most of the day in the house that fall. Theo read, talked on the phone with her sisters, her brother, our boys, and grandkids every day, and slept a lot. She never complained of the pain or became negative in any way.

Once, when I was preparing dinner for us, she said, "I'm sorry you have to go through this with me." That was as down as I'd seen her, and about a week later, she had such a dour expression that I asked her what was on her mind.

"What does it all matter?" she said, as sad and anguished as I had seen her. "It is all just air."

"What do you mean?" I asked.

"All that work," she said, holding her hands out and waving them. "All those years of work, and it is just air. None of it matters."

"Theo," I said. "It does matter. Through your work you helped thousands of people. You changed their lives, and who knows how many others were affected by your work? You have been an incredible force for good in the world."

She didn't answer, and her expression didn't change. I didn't know if there was any comforting her at that moment.

We spent long hours in the living room. I had bought her an electrically controlled, overstuffed recliner she said she didn't need, as she had said about the split king bed I'd bought that she could control to lift and tilt in various positions, but soon came to appreciate and love both. She would curl up with a blanket in the chair, find a comfortable angle, and sleep, read, or watch TV.

She especially enjoyed watching the Buffalo Bills quarterback Josh Allen play because he had played for the University of Wyoming, and she didn't think sports analysts would give him a fair shake because he had come from such a small school. She had seen similar scenarios, and it upset her. One analyst said he was a thrower, not a passer, that he could throw the ball long distances, but he was not accurate.

"He's going to eat his words," Theo said. She called him "Joshie," and would sit on pins and needles during his games, yelling, "Go, Joshie! Go!" when he ran the ball.

I dug out my old coin collections and began sorting through them to organize in sets as I sat with her. I had boxes of pennies, nickels, dimes, quarters, halves, and silver dollars I had not looked at in years. Theo once gave some Boy Scouts, who came begging at our door for penny collections while I was at the Bat House, a tall brass cuspidor full of Indian Head pennies I had saved. She had no idea of their worth — to her, they were one cent each.

I was angry with her for giving them away, but she wasn't too disturbed by it.

"At least they went to a good cause," she said with a smile.

I also had several rookie cards of athletes, like Michael Jordan's and Mickey Mantle's, and I had bought three Josh Allen's, two from UW. One was a "patch card," which had a small piece of his football pants inside. On her seventy-seventh birthday, I gave it to her with a card that said, "I know you have always wanted into Joshie's pants, so here you go."

She began spending hours in our upstairs sunroom, sitting in the chair she had for clients in her office, listening to guided meditations. I watched her from the doorway and knew she was in a deep state of relaxation. She would emerge from these sessions calm and serene.

We had a heavy snowstorm in February which dumped about two feet overnight, and while I shoveled our front steps and sidewalk, Theo put on her big down coat with a hood and shoveled the sidewalk to our garage. I took her photo as she stood smiling at me with Belle at her side, and in March, I took another photo of her in front of a massive redwood tree in Calaveras Big Trees State Park. She had felt good enough to fly to California to visit Matt and Kristin and their children. I recorded her in their backyard reading this story to the kids:

A man asked God to show him Heaven and Hell, and God presented to him two rooms. In the first, sickly people sit around the table, and in the center is a gigantic pot of delicious smelling soup. Each person can reach the pot, but their spoons are so long that there is no way to get them back into their mouths. Each tortured soul struggles in vain to get a bite to eat. They writhe in pain as they fruitlessly ladle and starve. This of course is Hell. And in the second room is the same table, the same soup, the same terribly long spoons. But this time, the diners, sated and happy, pour spoons full of soup into their neighbors' mouths. In Hell, we starve alone. In Heaven, we feed each other.

In the video, at the end of her reading, she looks up at the camera and smiles.

In May, she was raking leaves in the backyard and planting flowers along the west side of the house. She had lost her appetite for most any food I cooked except for sweet potatoes and was soon only eating a spoonful or two. On June 6, I took her to the hospital because her abdomen had filled with fluid. The nurses drained it, and our doctor said her internal organs were failing, and that she only had a few weeks to live. I called Bart and Matt, and they brought all the grandchildren to see her on June 11. They went home after a few days, and the boys returned on the sixteenth by themselves.

Her sisters, Marty and Susan, came to spend time with her, and her brother Matt wrote her a candid heartfelt letter which touched us all.

I was giving her morphine and fentanyl, and she became dreamy and hallucinatory. Once, when I put on latex gloves to change her fentanyl patch, she asked me if I had enough gloves. I said I had a whole box of them, and she asked why I wore them.

"The nurse told me if I got any fentanyl on me, I might turn into a zombie," I said.

"No one will know the difference," she said.

Bart's wife Janice came to help us, and after a few days, we decided to take her to Spirit Mountain Hospice, which her sister Marty had been instrumental in building. As we wheeled her in on a gurney, the nurse who received us began thanking her for how much she had helped her as one of her clients. Theo recognized her and wanted to know how everything was going in her life. The boys and I took turns staying with her, sleeping on a couch in the room. I brought Belle in for her, and she jumped up on her bed, landing in the middle of her and startling her into a big smile.

On June 24, as I was filling the car with gas before relieving the boys at the Hospice, I had a sudden feeling I needed to get there fast. On my way, I received a call from the Hospice nurse who told me Theo only had a few hours.

We stood by her as she took her last two breaths. I howled in grief, and both boys held me. It was the most painful moment of my life, but she was done with her suffering.

Grief

During the year before her death, Theo and I talked about everything we could think of. I told her I didn't know what I'd do after she was gone, that I thought I would just go around crying all the time. In her usual calm and professional voice, she said, "Well, you can cry for a while, but then go get some sunshine." She believed time in the outdoors, especially in wilderness, could soothe any emotional pain. But she had the ability to focus on the present, saying that happiness depended on redirecting one's focus to a flower, a bird, or light's play. I didn't.

"I don't know what I'll do without you," I told her.

"Keep writing," she said.

When she was under the influence of morphine and fentanyl, not herself and distant, I sat on the edge of her bed after dressing her in her favorite blouse and pants and began to cry. She asked me what was wrong, and I said I was afraid she was leaving me.

She immediately sat up and threw her arms around me, saying, "Oh Mike, I'm not leaving you." She held me until I stopped crying and sat back onto her pillows, seeming to believe she had resolved my fear.

After a moment, I realized she did not understand that I was afraid of her death. She thought I was afraid of her quitting our relationship, of ending our marriage. This minor shock made me realize she had already partially left me.

It became more evident when all the nieces and nephews

gathered in our bedroom to see her one final time. She was visiting with all of them and suddenly said, "Mike, what are you doing having everybody here? You'd think I was dying or something." Everyone grew silent and looked at me. I was speechless.

After they had gone, she said, "Everybody said I looked nice."

She wore a favorite green blouse, white caprices, and emerald earrings I had given her for an anniversary. "You do look nice," I said. "You are beautiful."

"You know just the right things to say," she said, and smiled.

When I asked her what she wanted me to say at her funeral, she said, "Just say that I was helpful."

I feared I would not know the right things to say and did not want to speak at it, but the boys insisted. I thought I would end up a blubbering mess, but I practiced what I wrote until I had it memorized. Bart and Matt and the grandkids all talked, as well as Kristin and Janice offering prayers, to an overflowing attendance. I felt like I had gotten through it but had only scratched the surface of her life.

She was cremated, and a woodworker friend in Montana made a beautiful urn from walnut and zebra wood. Another friend carved a dove to sit on top of it, which she had requested.

Matt took it to California, and the boys have spread some of her ashes in the Grand Canyon and in the Tetons. I ordered a tombstone with my name next to hers. Linda, the neighbor Theo walked with when she became ill, gave us two plots she had in the Cody cemetery.

For a year, I was numb. I stopped playing in my regular poker games and stayed at home most of the time. I suffered from debilitating pain in my left side and finally had an operation on my neck vertebrae that helped. I took the MGTD to Colorado to be restored and went through my coin collections. I read and learned to cook for only one person again. I didn't drink any alcohol as many friends feared I would, but I occasionally thought of suicide.

I would wake up in the middle of the night, reach out my left arm where Theo was supposed to be and realize she was gone. My right arm reached for the handle of the nightstand drawer where my .32 Colt semi-auto lay, and I considered opening it, taking out the pistol and ending how tired I was of living without her.

That period is a blur until March, when I went to the Mountain States basketball tournament in Las Vegas with Bob Anderson. I bought us two seats at midcourt, seven rows up, and we loved watching all the games. I won several thousand dollars at poker. I started my home game again, took my 1980 VW camper van to Salt Lake City to be restored, picked up my gun buying and selling hobby again and became interested in ancient coins.

When I flew to Baltimore for a coin exposition, I paid homage to Edgar Allen Poe by walking around Lombard Street where he was picked up by a friend outside a bar and voting place called *Gunner's Hall* before dying in the hospital. Like his mysteries, the cause of his death has remained clouded. Theories include tuberculosis, a brain tumor, voter fraud "cooping," and alcohol poisoning. The gloom of the street at night and his tragic life induced me to have a martini in *The Horse You Came In On Saloon*. At home, I began making myself a martini or two every day at 4 P.M.

I had told all five grandchildren after Theo died that I would take them anywhere in the world they wanted to go, and it would just be one on one. Sydney was first, and she wanted to go to Scotland, so I took her in May, stopping in New York for a few days to see the sites. Club 21, much to my dismay, had closed because of Covid, as many of the city's restaurants had. In Scotland, we contacted Theo's relatives in her grandparents' hometown, where they filled Sydney in on her ancestry, showing her a giant tombstone where many of her forebears were buried. I had a kidney stone decide to make its excruciating journey toward my bladder and I had to stay on codeine in Edinburgh while Syd traveled around with a girl she had met from Canada. She was adamant she would return to Scotland when she could. Feeling horrible that I hadn't been able to finish the itinerary I had planned, I thought I owed her a second trip. I bought several bottles of Scotch to bring home, and they didn't last long.

Mason came to live with me for the summer and work for HR's construction company. I took him fishing, and he became proficient with a fly rod. I enjoyed cooking for him because of his voracious appetite, and we played cribbage every day after dinner, when I had a martini, and sometimes two, three or four. I was in black and white survival mode.

My world was flat, devoid of feeling much for anyone for about a year. When I tried having a relationship, it failed. I had no idea of grief's depth and power. I was not ready for anything but Platonic relationships at best, yet I wanted to go all in without paying attention to that moment between stimulation and reaction, that pause at the end of an exhale. I believed I could quickly establish an interdependent relationship built on respect for each other's independence through trust and honesty, as Theo and I had, which had taken years to develop.

I stopped drinking alcohol, but I became more suicidal in the following months. I started seeing a psychologist whom Theo had supervised, and she encouraged me to keep writing, as Theo had. She helped me become aware that I had never fully grieved Theo's death before encountering another loss, and that I had merged them without separating either. I even combined their names in Freudian slips and dreamed they were one sleeping body I was trying to awaken. I kept a journal of these dreams that began to illuminate my confusion, but I struggled to separate the two. Bombs exploded in the middle of romantic walks in idyllic settings. Theo stood on a beach, her arms folded at her waist as she gazed at the sun setting into the ocean, but her back was toward me, and she would not answer my calling her. I was attacked by wolves in a football game I was quarterbacking. I was trapped inside a shower stall, Theo's face inches away on the other side of opaque glass, but she couldn't hear me. I had folded the two into one iron hard layer of grief.

Coming to these realizations took months of therapy. A colony of bats roosted in my skull, and they weren't about to evacuate congenially. One night I struggled to breathe, so I went outside to be in the fresh air, but my chest was ready to explode. It felt like I had dived to ninety feet and run my scuba tank dry. At that moment, as if my dive buddy had rushed to me with an auxiliary mouthpiece, Mike McIntyre called to say he had an odd feeling something was wrong. I told him what was happening, and after about five minutes, I gained my regular breath. I later learned "dying of a broken heart" is more than a cliché. It is an actual biologic effect of grief, the cause of many people's deaths soon after their spouse's. I had come close.

I drove to Salt Lake City to attend yoga workshops, where I found peace of mind while there, but on my way back to Cody, I drove dangerously fast and cried until I had to stop. On a bird hunting trip, I walked around in a snowstorm with my shotgun and wanted to kill myself, but the thought of someone having Belle who wouldn't hunt stopped me. I didn't even consider the pain I would cause my family until Matt made me aware of it. I couldn't sleep and began taking pills every night to get some rest. I was exhausted.

Thanksgiving was especially difficult, even though Layne, my niece in Jackson invited me there with Matt and his family. She was married to the game warden there, and he took Ollie out to get his first elk, which made me feel happy for him. Her sister Lindsay was there with her kids, and observing their high energy gave me a certain sense of loving history. I took all the kids to dinner at an expensive restaurant where they enjoyed themselves immensely, but I couldn't shake the depression. I bought three bottles of Talisker 18 Scotch, which had sold out in Scotland, at the liquor store there. It didn't last long.

Christmas with my sister comforted me, but I still felt a terrible loss. Mason, Oliver, and Alexander wanted to go deep sea fishing for their trip I had promised them, so I took them to Mexico at the end of the month. They all caught big marlin, and we filled the boat with mahi, tuna and bonita for four days. It was the best fishing I'd ever had in Mexico. On the second day, Theo's birthday, while returning to the harbor with six lines out, I was watching a bait on the starboard side when I had a premonition a marlin would hit it. Seconds later, one did, and Mason fought the 150-pound fish into the boat. All three boys said Grandma Theo had put it there, her own birthday present to us.

The captain and deckhand said the boys were the strongest clients they'd ever had to work so many fish. I was proud of their fit bodies and minds, that they all lived healthy lives and that they expressed their gratitude. On New Year's Eve I smoked a good Cuban cigar on my hotel room's deck and drank tequila with Mexican beer. I watched the fireworks in the harbor begin about ten o'clock and went to bed, satisfied and contented that the boys were so delighted with the trip, but as lonely as I had been since Theo's death.

Recovery

In January, a former colleague at the high school who was now part owner of a gym, asked me to teach yoga to the senior citizens she was working with. I taught two classes of chair yoga and was amazed at their abilities. One student was ninety-one and another was ninety-three. She had high school athletes and a trainer helping them with weights, so I hired the trainer, Aaron, to guide me in weightlifting. I had lifted in college athletics, but not with the structured, intelligent program he designed. It made a world of difference to be teaching yoga again and to be pushing my limits on the weights. I lost twenty pounds, then regained ten, all muscle, Aaron said, which made me feel like Superman. The more I read about the numerous benefits of weightlifting, and the more I practiced it with yoga, the better I felt mentally and physically, and I became dedicated to it three days week.

At the end of January, I returned to Mexico for a weeklong yoga teacher training retreat where the people were kind, loving participants, and the food was outstanding vegetarian fare. I drank a little wine with meals but felt so good that I didn't care for much alcohol at all. I had my coffee while watching the sun come up over the mountains every morning and then walked the beach where I followed migrating whales fifty yards away. Through the big windows of the third story yoga studio, I watched marlin leap ten to twenty feet out of the blue ocean, their sleek bodies shimmering in the sunlight, and I remembered the boys, their arms and backs aching after reeling them in. I returned to Cody and began teaching with a revitalized love of yoga, a mindful awareness of what I didn't know, and an open heart to new perception.

In March I flew to Las Vegas for another coin expo where my fascination in antique coins grew greater than the size of my wallet, but I rationalized my purchases by telling myself I had replaced what I normally spent on rare Scotch with coins that Jesus, Caesar or Alexander the Great might have held. I also bought a 2020 Bat Coin, an American Samoa quarter with two flying fox bats, a mother, and a pup on the reverse. Of course, I had to buy the most expensive one, a West Point mint with a V75 Privy mark, as opposed to the other three mints. Anything to honor the only US National Park that harbors the fruit bat. I thought Theo would even approve of my splurging, and remembering her love of National Parks, I drove to Death Valley where I walked for a while, wishing she could be with me before the heat began to scorch my brain. I could hear her telling me it was already scorched before I began walking.

I had been closely monitoring how much alcohol I drank, but on home poker nights, I sometimes had too much, so I quit entirely, keeping my trip with Melissa in mind. She was my last grandchild I needed to take anywhere in the world. Her choice was France.

When I asked her what she wanted to do there, she said, "Sit at a sidewalk café in Paris and watch people." I found it easy enough and more delightful than I'd imagined. She had taken one year of French as a high school freshman, and I had studied it on Duolingo for several months, so we at least found the best boulangeries and creperies. We arrived in June, the weather perfect and parts of our journey magical. We bicycled in the early morning and at night, took a cruise on the Seine, and got lost in museums. In Paris' Montmartre District, from a small hotel next to an apartment where Picasso had lived, our view of the city was fantastic at night, the Eiffel Tower lit below us. After touring the Loir Valley, we stayed in Normandy, where I found an uncle's grave in the American Cemetery. Imagining what soldiers had experienced landing on the beaches, especially Omaha, was overwhelming. Nevertheless, Missa left with a strong desire to live there. She had not seen *Saving Private Ryan*, and given her powerful capacity for visual memory, I did not recommend it.

With her father Matt, I took a thirty-five-mile backpacking trip in the Wind River Mountains in August, where carrying a thirty-seven-pound pack over high mountain passes tested my limits, but I made it without much trouble. The granite boulders and rock-strewn trails demanded constant attention to where and how I stepped, creating a walking meditation of five days. The various forms of granite, with mixtures of orthoclase, plagioclase, mica, quartz, and feldspar, fascinated me with their beauty.

I had read many definitions of "mindfulness" in my yoga studies, but the one I came to feel most deeply on the trip was "paying attention with an enduring faith in a kind universe." The magnificent peaks in that range emanated the mysteries of time and space, and every step among them simultaneously humbled and exalted me. I felt grateful for being there and believed whatever suffering I had experienced held meaning and purpose I had yet to discover.

Whenever I came upon a group of wildflowers, I was firmly aware of Theo's presence. Upon crossing Washakie Pass at 11,600 feet, with the wind blowing and gusting 60 to 90 miles per hour, a particularly large patch of yellow daisies greeted me, and I suddenly burst into tears that blurred my vision so completely I had to stop, take off my pack and recover. I knew I was suffering from hypoxia because I was dizzy and my legs trembled, but I also knew I was grieving Theo's death from as great a depth as I ever had.

It is now three years since she died after forty-one years of our marriage, and I am occasionally overwhelmed by grief and begin to cry, surprised at the triggers of such moments. Sometimes they are sudden minutiae like a memory of her voice, her laugh, a vision of her glance, a picture of her walking in the mountains, and sometimes their impetus lies in a feeling of regret, loneliness, or general remorse. I don't believe it will ever stop, that I will for the rest of my life be subject to such moments, and I have come to accept it. Perhaps they will diminish with time, I am not sure, but for the present, I let the loss wash through me and try to remember that she said, "You can cry for a while, but then go get some sunshine."

On summer nights I sit outside, enjoy a cigar and a glass of whiskey, and watch the bats fly around in my backyard. There are very few. White-nose syndrome was recently discovered in Montana's Pryor Mountain Mystery Cave, yet I am hopeful they will survive it as they have so many other viruses. I believe they will thrive on Earth long after humans are gone, and in that belief, along with being open to what next the universe will bring, I find some pleasure and contentment.

Acknowledgements

Thanks to: Rick Stonehouse, Bob Anderson, Bruce McCormack, Gordon Dean, Vicki Gill and Julia Hoskins for their careful readings of the early manuscript; the Lloyd family for their helpful details; Raina Plowright, Sarah Olson, Matt Lyman and Bryce Maxell for sharing their expertise in bat research; Mark Leichliter for his editorial expertise; Renée Tafoya at WordsWorth Publishing for her keen editing and creative design; and Dr. Esther Saville for her loving therapy sessions that gave healthy perspective to the bats in my brain.

Note from the author

As a high school sophomore, I began keeping a diary, and I maintained the practice through the years, including the time I was working on the Bat House. When I retired from teaching in 2014, I began this memoir, calling it *The Bat House Chronicles* and writing in present tense. I mention this for three reasons:

First, because sometimes when I read dialogues in the text I must remind myself of their accuracy, taken from my journals and not memory; however, given some of the late hours I wrote in my journal, and some of the states of mind I was in at various times, I still wonder at their complete accuracy. If I failed at that, I hope those whom I have quoted are not overly offended and will forgive me. I have heartily attempted to convey what did happen from what did not.

Second, Richard Ford, the Pulitzer Prize winning author, reminded me of Northrop Frey's distinction between fiction's and memoir's arrival at truth, that "memoir arrives at truth on facts; a novel arrives at truth by reliance on imagination and artifice. Fiction relies on a *disinterested* use of words. You must have nothing riding on the outcome." I have tried to rely on an *interested* use of words by which I have *everything* riding on the outcome. My journals often provided me with the facts—it will be for the reader to determine at what truths the memoir arrives.

Third, in studying the best of memoir writing, I found Vivian Gornick's claim in *The Situation and the Story: The Art of Personal Narration* that "a memoir is a work of sustained narrative prose, controlled by the idea of the self, under obligation to lift from the raw material of life a tale that will shape experience, transform event, and deliver wisdom." I walked around in my sleep reciting this for months until I began to comprehend it, finally realizing I was shaping my experience from my journals and transforming the events by selectively presenting them in past tense. Whatever wisdom might be delivered, I again leave to the reader. I hope there is some.

Resources

Bat Conservation International (batcon.org). "Conserving the world's bats and their ecosystems to ensure a healthy planet."

Organization for Bat Conservation (batconservation.org) "Founded in 1992 in Michigan with a small team offering live bat programs to schools, nature centers and museums."

Graham, Gary L., Ph.D. Bats of the World. *St. Martin's Press*, New York, NY. 1994.

American Bird Conservancy (abcbirds.org). "We believe unequivocally that conserving birds and their habitats benefits all other species — including people."

American Birding Association (aba.org). "The ABA's education programs promote birding skills, ornithological knowledge, and the development of a conservation ethic."

"Multiple Mortality Events in Bats: A Global Review." *Mammal Review*, January, 2016.

Drouin, Roger. "3 Ways to Keep Bats Away from Wind Turbines." *Scientific American*. September 1, 2014.

Russo, Danilo, et.al. "Bats mimic hymenopteran sounds to deter predators." *Current Biology*, May 9, 2022.

www.ingramcontent.com/pod-product-compliance
Lightning Source LLC
Chambersburg PA
CBHW071000160426
43193CB00012B/1853